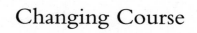

Changing Course

Changing Course

The wartime experiences of a
member of the Women's Royal
Naval Service, 1939-1945

Roxane Houston

GRUB STREET · LONDON

Published by
Grub Street
4 Rainham Close
London
SW11 6SS

Copyright © 2005 Grub Street
Text copyright © 2005 Roxane Houston

British Library Cataloguing in Publication Data
Houston, Roxane
Changing course: the wartime experiences of a member
of the Women's Royal Naval Service, 1939-1945
1. Houston, Roxane   2. Great Britain. Royal Navy.
Women's Royal Naval Service   3. World War, 1939-1945 –
Personal narratives, British   4. World War 1939-1945 –
Participation, Female
I. Title
940.5′45′941′092

ISBN 1 904943 10 1

Typeset by Pearl Graphics, Hemel Hempstead

Printed and bound in Great Britain by Biddles Ltd, King's Lynn

CONTENTS

For my grandchildren,
Alexander, Olivia, Matilda and Willow

In memory of David Arthur Houston, Midshipman RN

"See that ye hold fast the heritage we leave you,
yea, and teach your children its value,
that never in the coming centuries
their hearts may fail them
or their hands grow weak."

after Francis Drake

(Inscription on the memorial to the Fallen
of the Second World War,
in Dartmouth Royal Naval College)

ACKNOWLEDGEMENTS

My most sincere thanks go to David Radford for his invaluable help and endless patience in the research, editing and preparation of the final manuscript.

Also to Julian Fellowes for encouragement and advice, and an excellent foreword.

And to Jane Buchanan (née Price), Joy Baker (née Heward), Audrey Hewett (née Clarke), Captain Derek Napper RN and Isobel Napper (née Cowie) for their useful advice and accurate memories when mine faltered.

AUTHOR'S NOTE

Writing this book has meant a journey back in time – sixty-four years in fact – to a point beginning in late May 1940. While working on a mobile canteen which visited outlying anti-aircraft sites some distance from my home in Cheshire, we went to help survivors from Dunkirk who were being deposited in the grounds of a big house. The shocked countryside erupted from its comfortable slumber to rush to their aid with food, clothing and blankets, while we served strong, sweet tea, custard tarts, doughnuts and chocolate biscuits throughout that interminable day. The men were in a wretched state, totally exhausted, but still showing their indomitable spirit.

That unforgettable experience led to my decision to join the WRNS for the duration, and by August 9th I was on my way to a Royal Naval Air Station in Cornwall, and to six years of a new life of changing places, values and outlook.

I never regretted that decision. It seemed then as if I was living in a real time, quite unlike my former life, one which still stands out so clearly and vividly in my mind that its resurgence now has presented little difficulty.

Although I have dedicated my book to my four grandchildren, it is also a memorial to my young brother David, aged eighteen and a half, when, as a midshipman aboard the cruiser HMS *Neptune*, he was lost with the entire crew, except for one survivor, when it was sunk off the coast of Tripoli in December 1941.

Apart from being a very dramatic point in history,

leading to widely-changing attitudes throughout post-war Britain, those six years represented an important part of my early life, which I have now been able to retain as a permanent record of the incredible courage and endurance of so many people, as well as the laughter and companionship of good friends and colleagues, whose presence I was always able to conjure up during the following years.

FOREWORD

You may think that we are not, as a generation, short of war stories. Even today when the fashion for them is not as great as it was forty years ago. You may feel that you have seen enough heroics played out on the big and small screens and you may argue that these days we are all, to a degree, aware of the tremendous sacrifices made by the few to ensure and protect the freedom of the many.

Maybe. But I think we are in danger of missing and, as the years go on, of losing the sense of what the Second World War meant for the thousands of ordinary men and women who were pulled away from their lives at every level of our society to play their part in a struggle that was not of their making. They may not have been Dam Busters, nor even the code breakers, but they were, nevertheless, decent, normal people, much like you and me today, who had no choice but to give up their plans and ambitions, private and public, to dedicate six long years to their country's good.

This is the story of just such a woman. Roxane Houston was a pretty, lively and talented girl, raised in a comfortable and loving home, whose big excitement was gaining a place to study singing at the Royal Academy of Music. Except that Hitler decided to invade Poland and everything changed. By August 1940, she was in the navy and by the time the war ended, she had travelled the Mediterranean and the Middle East, survived shot and shell, and lost her young brother when HMS *Neptune* sank off Tripoli. In short, in those six years she survived grief, love and danger and it was a very different young woman who arrived at the Royal Academy in the autumn of 1946 to begin what would prove to be a distinguished career. I don't know if her experiences added depth to her singing although I rather suspect they did. What I do know is that they altered her view of life and that breezy young girl from the 1930s, without a care in her privileged world, had gone and would never return.

Those men and women fighting that war were our parents, our mothers and our fathers, and we are entering the final years when they will have the chance to tell their story. We owe them that chance and we owe them our attention. Indeed, we owe them all, each and every one of them, a debt we can never hope to repay.

Julian Fellowes, 2005

I

TUNING UP

July 28th 1939   *Aldeburgh, Suffolk*
The news from across the Channel was disturbing, and our
parents took to listening to every news bulletin on the
wireless, becoming increasingly anxious. My father, fearing
it might be the last holiday we would spend together for
some while, had decided to take us earlier than usual to our
favourite holiday haunt, the little seaside town of
Aldeburgh in Suffolk. If older people felt such anxiety it
was not the same for our generation. We were young and
strong and optimistic with a shared disbelief in any such
dark future. This was our third holiday in Suffolk, and we
had made many friends there. With my two brothers, Tony,
aged twenty-one, newly down from Cambridge, and
David, aged sixteen, in his final year at the Royal Naval
College at Dartmouth, I spent the carefree days mainly at
nearby Thorpeness playing tennis, swimming, boating on

the Meare or dancing at the Country Club. Quite a few engagements were celebrated, Tony's among them, having met his fiancée Margaret on the dance floor.

My parents gave an enormous party for them at the mock Tudor house they had rented in the Aldeburgh High Street, very close to the sea, where my father always preferred to stay during our holidays. He said it was less hectic and noisy than over at Thorpeness. He was always taking photographs, and there was one of us all together, looking happy and relaxed, which I cherished particularly.

Still blithely unaware of the true threat to Europe and possibly to ourselves, we didn't see, as our parents undoubtedly did, the ominous grey shadow lurking in the wake of our thoughtless pleasure. All that mattered to us just then was the enjoyment of a present when problems could be shelved and decisions left unresolved, and we took full advantage of that.

But not for long.

The true present caught up with us as the political situation worsened, and cold reality struck us like a body blow as the tennis courts gradually emptied and young men began to drift homeward to prepare to enlist in the various services, while the girls bravely went through the final motions of holiday without them. While at Cambridge Tony had joined the Territorial Army in the Royal Engineers, and now, expecting to be called up for active service, he decided that he and Margaret would be married much sooner than originally intended. This had become a poignant time, and like many of the other families we finally decided to return home before our holiday month was up, all of us now on edge as the hideous cries of 'Sieg Heil' grew louder and more triumphant, and twenty miles or so of English Channel didn't seem much protection.

August 17th 1939   *Sandiway, Cheshire*
On arriving home in Hartford, Cheshire, we heard that the police at nearby Sandiway had been looking for volunteers to help man the small station in the event of a declaration of war and possible air attacks to follow, and I joined two of my friends who were keen to offer their services. The work was easy, based on a four-hour rota system which was quite pleasant during the day, though being collected at four in the morning by a police car needed some getting used to. Apart from learning the required routine in the event of a national emergency, there wasn't much to do except listen in constantly to the wireless, drink endless mugs of strong tea or cocoa, and play cards till eight o'clock, when I'd be driven home for breakfast. On the whole, it was all rather fun, particularly learning to play poker. The sergeant in charge, a pleasant, middle-aged man, told me I was his star pupil, which was praise indeed since he always won every game. I decided I'd have to try to cultivate his poker face, as he always seemed to know exactly what I was thinking.

September 3rd 1939   *Sandiway*
As the placid routine continued, we began to wonder if this rather casual vigilance was really necessary, since nothing ever seemed to be happening, no sudden red alert from Chester, nothing. Then, just after eleven o'clock, during a particularly tense moment in our poker game, the sergeant suddenly hissed for silence and we all froze. A special announcement was coming over the wireless, and as we listened to Neville Chamberlain's tired, disillusioned voice telling us we were now at war with Germany, we just sat there, stunned, our cards still in our hands. In spite of having feared this possibility, the reality still came as a shock. I suppose we'd all been hoping that something might happen to prevent it, but the Fates decreed otherwise. No peace in our time for us – at least,

not in the foreseeable future.

Then with a long drawn out sigh that seemed to travel up from his feet, the sergeant stirred and glanced round at us. All at once he appeared to have grown older, his face fallen in.

"Well, that's that, then," he said quietly, and as if this were a signal we all came to life and went to our separate stations of duty, though what exactly we expected to happen at that moment none of us knew. As I looked out of the window I couldn't believe this was really happening. The Cheshire countryside looked as normal and peaceful as ever on this cloudless Sunday morning, though I noticed that no church bells were ringing for morning service.

As if he read my thoughts the sergeant looked across at me. "We won't be hearing any bells from now on," he said, "not unless there are German parachutists being dropped – or till the war's over."

He had hardly finished speaking when a new and sinister sound could be heard in the background over the air – a weird undulating howl almost blotting out the announcer's voice.

"Christ!" he muttered under his breath. "They've started already!"

"What is it?" one of the volunteers asked, frowning anxiously.

"It's an air raid siren. They're bombing London."

We sat in petrified silence. Bombing London? It wasn't – it couldn't be possible! I felt the muscles in my stomach tighten into an uncomfortable knot as we listened to the announcer's excited comments. But nothing more happened, and a little later someone came on to say it had been a false alarm.

There was a momentary sense of anti-climax, then later it was time to go home to lunch with my anxious parents, though I had never felt less like eating.

September 4th 1939   *Oaklands, Hartford, Cheshire*

And that, though perhaps none of us quite realised it, was the beginning of the end of an entire way of life. I supposed it must always be disturbing and uncomfortable to live through the tail end of an era, and find that all the well known landmarks which had previously informed one's judgement would suddenly, in the light of coming events, count for nothing. Of course, this affected my parents' generation more than mine. Their once familiar road had without warning completely changed character and direction with no signpost anywhere in sight. Having been cosily enshrined in the comfortable confines of their class with all its behaviour patterns and prejudices, it would take time for them to adapt to the inevitable changes. But for my generation it was different, an exhilarating plunge into the unknown. I began to realise I'd been clinging to ideas and judgements that now seemed obsolete and nothing to do with me.

I had left the Downs School at Seaford in Sussex, having successfully passed my Matriculation examination, and from January 1937 spent six months at a domestic science 'finishing' school in Switzerland, accompanied by a school friend from the Downs. Villa Brillantmont was situated in Lausanne with a breathtaking view of Lac Léman and the majestic Dents du Midi rising icily pure and aloof beyond it. This was where we were to be 'finished off' – that is to say, to be turned out as young ladies armed with all the social and domestic graces thought necessary for our future stations in life, after which we were supposed to be able to run great houses or estates with maximum efficiency. Not only that, we should be able to hold our own as hostesses or guests at any great social event, indulge in witty and well-informed conversation, (preferably also in French or German as well as our native tongue!), and be critically knowledgeable of the arts in general and an accomplished performer in one of them in particular.

This was all quite interesting, although I found the domestic side of it utterly boring. If it had not been for my piano lessons with an eighty-year-old ex-pupil of the world-famous concert pianist Walter Gieseking, and my German lessons (conducted in French), I might have given up altogether and fled homeward. I had been learning the piano since I was five years old, often playing at various school concerts, so this wonderful old teacher was an absolute godsend. She was horrified at the thought of my giving up, and as the Easter holidays approached, I allowed myself to be persuaded to remain. During the three-week break, many of the girls had elected to spend the time skiing up at the enchanting little mountain village of Chesières, high above Vevey where, of course, we all fell in love with our dashing ski instructor, René Ruchet.

Our chalet was warm and comfortable, and had been sold to our school by King Leopold of the Belgians. Food was plentiful and delicious, and we, thank heaven, didn't have to cook it!

Villa Brillantmont was full of interesting pupils. There were daughters of international politicians, diplomats and foreign royalty, such as the incredibly beautiful Indian princess, Ayesha Devi of Cooch Behar; the equally beautiful future American film star Gene Tierney; Anne Phillips, daughter of the American ambassador to Rome, as well as Marlene Dietrich's daughter Maria Sieber and others from equally glamorous backgrounds. Mademoiselle Heubi ruled us all with an iron hand in a velvet glove, a necessity when dealing with girls of sixteen and seventeen, who were highly sophisticated and very used to having their own way, and who thought nothing of climbing out of windows at night to keep their rendezvous with male acquaintances. There was one very attractive French girl called Monique whose nocturnal escapades were never discovered, and who made a lot of us feel dull, gauche and unadventurous. How I wished I had the nerve to venture out after her, but of course I never did!

Then it was July, and Mademoiselle Heubi and her staff bade us all an almost tearful farewell as they saw us off to our real worlds. It was time now to come out of my shell. One couldn't hide away from life forever, and I decided now that whatever was in store for us all, I, at any rate, was going to make sure I had a hand in it, however small and insignificant. That way I would at least be a contemporary part of a vibrant present, whether unpleasant or even dangerous, and not be trapped in what I had come to see as an outworn style of living. The gentler sounds of my youth were giving way to discordant and ominous over-tones, which were to reverberate worldwide in a crescendo of horrifying clamour that would eventually overtake and drown all others.

September 19th 1939   *Oaklands*
Things seemed to be moving very fast, and we were all rather confused and bewildered. Tony and Margaret got married in a Cambridge Registry Office, and went off for their brief honeymoon before Tony was posted to the Officer Cadet Training Unit at Aldershot. My mother seemed particularly bewildered by the speed of all this. Tony was only twenty-one, Margaret a year or so older.

"They're so young," she almost wailed. "It's all been so sudden!"

Added to this, our three domestic staff had given notice in a body, and gone off to work in a nearby munitions factory, and my mother, never having even boiled an egg in her life, had been suddenly left to cope with the running of a large house. Luckily Nanna, (the monthly nurse who at the age of seventeen had come to look after me at birth and stayed on ever since as general help and friend to us all) had elected to remain, and was solely responsible for instructing my mother in the art of cooking and domestic management.

I wasn't much help, even after my six months domestic science course at Villa Brillantmont, since all our cooking there had been on a most lavish scale, with litres of cream and pounds of butter added to most of the recipes with such abandon that I found I had put on almost a stone in weight on my return home.

But this was not to be the end of our trials. Worse was to come. Our hitherto comfortable existence was rapidly falling apart.

October 8th 1939   *Oaklands*

Coming down to breakfast, I found my father frowning over a letter in an official-looking buff envelope. It was informing us that a family of evacuees, Mum and two children, were to be billeted on us for an indefinite period, since the long-standing plans for evacuation of children from city areas were now in effect, and we had a suitably large house. The family would therefore be arriving from Bootle in a week's time.

"Oh heavens!" my mother cried. "How are we ever going to manage? And where on earth *is* Bootle?"

"It's one of the poorer areas of Liverpool," my father replied, picking up his morning newspaper.

My mother glanced round at us distractedly. "But where can we put them all?"

"There's plenty of room now that Cook and the others have left," I reminded her, soothingly.

Her face cleared. "Of course," she said, looking relieved. "I was forgetting."

Our visitors duly turned up, and I think this was one of the greatest shocks we'd ever suffered. The mother, a blowsy, rather aggressive woman, probably still in her thirties, though so gaunt, exhausted and careworn that she seemed much older, stood in the hall clutching her two children's hands, while the lady who had driven them from Liverpool collected their pathetic bundles of clothing from the boot of the car. A pungent smell arose and clung to everything, while we stood there, momentarily stunned. Not only were our guests clad in the poorest and most inadequate of garments, but all three were absolutely filthy, and before very long we became aware that the heads of the two children were alive with lice.

The arrival of other evacuees in the neighbourhood was a similar shock, and prompted frantic activity on the part of their various hostesses. To think that anyone – especially children – should exist in such appalling squalor! There was a bathroom next to the maids' bedroom which we now allotted to our evacuees, and although Nanna and I dealt ruthlessly with the hygiene of the two young children, this was not at all to the liking of their mother, who became quite indignant at this treatment. My mother, however, showing unexpected firmness, laid down a rule that the children, at least, were to have a bath every evening. Their mother reluctantly gave in, but there was nothing we could do to persuade *her* to have a bath. She was not used to it, she said, she would catch a chill. So, like all our friends and neighbours in a similar situation, my mother and I ransacked the house for spare clothing before driving into Chester to buy other items, including hair and tooth-brushes and the other necessary requisites for hygiene. The children, Billy and Susie, thrived under this treatment, sleeping long hours and waking refreshed and ravenously hungry for country fare, but their mother seemed unhappy. She couldn't get used to the silence. It kept her awake, she said, and there were no neighbours to talk to. She was lonely and wanted to go back home. No bombs had fallen on Liverpool, so what was the point of everybody being separated from their families? And so on.

We got used to the daily moan, but after about three months things came to a head. One of the other evacuee mothers whom she had met at our local shops told her she was returning home, as she'd had a letter from one of her neighbours telling her that her husband had been seen in the local pub with another woman – and mighty friendly from the looks of them! She wasn't going to put up with that, not she! Stan was too good-looking, he was always being chased after – a real pushover when it came to flattery, Stan was.

That was enough for our evacuee mum. She was also going back home and nobody was going to stop her! My mother did her best to try and persuade her to stay for the children's sake, but she was adamant, and after a few more days they were all seen off on the train, wearing their new clothes, with other belongings packed inside two of our larger suitcases. Both children were clutching teddy bears and carrier bags filled with smaller toys and chocolate bars, while their mother, her gaunt face now filled out with adequate rest and nourishing food, held yet another carrier bag bulging with groceries, and a new handbag with five pounds in it.

She was actually smiling in anticipation of going home, but the children appeared rather sorry to be leaving. It seemed a pity. They both looked so rosy and healthy, having run wild about the garden, even making friends with our gardener who had taught them the names of the flowers and allowed them to pick a few for their room.

We were really concerned for them. "Well, maybe Liverpool won't be bombed after all," I remarked hopefully as we waved them goodbye.

My mother sighed and shook her head. "It's very unwise of her," she said, then her expression changed, suddenly becoming unusually determined. "That bedroom will have to be fumigated," she added. "Think of it – three months without a bath, and I don't believe their window has been opened once all the time they were with us!"

And so it seemed when, with our two helpers from the village, we went inside it ....

February 27th 1940   *Oaklands*

It was a strange feeling knowing that war had been declared in Britain, yet nothing in the way of enemy action had actually occurred. Hitler was on the rampage through Europe and no one seemed able to stop him. But at least this peculiar, so-called 'phoney war' was giving us much needed time to prepare for what must surely descend on us soon. Most people were galvanized out of their false sense of security following Neville Chamberlain's 'Peace in our time' announcement, but there were others among our parents' older acquaintances who thought differently. When notices began to appear saying 'Careless talk costs lives' or 'Walls have ears', opinions were expressed that this was merely hysterical reaction, or spy mania. After all, what would spies be doing in this totally unexciting part of Cheshire? No, these complacent folk argued, we don't think we really need to worry about spies here.

They were to be proved wrong in a highly unpleasant and sinister manner. It was the custom on Sundays, after morning church, for friends and neighbours to foregather for a cocktail in each other's houses, at times bringing any of their house guests with them. On a certain occasion one of my father's friends, James Glanville, brought two extra guests with his family to our house – an attractive dark-haired girl named Edith, and Olé, a tall, fair young Norwegian, both of whom proved to be lively and amusing additions to the party. Naturally, no one attached any importance then to the fact that both James Glanville and my own father were management officers of Imperial Chemical Industries (ICI), whose main works were situated close to our neighbouring town of Northwich and the nearby salt flats; nor indeed saw anything sinister in Edith and Olé being invited to dine at Winnington Hall, the elegant building close to the tennis courts, adjacent to the main works complex, for the use of members of staff.

Later, we heard to our horror the chilling rumour that

not only had Olé been one of that infamous band of Norwegian traitors known as Quislings, but that Edith herself was German, and that both had been caught and subsequently shot as spies. This last part of the rumour, however, had not been confirmed. Maybe it was just spy mania, but it was disturbing all the same.

It was then, rumour or not, that the true seriousness of our situation was fully brought home to us. Shocked and stunned, my mother said vehemently that she wished there could be some way to fumigate our house, though what disinfectant could ever eradicate something as intangible as treachery? How trusting and gullible we'd all been! But then, I suppose we weren't used to suspicion and hadn't yet learnt to detect danger beneath a smiling surface. At least, I thought, the ICI works hadn't been sabotaged. Security would certainly now be increased, and we ourselves would have to be much more on our guard since this 'phoney war' wasn't going to continue for ever.

Not surprisingly, I didn't sleep very well for some nights afterwards.

March 31st 1940   *Oaklands*
As the so-called 'phoney war' persisted, I became restless and depressed, feeling I was no use to anyone. Tony was still at Aldershot, my younger brother David, now seventeen, was in his final year at the Royal Naval College at Dartmouth, while most of my friends had joined one or other of the services and gone off to various places. But what was *I* doing? Very little apart from listening in, with my worried parents, to every news bulletin on the wireless, helping to man a small police station in the expectation of air raids which never came, or with several hundred other volunteers spending days in a large factory over at Crewe, learning to assemble thousands of gas masks. I couldn't even go to London to study singing at the Royal Academy of Music (always my ambition), in case it might be bombed,

so had to make do with studying privately at home, fortunately with an excellent teacher, Mrs Florence Hindley, who came once a week to relieve my growing boredom and frustration.

April 15th 1940   *Oaklands*

Something useful turned up at last! Mary Hamer, one of my mother's younger tennis-playing friends, asked me to join her on her mobile canteen, taking refreshments to outlying and isolated anti-aircraft sites. I accepted at once, and went to say goodbye to my colleagues at the police station, who all said they'd miss me, adding pointedly that they hoped I'd visit them some time on my rounds. It meant getting up at six o'clock every morning, eating a hurried, scanty breakfast, and going off with Mary to the local bakery. The extra staff must have been working like mad every night to supply us with the hundreds of doughnuts, biscuits and custard tarts we needed. After that we had to drive to the nearby dairy to collect the milk for our two enormous urns of incredibly strong, sweet tea, and while Mary drove down countless narrow country lanes I sorted out our provisions into some kind of order. During these early morning drives I thought what a lot we missed through normally getting up so late. It was remarkably warm that spring, and at that hour the air was wonderfully fresh, the scent of grass and early flowering hedgerows giving a feeling of tranquillity totally at odds with these preparations for conflict and tumult.

It was a struggle to arrange the refreshments as we lurched over rough and bumpy fields. The eatables were supposed to be neatly laid out on trays on top of and below the serving counter, with the thick, clumsy mugs set out as close to the tea urns as possible, but nothing seemed to stay put. I don't know how many fragile custard tarts slid to the floor and were squashed underfoot, but despite these difficulties I was happier than I had been for months. Mary was a delightful companion on these trips, well able to cope with any disasters en route. She was about ten years older than me, and I never knew her cool, rather detached manner to desert her under any circumstances, even when our van almost overturned in a deep rut and once again sent all my carefully displayed refreshments flying in all directions. She seemed to find it rather amusing and obligingly stopped and helped me to put them all back in place. There was nothing else we could do as we had almost reached our destination. (I hoped the floor of our van had been as clean as it looked!)

As we arrived, eager customers emerged from the meagre huts and gun emplacements and surged round our van, demanding we open at once. I think they looked on us not only as bringers of refreshment but also as entertainment, a welcome break in the monotony of their solitary daily routine. I, of course, was an easy butt for their occasionally ribald form of wit, though Mary gave them the cold shoulder when their jokes became too risqué – those I understood, that is. Some passed me completely by, and I had to ask Mary for an explanation of any she considered suitable for such an over-protected fledgling to hear.

May 20th 1940   *Oaklands*

By now my father was beginning to suffer from the same restlessness that had previously attacked me, and we weren't at all surprised when, with many of his contemporaries, he applied to join the Home Guard which was just then being formed. Since his work at ICI was both important and demanding, my mother was very concerned about him creeping around the countryside at all hours of the night on the lookout for enemy parachutists. But he was adamant. Having received the Military Cross during the First World War he bitterly resented being considered too old at the age of fifty-six for any active service, and I think he really enjoyed being of some use. At any rate, he became more buoyant and enthusiastic, and I caught glimpses now and then of what he must have been like as a young man.

May 30th 1940   *Oaklands*

Things began to warm up with a vengeance. The news was bad on all sides. The men of the British Expeditionary Force were in dire trouble, fighting a desperate rearguard action towards Dunkirk against overwhelming odds. Their epic rescue by the Royal Navy and hundreds of ships of every description, even down to tiny rowing boats, was in progress, when a sudden late evening call came through for us to load up with as many stores as our mobile canteen could carry, and proceed very early next morning to a certain large house off the Chester Road where our presence would be urgently needed. A contingent of troops would be arriving at that time, we were told, and although we had a vague idea of who they might be we were certainly not prepared for the reality of the situation that would face us.

I knew the house quite well, having been invited for tennis and cocktail parties on several occasions, but on that particular morning the place was almost unrecognisable, every door and window wide open, while some sort of frenzied activity seemed to be going on indoors.

A purposeful young Army officer came over and instructed us to park on the edge of the spacious lawn outside the front door. It seemed like sacrilege to ruin that perfectly kept grass, but we soon saw the reason for this when several ten-ton Army lorries lumbered up the winding drive and proceeded to disgorge what seemed like hundreds of soldiers. As officers and men hurried forward to direct them towards the empty lawns and tennis court, we saw that some of the men were in a pitiable condition, obviously completely exhausted. Once on the soft grass they dropped where they stood, several appearing even to fall asleep. That magical early summer which had so assisted their escape from Dunkirk still held, and although the early morning must have been a cool blessing for some, there were others who were shaking with the chill of deferred shock and incipient fever.

Soon all over the lawns and grass tennis court there wasn't a single patch of green to be seen beneath the wave of khaki and sunburnt limbs, and after a moment of stunned amazement Mary and I hurriedly opened up the canteen and prepared for the expected onslaught of customers. Piles of jam doughnuts, row upon row of bright yellow custard tarts, pies and biscuits, every possible variety of chocolate bar, gleaming white mugs and steaming urns of tea awaited them, yet there was no immediate rush. At first, no one moved. We looked at each other in surprise, then, undaunted, Mary leant out of the window and raised her voice.

"Come and get it, boys!" she called. "Your tea's getting cold!"

That had the desired effect. Many, who before had lain as dead, now rose painfully to their feet and dragged themselves towards us as if they couldn't quite believe their good fortune.

Then, gradually, word got round, and for the next few hours we worked non-stop. The tangled activity going on inside the house continued, as local people rushed to help, bringing with them food, blankets and clothing. Our tea urns were refilled again and again from the house, and by late morning that beautiful garden began to take on an almost festive air. Amazing, I thought, what a mug of strong, sweet tea can do to restore the balance of the average Briton! Talk, even bursts of laughter, broke out as men sat in groups, recalling details of their hazardous escape. Some even began to crack jokes with us instead of the muttered thanks we'd received at first, and a sort of cheerful acceptance of their appalling experience began to permeate through that vast crowd. You could actually *feel* the change of mood, the lifting of spirit, almost *see* them thinking that at least they were back home, admittedly not in very good nick, as they put it, but at least in one piece – and they'd done their best. What more could anyone ask of them? Now, they'd just have to pick up the bits and go on from there. The people in charge would have to decide the next move. Meanwhile, they were resting their tired bodies on the soft, green grass of an English garden, drinking a real English cup of tea, and for the moment everything else would have to be put 'on hold'.

So that was that – and what had been a disastrous defeat was somehow turned into a sort of Pyrrhic victory. What a crazy lot we are! I thought. Here is our sceptred isle in severe and terribly real danger, yet we're all so perverse as to feel a totally irrational sense of *relief* that we're completely on our own, bereft of allies, convinced we can face an overwhelming and ever more powerful enemy! This was surely carrying optimism too far, yet curiously I felt the same as everyone else. We could rely on ourselves, even in the face of Hitler's possible invasion. Extraordinary recklessness really, for what an easy conquest this small island would be, with twenty or so miles between it and the French coast being little more than a castle moat! Yet there it was.

"At least we know where we stand," the grocer commented philosophically. "There's no one to let us down now," said my friends at Sandiway police station. "Don't you worry, miss, we can rely on ourselves," declared the postman. We heard these sentiments everywhere, and they were only further strengthened by Churchill's fighting speeches over the wireless, to which we all listened avidly. A sort of latent aggression began to stiffen our spines and set our minds to working out how and with what weapons we might shortly be called upon to repel possible attacks on our homes – and suddenly it seemed as though the whole country was welding itself into a single determined state of mind. I imagined that this mental attitude must have been deeply familiar to those other countries over in Europe who were now under the Nazi yoke, but naturally, since none of us in Britain had any recent experience of this, the primitive killer-instinct lurking in all of us when facing a threat of attack had lain dormant. Its sudden awakening was strange and rather frightening. Even our vicar, the calmest and most gentle of men, seemed to be assailed by it. For him 'militant here on earth' took on an entirely new meaning, and there was a certain glint behind his hitherto mild gaze that had nothing to do with turning the other cheek.

Suddenly, no one made gentle fun of the Home Guard any more – in fact, its numbers increased dramatically. Everyone in Cheshire seemed to be gearing up into a state of frenzied expectation. All the big towns were going to be flattened by German bombers – there would be invasion all along the south coast – enemy parachutists would come floating silently downwards on to the sleeping countryside and make their insidious way towards designated targets: they might even be found, armed to the teeth, lurking among the shadows of our own gardens, ready to pounce – and, of course, few of them would be easy to spot beneath their various disguises. Nuns, of course, were particularly under suspicion. So simple to conceal deadly weapons, portable wireless sets and other equipment under their loose robes. If you met a nun in what you considered an unusual place for her to be, that's when you had to be on the alert. Approach with caution! Always look at their feet, the knowledgeable advised, the size of shoe was sure to give them away.

June 10th 1940   *Oaklands*
Other friends of mine were also becoming increasingly frustrated at home, but it wasn't until a bridge-playing

friend of my mother's took me aside and asked me what I was going to do with myself now that the Royal Academy of Music was out of the question, that I finally came to any decision.

"I really don't know," I answered despondently. "My parents want me to join the ATS in Chester – but that means I'd still be at home doing nothing when not actually on duty."

She saw the force of this objection immediately. "Well, you could join one of the services which are stationed elsewhere," she suggested. "After all, I expect you girls will be called up before long, anyway, and then you'll have no choice. You may as well volunteer now for whichever service you think you'd prefer."

We were silent for a moment, then she added in her quiet voice, "Your younger brother's in the Navy, isn't he?" And all at once my decision was made for me, clear-cut and irrevocable.

To be by the sea! To watch ships coming and going, even perhaps to go on board! Why ever hadn't I thought of this before?

I thanked her profusely, and much to her amusement said I must go at once and fix it all up before anyone stopped me.

June 12th 1940   *Oaklands*

After that things moved rapidly. I rang Joy Harper, a friend who lived quite near by, who I knew was as bored and frustrated with home life as I was, and she jumped at my suggestion. We agreed not to tell our parents till it was all settled in case of opposition. I rang the WRNS Head-quarters in London, and was told to go and volunteer in Manchester, where we would also have a medical exami-nation. It all seemed too easy, but I was worried about my short sight. Did the Navy take anyone who needed glasses?

I needn't have worried. The doctor was quite encouraging.

"Your eyesight's all right for clerical work," he told me. "You can join under the category of Wren Writer. Of course, you won't be able to do anything very active in case you lose your glasses, but otherwise you'll pass."

On our way home we were jubilant. We'd been accepted, and would be called up within the next few weeks.

"In the meantime," I said, rather uncertainly, "we'll have to tell our parents."

"Well, they can't do anything about it now," said Joy firmly. "We've signed on for the duration as mobile Wrens, so they can send us anywhere they want."

"I hope it won't be too much of a shock," I said, suddenly thinking of my mother with all three of her children liable to be ordered anywhere. "Still, I suppose we'll get leave."

Our misgivings were unnecessary. After the initial shock had worn off both our families accepted our decision and even seemed rather proud of our independence. One or two of our friends, however, sounded dubious.

"It'll be horribly uncomfortable," they warned us. "You'll probably have to share a room with heaven knows who, and have people order you about – and wear uniform and clumping shoes – and most likely, thick black wool stockings. How can you bear the thought? You'll hate it!"

But none of these arguments swayed us. They couldn't now, anyway. We were in the women's Navy for better or worse, and had to make the best of it. Neither Joy nor I cared if we left our safe and comfortable, if rather dull homes (ungrateful pair that we were!). We were about to take the plunge into a totally different kind of life, and we didn't mind *how* different just as long as it *was* different.

Two weeks later we received our marching orders, and were relieved yet surprised to find that we were both being

sent to a Royal Naval Air Station at St Merryn, near
Padstow in north Cornwall. What, no ships? And would
there be any sea to look at? The air station was known as
HMS Vulture, and we later learnt that all naval and air
stations were named as if they were one of His Majesty's
ships. We were ordered to report on August 9th in London,
at Paddington station, to catch the 1200 hours train to
Padstow, and would be met on the platform by Second
Officer Johnson WRNS.

After we informed our friends of our imminent
departure their compassion and apprehension exceeded all
bounds. We were given farewell parties, farewell presents,
farewell admonitions and commiserations until you'd have
thought we were going to the moon. None of them
seemed to understand the sense of excitement we felt, or
the expectation of things new and demanding which were
waiting for us. Perhaps some of them may have envied us a
little, but lacked the adventurous spirit to join up too.

August 9th 1940   *en route for Royal Naval Air Station*
                    (RNAS), St Merryn, Padstow, north Cornwall
Our parents wanted to see us off from Paddington, but this
Joy and I firmly vetoed, afraid of a tearful farewell scene, so
they agreed to accompany us only as far as Chester. It was
just as well, since my mother had last minute qualms.

Arriving on the station platform at Paddington, Joy and
I found ourselves among a large group of girls and quite a
few older women, whose names were being ticked off on a
long list by an efficient looking WRNS officer in a neat
dark blue uniform and attractive tricorne hat, on the front
of which was the naval crown, picked out in red and gold
above an anchor surrounded by blue leaves, the same
colour as the two sleevebands denoting her rank. After our
names had been noted down we all stood around, glancing
appraisingly at each other. None of us, of course, were in
uniform, and there was a noticeable difference in the style

of our civilian clothes and luggage. It was a blazingly hot day, so most of us were wearing light summer dresses, carrying jackets or coats over our arms; but there were others whose shabby garments and dilapidated suitcases spoke clearly of deprivation, and who tended to huddle rather anxiously together as if for support amongst those whose appearance matched their own. How true about birds of a feather!

Joy and I instinctively drifted towards the girls who looked and spoke as we did, and travelled down with several kindred spirits in whose company we quite enjoyed the long trip. But even the most comfortable train journey can pall after some time, and we were all relieved when we finally pulled into Padstow station, and were able to get out and stretch our cramped limbs. The carriages had all been full of service men and women as well as civilians, and our only diversion had been a visit to the dining car for sand-wiches and coffee (our travelling expenses were paid for) and short periods of standing in the corridor by an open window, staring out at the magnificent panorama of countryside, inhaling the fresh air which later held a tang of the sea.

Once at Padstow, as we sat amongst our luggage on the low wall round the little harbour, waiting for some form of transport to take us to St Merryn, I began for the first time to have doubts. Perhaps it was because I was tired. It had been a long day for we'd caught a very early train that morning from Cheshire. Now, as I looked round at my companions I wondered suddenly what on earth we thought we were going to achieve. How could girls of our age and inexperience make the slightest difference to the course of the war? It was ridiculous, the whole business. Absurd.

Then I noticed small groups of holidaymakers further round the quayside gazing at us with a sort of amused interest, as if wondering what so many of us could be doing there, wasting a wonderful sunny afternoon. I turned away from them to stare down at the shimmering blue water, the fishermen's small boats floating lazily at their moorings, and the pretty, white-painted houses and shops surrounding the quayside and thought suddenly, you'd never know there was a war on.

Then there was a sudden disturbance, and everyone gathered up their belongings as two enormous lorries lumbered towards us and ground to a noisy halt. I didn't quite know what I'd been expecting, perhaps a fleet of smart buses or comfortable coaches, certainly not these ungainly monsters that had surely seen better days.

One by one we were helped, or rather hauled up into the smelly interiors by several sturdy young sailors, who looked us over with appreciative eyes and cheerful grins before obligingly seizing our cases and slinging them in after us. We couldn't see anything ahead of us, but from the back the countryside was bathed in sunlight, so calm and peaceful it seemed a thousand miles from anything to do with war. A heady scent pursued us from the flowering hedges on either side of the road, where I could make out foxgloves and honeysuckle, and beyond them, in the quiet fields stooks of hay already stood in neat rows awaiting collection. My tired spirits rose. After all, this was why I'd joined up – for something different, and as we lurched and jolted our way along the narrow winding road, I knew for certain that everything was going to be very different indeed, though I was far from realising how soon Britain would be waking up to the unwelcome intrusion of a present which promised only blood, sweat and tears.

II

DRUM ROLL

August 9th 1940   *Royal Naval Air Station (RNAS),*
                           St Merryn, Padstow, Cornwall (HMS Vulture)
All at once the lorry ground to a shuddering halt, voices
were heard for a few moments, then we rumbled slowly
through a wide gateway with high wire fencing on either
side of it. Just inside was a low concrete building, in front
of which stood an armed sentry trying hard to preserve his
dignity as some of the girls shouted out a raucous greeting
to him. Ahead, beside a wide roadway, lay a collection of
other low buildings, some concrete, some flimsy-looking
rectangular erections of corrugated iron, which we later
learnt were Nissen huts. Outside one of the concrete
buildings we came to a sudden halt, and the driver and his
mate leapt down to open up the wooden flap at the rear of
the lorry to let us out, and we were able to get a closer look
at our unprepossessing new home.

Several WRNS personnel came out to meet us, and briskly instructed us to carry our suitcases into the various concrete huts as our names were called out. Joy and I and several of the girls we'd travelled down with were shown into the first of these, and hastily appropriated the beds nearest the doorway, looking round us with distaste.

"Blimey!" an awed Cockney voice muttered somewhere behind me. "Look at all them beds – must be twenty at least!"

Twenty? No, eighteen. Nine a side. Narrow little iron beds with only a narrow strip of dingy carpeting and a narrow locker dividing each from its neighbour. Everything narrow, meagre, impersonal, small worlds of isolation.

Although it was a very hot day all the windows were closed, and there was a curious smell of dusty concrete and new fittings. For a moment I stood transfixed, thinking this must be what an early nineteenth century workhouse could have looked like. The contrast with my comfortable bedroom at home couldn't have been greater. Was this what I had so blithely let myself in for? But then, of course, as Captain Bligh of the *Bounty* would have put it, a WRNS rating was probably the lowest form of animal life in the British Navy, so what more could we expect?

"My God!" an appalled voice spoke nearby. "What *do* they expect us to do with all our things?"

The girl standing at the end of the next bed to mine was staring at the locker beside it, frowning. I glanced at her with sudden interest. Someone else with short sight! Her eyes, behind even stronger glasses than mine, looked round at me, registering my glasses for a moment, then she dropped her suitcase, dumped her coat and handbag on to the bed and collapsed on to it with a resigned sigh.

"I have a feeling we're going to need a very strong sense of humour in this place," she remarked to no one in particular. "Why ever did I leave my job? I must have been mad to volunteer!"

I wondered what her job had been. She was obviously several years older then the girls I'd travelled down with, and her forthright manner of speaking argued a certain built-in confidence. She looked competent enough to deal with anything.

Joy had taken the bed on the other side of mine, and gave me a relieved grin as she flung her belongings down on it. I was glad to have her around. She had a definite mind of her own, with an impish quality that gave her a sense of enjoyment in everything she did, always able to see the funny side of things. She was certainly well named.

One of the beds opposite us was occupied by Elizabeth Welburn, known as Liz, possibly the most beautiful girl I'd ever seen, with brilliant large eyes that looked almost green in certain lights, and luxuriant auburn hair down to her shoulders. (Pity she'd have to cut it shorter, as it was a stern rule that once in uniform our hair was not permitted to touch our collars.) Not that that would make any difference to someone like her. Men, it seemed, had only to look at her once to fall madly in love with her, and part of her attraction was that she appeared to be quite oblivious of her looks, and never did anything to seek attention.

Next to her was Peggy Caunt, tall and vivacious, with a mass of curly dark hair framing her lively face, and a mellifluous speaking voice that was rarely silenced. Even after the most tiring night watch when most of us would be totally exhausted, she never seemed to lack energy. I wished I had as much.

As for me, I supposed I was probably what the French charmingly refer to as 'jolie-laide', which literally translates as 'pretty ugly' (meaning, I believe, someone with more style than beauty), but which has another interpretation in English that's anything but complimentary! I was always told by various terrifying great-aunts that wearing glasses didn't help, (at least, if in pursuit of social success!) and finally, in despair, my mother bought me for my seventeenth birthday a delicate pair of silver-framed, folding lorgnettes, so that I should be able to find my way surreptitiously around a ballroom and its necessary environs without disgracing myself by tripping over something or falling down a flight of stairs. After this, of course, my friends naturally christened me 'the Duchess'. I was certain my short-sighted neighbour Celia Allen wouldn't have let such a trivial thing irritate her, and of course, once in uniform none of that nonsense would apply anywhere in His Majesty's Navy.

I'd never been very introspective about anyone I met. Ever since my father gave me a Baby Corona typewriter for my tenth birthday, (he and I always communicated in verse on important occasions), I had made up stories about people. The ones I've really known and liked had all been products of my imagination, created by me to feel and behave exactly as I wished them to, and who never argued or answered back or asked anything of me. In that way, I was never disappointed or let down. How different things were now! Having to live so closely with such a varied crowd, I'd be forced to see them as real, with very different attitudes and perceptions to mine. It was high time I left my little fantasy world and came down to earth with a bump. Very salutary!

Giving myself a mental shake, I became aware that all around us were comments of surprise or disgust, hastily suppressed as the WRNS petty officer assigned to our hut came to show us the general layout of our future home.

She explained to us that each hut was named after one of the commanders on the station. Ours was Bruce Hut, after Lieutenant Commander Merlin Bruce whom we would see before long.

Obediently, we followed her down a narrow corridor into the ablutions hut, a bit basic but at least clinically new and shiny, then out into the corridor again to the main recreation hut and the vast dining room, which she called the mess. Both were of the same unprepossessing type as Bruce Hut, with windows down each side and doors at both ends. Not so bad in this marvellous weather, I thought, but whatever shall we do in the winter! Then I noticed the endless lines of piping throughout the buildings which could only be for heating, so that was one major problem solved.

At the end of our guided tour the petty officer glanced at her watch. "Pity you all arrived so late," she said. "Supper's usually at six and it's already nearly seven. You'd better go in straight away or it'll all be cold."

It couldn't have mattered very much either way. The stew which served us was little short of revolting, lukewarm and swimming in grease, with potatoes and carrots only half cooked and some chunks of indefinable meat hidden under dark brown clotted gravy. I'd never been very fussy about what I ate, but my appetite now deserted me entirely, and I made do with a couple of thick slices of bread with margarine and an enormous mug of strong tea with tinned milk and far too much sugar. It was even worse than the vilely sweet tea we had served in our mobile canteen, but then I'd ceased to care. It was better than nothing, and now that so many female cooks and stewards had arrived perhaps the general standard of nourishment would improve.

August 10th 1940   *RNAS St Merryn*
That first week was to be the strangest I'd ever lived through. There were so many things to get used to, the most difficult being our sleeping quarters. The beds felt as if the mattresses had been stuffed with potatoes, so narrow, lumpy and uncomfortable it was many nights before any of us could sleep for long, while the barrage of snoring from certain areas of the hut rendered parts of the night hideous. And as if this were not enough we had to endure an entirely novel way of being woken up. About six o'clock on

that first morning I had expected loud ringing of bells, but instead, we heard rough voices overhead uttering jovial shouts of "Wakey, wa-a-akey!" followed by "Show a leg there! Show a leg!" and in sleepy amazement looked up into grinning faces staring down at us from a gaping hole in the roof. Apparently they were ship's carpenters sent to mend it after it had been damaged in a brief air raid several days before our arrival. None of us had realised that so far our only protection from the elements had been a thick strip of tarpaulin nailed across the gap! Obviously, by some oversight, the repair work had been forgotten, probably in the bustle of our arrival.

The sailors were given very short shrift as furious voices told them exactly where to go and to be quick about it. At first they were inclined to argue, saying they'd never get the job finished at this rate, but eventually they withdrew reluctantly, and we were able to start getting up. Fortunately, our efficient WRNS petty officer, on hearing of this unwelcome visitation, promptly set the wheels in motion for the completion of the roof at a more appropriate time.

It took some time to get used to calling the floor the 'deck', the walls 'bulkheads', the dining room the 'mess' and even, when we left the camp by the inevitable ten-ton lorry, to refer to 'going ashore' by the crowning misnomer of the 'liberty-boat'! I hoped no one would expect me to call my handbag my 'ditty-box', the receptacle which contained all a sailor's personal papers, paybook and letters, (what Chaucer might have termed a 'bag of needments'). I began to feel I was living in a sort of looking-glass world, and wondered if I'd ever fit in.

August 11th 1940   *RNAS St Merryn*

Our first officer in charge, a tall, smart woman of about forty-five, summoned us all to the recreation hut for some general instructions about what the Service would expect from us. She began by informing us that WRNS officers were to be addressed as 'Ma'am' by all naval ratings, and ended her talk with a pointed diatribe about class.

"There is no such thing as class here," she stated firmly, stressing the word while glancing momentarily in our direction. "As Wren ratings you are all equal, and I will have no distinctions between any of you. Naturally, you will take orders from a Leading Wren, but that will be on account of her seniority in rank and for no other reason." She allowed this to sink in for a few moments, then added, "We're all in this together, don't forget. And it's not going to be a picnic."

This lecture was probably necessary as the differences in background were palpably obvious, and to begin with I don't think some of us were too tolerant of the behaviour of several of our hut mates. We didn't openly make fun of them, though much that was natural and unremarkable to them seemed funny, even rather embarrassing to us.

Their nightly salutations of "G'night, 'Enery!", "Night, night, Stan!" as they fondly kissed the bedside photographs of their various boyfriends, were frequently interspersed with endearments of a more intimate nature, while their sense of humour was ribald in the extreme. We learnt some quite unrepeatable jokes which, when we finally understood the allusions, reduced us to smothered laughter in the face of the shocked stares of some of our more strictly reared companions. Our vocabulary, also, was being rapidly enlarged, though it was questionable whether that would have pleased any of our parents.

I'd never thought about this before, but I began to realise that it wasn't altogether easy for women to live peacefully in such close proximity with each other, and never to be alone when they wanted to be. Even at boarding school at Seaford, as a sixth former, we'd only shared two to a bedroom. Women of the same background, whose style of living bore some resemblance, might enjoy the company of likeminded souls, but for girls of different backgrounds it was difficult to cross the divide. So much we took for granted was far beyond any of their expectations, and the confidence we'd automatically gained from comfortable surroundings, affection and solid family support was probably unknown to many of them. At first I felt we were viewed with slight awe, even envy or resentment, our accents and behaviour covertly ridiculed behind our backs, but since we were all now in the same melting pot we'd just have to make the best of it.

August 15th 1940   *RNAS St Merryn*
For those of us who were watchkeepers in the Signals Distribution Office (the SDO), it was necessary between watches to sleep during the daytime. At first this was impossible with all the comings and goings of the WRNS stewards who came to clean the hut each morning, chatting loudly as they did so. They didn't seem to understand why the watchkeepers seemed to be allowed so much time off duty during the day, and rather sarcastically christened us the 'Intelligence Squad'. But after a while, when they saw how genuinely tired we were, particularly after the long night watches, they took pity on us and began to be quieter, and to show us little acts of kindness by surreptitiously bringing us our lunch in bed so that we didn't have to get up and dress after only a few hours sleep in order to go and eat in the mess.

This was greatly appreciated, and we began to respond. We had just learnt that the factory which had been turning out our WRNS uniform, having been bombed back in late July, would be unlikely to be able to send us any for the time being, so we were still in summer dresses. This slightly pierced our complacency and made us feel rather guilty. A few of the girls and older women who had joined up as cooks and stewards obviously came from very poor families, and we heard that some of them had brought hardly a single change of clothing with them. I was forcibly reminded of our evacuees from Bootle, and looking at the array of dresses and underwear I and my immediate neighbours in Bruce Hut had brought with us I was suddenly smitten, as were they, with a feeling of guilt, that it was rather unfair and we ought to do something about it.

There was one particularly sad member of our hut, whose bed was just two away from Joy's, a pale, nervous little thing named Ada, who gazed at us all with red-rimmed, apprehensive eyes, and hardly dared to speak. Apparently she was eighteen-years-old, but so thin and undernourished and lost looking she seemed about twelve. After three days it was noticed that she seemed to live night and day in the same clothes and was never even seen to wash. Not surprisingly her immediate neighbours began to make remarks about the smell that arose whenever she prepared to go to bed. As a result, after some guarded consultation, a number of us were suddenly seized with enthusiasm to see what could be done for our Eliza Doolittle. Peggy's neighbour, Maureen, who had been a hairdresser in civilian life, offered to cut and restyle Ada's hair, after a sympathetic older woman had agreed to supervise a very thorough bathing session. Not to be outdone, we contributed our most highly scented toilet soap, bath salts and talcum powder, as well as face flannel, toothbrush, toothpaste and several hair combs. After Ada's hair had been cleverly cut into a short, easy curly style, Maureen, in a further fit of enthusiasm, presented her with a brand new hairbrush with strict instructions how and when to use it. Throughout all this our victim remained silent and passive, seemingly unable to take in what was happening to her.

There was to be a further benefit from our enthusiasm. One of the Wrens in Bruce Hut who worked in naval stores, came up trumps with underclothes and nightwear not only for Ada, but also for any of the others who had no change of clothing with them. You have to say it for the Navy. They were nothing if not severely practical.

Ada's transformation was startling. We'd had a general

whip round with the result that she was now attired in a pretty flowered cotton skirt, white blouse and navy blue cardigan, together with white socks and a pair of navy gym shoes from naval stores. We were all naturally very proud of our achievement. From the drab, unhappy waif there now emerged a smart young girl, quite good looking, who stared round-eyed at her image in the inadequate mirror over her locker, and was seen to smile tremulously for the first time before finally bursting into tears of gratitude.

After that there was no stopping anyone. The ice had been well and truly broken, and before long some of us began to be besieged with questions asking our advice about general appearance and grooming, while Maureen had probably never been so busy in her life.

Amazing what a bit of encouragement can do! Once they'd discovered that the potential for good looks wasn't the prerogative only of rich girls, the younger, less well off ones took to all this like ducks to water, and although the older element tended to look on indulgently, it wasn't long before they too were tentatively asking Maureen to show them how to do their hair. There seemed to be a general feeling that all of us had to be able to do justice to our uniform, though no one had any idea how soon this would arrive.

August 17th 1940   *RNAS St Merryn*
There was no getting away from it. Brightly coloured summer dresses and light summer sandals didn't look right on a parade ground, and we were all horribly self-conscious and uncomfortable during our daily torturous drill sessions. No matter how often we marched obediently up and down the concrete strip we felt more and more ridiculous, as our unsuitable footwear made it impossible to match the expected long stride of the Royal Navy. Worse still, the increasingly rapid click of our heels was greeted by smothered guffaws from watching ratings, who seemed to

view us as entertainment. As we struggled to obey the crisp, well-articulated commands of our unfortunate WRNS officer, her shouts of 'Left, right! Left, right!' rose in pitch and speed until she was forced to call a halt for lack of breath. Luckily, no one insisted we salute officers until we were in uniform, for which we were all deeply thankful. There was a limit to absurdity.

"How often do you think we'll have to go through this damned rigmarole?" Celia demanded crossly, gently massaging her feet back in Bruce Hut after that first disastrous session. "No wonder those sailors were laughing. We must have looked absolute idiots!"

"All women look silly marching," said Joy, kicking off her shoes and carefully inspecting them. "Oh, God, look at that! My sandals will never stand up to this."

Peggy, lying back on her bed, laughed suddenly. "That poor woman! She'll have no voice left if she goes on shouting like that. Thank God I'm not an officer!"

Liz yawned and stretched herself on her bed. "We'd better wear tennis shoes next time," she said. "I wonder why it's necessary for us to do drill, anyway. I mean, where are we ever going to march to?"

"Church parade," said Celia, laconically. "Petty Officer Jones told me we have to march up to the church service here on the camp. The Roman Catholics take the transport over to the Catholic church at—"

"The liberty-boat!" we corrected her with one voice.

"Oh hell!" said Celia, and sighed. Life was sometimes very hard.

And yet, I had to admit that I was beginning to enjoy being here. At home there had been hardly anyone of my own age except Joy to talk to, certainly few people to laugh with, whereas here we laughed a lot. So many things seemed to be funny, and our officers, both male and female, were pleasant and helpful.

I particularly enjoyed the aircraft recognition sessions,

learning to differentiate between the shape and sound of
our own planes, and the outlines and heavy throbbing
sound of the German engines. There was more to amuse us
when we were given physical training instruction. This
included some unexpected methods of incapacitating
enemy parachutists should they approach near enough for
us to do so – presumably before they could shoot us! If the
WRNS physical training instructor hadn't taken it all so
seriously this wouldn't have been greeted with such gales
of laughter, but the very thought of it being even faintly
possible was too much for us.

"If me mum could see me now," commented one of the
girls from our hut between shock and amusement, "she'd
'ave a fit, she would!"

That thought had also crossed my mind, and struck me
again, more forcibly, when we were learning to shoot,
staggering under the weight and vicious kick-back of the
.303 rifles against our shoulders as we fired.

The sergeant of Marines who instructed us was a brave
man to stand anywhere in our vicinity, since it proved
impossible for even the sturdiest among us to hold the rifle
completely steady when trying to take aim. It waved
drunkenly about from side to side, and after a while he
called a halt, and stood looking down at us in resigned
silence.

"It's no good," he said at last. "You'll have to do it on
your stomachs."

So we all lay down on the dusty concrete, feet widely
outspread in an inelegant and uncomfortable position,
though it somehow anchored us firmly enough to take
more accurate aim. I was far more successful with the .45
Webley Scott revolver. At least we could stand up to fire,
and poor eyesight or not, both Celia and I managed to hit
a matchbox from a respectable distance.

This brought with it a rather disturbing thought. The
camp was still unfinished and exposed on part of its

perimeter, particularly the part facing Porthcothan Bay, only a short way across the fields, and suddenly it struck me that what seemed rather an amusing pastime, might one day really have to be put to the test. For the first time a faint shaft of apprehension went through me as I visualised the enemy's approach, shadowed and silent, perhaps by sea or parachute, figures creeping stealthily out of the darkness or the early morning mist, to take command of the whole station. Was it really possible that we might have to play a part in its defence? That spelt responsibility, something I'd never experienced. Since I was born there had always been someone else to take responsibility for me. But now, suddenly, I could find myself facing a situation when something or someone might actually depend on *me*, on my own reaction and response. If I held a gun in my hand it might even have to be my own decision to use it. No hiding behind anyone else. There were a few armed sentries stationed at various points, also a small number of soldiers from the Pioneer Corps, mainly rather elderly from what we saw of them, who were installing pom-pom guns here and there, one just outside the far door of Bruce Hut. Our air defences were even more inadequate. Most of our aircraft were Rocs, Skuas, Fairey Fulmars and the reliable Swordfish (affectionately known as 'Stringbags') and Albacores. But all this didn't seem to add up to very much against a determined enemy attack. The chilling reality of our situation was now brought home to me with unpleasant clarity. Cheshire seemed a long way off.

August 20th 1940   *RNAS St Merryn*

The SDO was in a long, low concrete building situated up a slight incline about five minutes walk from our quarters. On one side of the SDO was a small room housing an erratic and unpredictable machine known as a teleprinter, and next to it was the telephone exchange with the all important switch for the air raid siren for use immediately a red alert message came from Plymouth. Beyond this lay the boiler room and usual amenities, and behind these the WRNS administration office and cypher office for top secret signals. On the other side of the building were the duty officer's cabin and the Captain's day cabin, and in the daytime the whole place hummed with activity. It was strangely quiet at night, for only the communications offices and duty officer's cabin were inhabited.

I always enjoyed that walk up to the SDO for the long night watch. The heat of the day left a wonderfully fragrant residue in the night air, and when the moon rose the fields and distant low hills gradually emerged from the shadows, and the whole station behind us was brilliantly illuminated, the tops of the buildings, hangars and runways streaked with silver. This was not to be such a welcome sight later on as it made us so vulnerable to air attack.

The Chief Petty Officer in charge – or to give him his full title, Chief Yeoman of Signals – was a true yeoman of England if ever I met one, solid, competent and reliable, a big burly man with a kindly twinkle in his eye and an inexhaustible fund of patience where his new staff was concerned. He needed it, for our inexperience and initial tendency to muddle might have driven a lesser man mad, but he took it all in his stride. I suppose after having had to cope with dangerous situations at sea, handling raw female recruits might have been considered a walkover, but I think even he was a bit disconcerted at first when he began to be affectionately addressed as 'Chiefy' – one of us, I forget who, in a moment of high stress, going so far as to call out, "Chiefy darling, what the hell do I do with this?" And it was not unusual when someone, having struggled vainly to make sense of a hopelessly garbled teleprinter message, finally burst into tears of frustration, to see him put his arm comfortingly round her shoulders, saying soothingly, "No need to worry, lass, we'll call back for clarification. Look – like this." And he would take her place at the infernal machine and show her once again how to ask for a repeat of the message.

Under his guidance we gradually developed into a fairly useful team. Now and then Lieutenant Commander Merlin Bruce (the same officer after whom our hut was named) would breeze into the SDO when he was duty officer, to look through the signals, unobtrusively observing us all from a pair of alert blue eyes that missed nothing. Everything about him bespoke energy, force and drive. He was one of those neat, smallish men, well-proportioned and compact, who seem to be found in the forefront of every activity they undertake, and though not particularly good looking with his pale reddish hair and brows, was blessed with considerable charm, and we were always on our toes to please him.

August 28th 1940   *RNAS St Merryn*
By now we had begun to settle down into our new routine. The so-called Intelligence Squad had joined up under the category of 'Writer', a naval term for secretary or clerk. St Merryn was not an operational station, merely training, and our job was the receiving, processing and sending out of signals to do with the running of the air station, movement of planes and personnel, weather reports and general information.

We worked a three-watch system over a period of four days, and although this routine took some time to get used to, it had its advantages, since it gave us the opportunity to enjoy the continuing glorious weather during the day. After the long night duty ending at eight o'clock, Liz, who was also on my watch, suggested that we had a quick breakfast, and instead of going to bed walk down to nearby Treyarnon Bay, to swim or stretch out on the warm golden sand and sleep under the shade of the surrounding high rocks. It was like being on our own private beach, since all the holidaymakers seemed to have left.

Later we would go up to the little café at the top end of the beach for a snack or a delicious Cornish cream tea, food rationing not yet having been introduced in this part of England. This more than made up for the deficiencies of the camp cooking, though even that was now beginning to show signs of improvement with a few professionals in the kitchens. Many of the cooks and stewards had come straight from domestic service in big houses, and knew how to make the best of available provisions. Despite this improvement, however, those of us who were not wholly dependent on the princely sum of twelve shillings and sixpence a week offered us by Their Lordships at the Admiralty, usually went into Padstow when off duty in the evenings, to a modest café by the harbour where, for about two shillings and sixpence, we would supplement our naval diet with huge helpings of fried eggs, bacon, sausages and chips. Afterwards, while waiting for the 'liberty-boat' to take us back to camp we would sit on the low harbour wall and chat to the friendly Cornish fishermen, while gazing out across the sparkling water as it gradually lost its brilliance in the gathering dusk.

August 30th 1940   *RNAS St Merryn*
Despite the dictum about there being no difference of class, difference of rank in the camp was still strictly adhered to. Wren ratings were not allowed to go out with officers, and for some of us this might have led to a life totally devoid of social contact, since the naval ratings were adamant in dubbing us 'officers' girls' and never once attempted to invite us out anywhere. They were usually willing, though, to help in any way that was needed, and were always mending our bicycles whenever we got a puncture. By the second week many of us had sent for these from home. Mine was an ancient affair, a sort of 'sit-up-and-beg' type of machine which had been in our cellar for heaven knows how long after we'd ceased to use it, but which was given

a new lease of life by a sailor named Stan who was a wizard with anything mechanical.

The situation over differences of rank was soon smoothed out. There were many officers on the station, and in some mysterious fashion it wasn't long before we got to know one or two of the younger pilots; and after that it was easy, except, of course, that we had to meet them away from the camp (I mean, ashore). We'd learnt that once in uniform we wouldn't be able to accept invitations to dine or dance at hotels or restaurants unless we wore 'civvies' so that our lack of rank wouldn't be noticed, and as long as we were discreet this worked very well, since naturally the officers themselves conspired to make this possible. Very soon, swimming parties with pilots from the various squadrons became a routine outing, either at Porthcothan or Treyarnon Bay, as well as evening trips over to St Izzy, to a quaint little pub called The Ring o' Bells. There was an ancient and horribly tinny piano on which I was always ordered to play and sing some of the songs I'd brought with me to Cornwall. The evenings usually ended with raucous choruses of well-known tunes, though with very different and distinctly bawdy words which fortunately amused the landlord and other customers. After that, it was a repeat of the hazardous journey we'd experienced on the way from St Merryn. Thirteen of us had begged a lift from one of the RNVR lieutenants who owned a sturdy little Morris Cowley. How he managed to drive I'll never know, with bodies clinging like limpets to every possible handhold on the outside of the car or packed inside like sardines. There was a lot of noise and laughter, and we were lucky not to meet any higher ranked personnel as we approached the camp, surreptitiously disembarking some way from the entrance and disappearing like wraiths into our various quarters after our whispered goodnights.

September 1st 1940   *RNAS St Merryn*

This pleasant, almost holiday atmosphere was not to last much longer. On a perfect sunny afternoon when Liz and I and some other off-duty Wrens had gone to swim at Porthcothan Bay with some of the pilots of 811 Squadron, it was shattered once and for all. We'd been in the warm water some time and were lazily drying ourselves, stretched out on the sand and thinking about a cream tea, when an unusual sound overhead caused Mike, one of the pilots, to hold up his hand for silence and glance quickly up at the sky. We all sat up then and strained our ears.

"Messerschmitt," he said briefly, and a moment later someone else added, "And a Spitfire."

Then, as the sound of the aircraft grew suddenly nearer, it was followed by the sharp, staccato rattle of machine-gun fire, and there were shouts of "Quick! Take cover!"

Scrambling to our feet we made a dash for the fallen rocks at the base of the cliffs and dived between them, cowering there as all hell appeared to break loose over our heads, with bullets spattering past us in all directions. We had a rather too clear view of the dogfight, the only one I'd ever seen. Although the bombing had begun in July down in the south of England there had been no raids at all up in Cheshire, so this was a sudden and most unpleasant shock. I glanced round at my companions. All the pilots, even the squadron leaders, were young, some only a few years older than Liz or Joy or me. Youth was no protection then. We all had lives to lose, perhaps not even from having to risk them up in an aeroplane. Easy enough to be killed here on a sunny beach by a machine-gun bullet that wasn't even intended for any of us in the first place. I suddenly felt cold.

We waited tensely for the crash that would indicate the end of the dogfight, but none came. All we heard was the sudden sharp whine of the engine as the Messerschmitt made for the open sea, followed by the swift acceleration of the Spitfire in hot pursuit. Then both sounds gradually died away and we emerged rather shakily from our rocky haven.

"Do you think they'll come back?" I asked, then thought, what a stupid question, how could anyone possibly know? But Mike only smiled reassuringly at me and replied: "Shouldn't think so, but there may be others. This beach is rather exposed if any German pilot wants to do a spot of machine-gunning and you just happen to be out here lying on the sand."

We stared at him with shocked expressions. Surely nobody would—?

His face hardened. "Just be ready to take cover, anyway. Don't sit too far from the cliffs." Then he added slowly, "They've already had something like that over at St Eval – before you lot arrived. Several of the WAAFs were wounded. The RAF station is only two miles or so from St Merryn."

As the implication of this sank in, his mood changed and he smiled.

"Well, at least this isn't going to stop me having one of those cream teas. We'll probably be as safe inside that café as anywhere else."

Safer perhaps. Safer than on a naval air station not far from an RAF bomber base which had already been shot up.

September 2nd 1940   *RNAS St Merryn*
Things were hotting up. As if that dogfight had been a foretaste of things to come, St Merryn suddenly became a target for a series of day and night bombing attacks for which we received no warning until well after the first bomb had landed with a heart-stopping crash. By the time the red warning from Plymouth had come through to our telephone exchange and the camp siren set to its eerie wailing, we were usually down in our air raid shelter just outside the far end of Bruce Hut. The first night attack caused chaos, since we had had no opportunity to get used

to the routine with which we were to become so familiar later. At the first indication of trouble we were supposed to roll out of bed, throw on tin hat, coat and shoes, grab torch, pillow and rug from our beds and make a dash through our outer door to the shelter, bent almost double beneath the fire of the pom-pom gun just outside it. Unfortunately, what with the noise of the attacking aircraft, warning shouts from various WRNS officers and cries of pain as we stumbled through the darkness down the awkward shelter steps, the poor old chap from the Pioneer Corps got thoroughly over-excited and ended up losing control of his gun, letting its head drop downwards, and shooting off his own big toe after missing some of the fleeing Wrens by inches.

This was the beginning of an exhausting period which seemed to go on for ever. A slightly younger man took over the pom-pom gun, though I never knew if he actually hit any enemy aircraft with it, and we all became accustomed, though still half asleep, to the rapid nightly retreat to our uncomfortable shelter. It was two thirds underground, with latticed wooden flooring placed directly over the earth which even after the lightest summer shower became unpleasantly damp and muddy.

As the attacks grew more frequent and lasted longer all kinds of creature comforts began to appear. Apart from torches and books, several of the girls brought out yards of knitting which grew in length and inaccuracy the fiercer the raids became. But there was one night when the crump-crump was much too close for comfort, and everyone raised their heads from their books or dropped a few more stitches, staring at each other in alarm. We waited, tense with anticipation.

Surely the next bomb couldn't miss—! I became aware of Peggy nudging me and turned my head.

"Sing something," she muttered.

I stared at her in dazed disbelief. "*Sing*—? What, *now*? I can't! It's the middle of the night!"

She nodded urgently. "Never mind! Go on! It'll give everyone something else to think about."

"More likely give them hysterics," I whispered back, glancing across at two of our opposite neighbours, who were clutching each other frantically as if about to give way to panic.

Peggy nudged me again. "We must do *something*. We can't just sit here and *wait*—!"

"Oh, all right," I said, too tired to argue. "What the hell—! What'll you have – Verdi – or Puccini?"

"Sing 'I'll walk beside you'," she hissed in my ear. "The song you sang last week at The Ring o' Bells at St Izzy, the one everyone liked."

"Well, you've asked for it," I said, "but do remember this isn't exactly the best time for singing."

Clearing my sleep-ridden throat I began to sing very softly, unsure of my reception, but apart from one or two terrified squeaks from opposite me whenever a bomb fell rather close by, everyone seemed to be listening, and at the end several voices asked me to sing again.

What a strange night that was! I must have sung at least five songs and arias, gradually becoming almost oblivious to the pandemonium raging above us. I suppose I was luckier than some of the others, since music could always take hold of me in this way. By the time I had reached the final passionate phrase of Madam Butterfly's 'One fine day' with the orchestra at full throttle, I was miles away from St Merryn, and therefore it was all the more infuriating when there was a piercing whistle and a bomb landed so close to us that the walls of the shelter shuddered violently, and the pale blue emergency light over our heads went out with a protesting splutter. Almost everyone gasped or screamed, cowering with their arms above their heads. In the thick darkness Peggy and l grabbed each other, and at that moment anger shook me out of my fear. To a musician it was unthinkable that such an aria should be deprived of its ending, and I knew I'd be haunted for the remainder of the night by those last unsung notes. It never occurred to me that perhaps none of us might be there by morning if the bombs got any nearer. All I knew was that Madame Butterfly was going to let fly her final ringing top B flat, bombs or no bombs, and let fly she did! I don't think I've ever sung a more electrifying high note than I did then, and afterwards there was a sudden complete silence in the shelter. Then, out of the darkness a voice spoke. "They must have heard you," and there was a shaky laugh. A little later in the distance the All Clear sounded, and we threaded our way cautiously outside, stepping carefully over mounds of shattered glass from some of the broken windows of Bruce Hut. It wasn't possible then to see what damage had been caused elsewhere, though the early morning light revealed a scene of disruption and chaos. The runways were pitted with craters, some of the aircraft were destroyed, and the roof of one of the hangars hung crazily over the side of the building as if it had been lifted off and deposited there again by some giant hand. Several of the other buildings on the camp had been damaged and there didn't seem to be a single window left intact. Fortunately Bruce Hut was otherwise untouched and the control tower and SDO had miraculously been missed altogether. But the most curious thing was that no one had been hurt.

"Pretty poor aim!" commented Lieutenant Commander Bruce sardonically, when he came into the SDO next morning.

September 4th 1940   *RNAS St Merryn*
After that there was little peace. Without warning, three or four times a night and even often during the day, out of a cloudless blue sky the Messerschmitts and Dorniers would sneak in directly from the sea, flying low, sometimes chased by those fiercely graceful Spitfires, or stealthily on their own, unloading the odd bomb or shooting up the camp

with machine-gun fire; and often during the night, taking their pick of targets defined with relentless clarity by an enormous, silver-circled moon that lit the camp as if it were day. Mostly they continued to go for runways or hangars, but after a while they would also roar down upon anyone out walking or on a bicycle, either on the camp or off it. Going to and from our various places of work became really hazardous, and there seemed to be no opportunity even to eat our meals in peace before the throb of enemy aircraft shook the air, and we had to rush down to the nearest shelter, balancing our food precariously on our lurching plates. Time after time, when bicycling back to camp after an outing we'd hear that ominous sound and have to throw ourselves off our bikes and into the nearest ditch or behind nearby trees.

One sunny morning, returning alone from a trip to Padstow, I was approaching the small hotel called the Cornish Arms, when a plane came screaming out of the sky behind me, the pilot firing furiously in my direction. Luckily, his speed sent the bullets whipping over my head as I flung myself from my bicycle into the ditch at the roadside, but not before I'd had a split-second glimpse of his face. He was very young with very fair hair, and he was laughing, his whole expression one of triumphant exultation. There was something vaguely familiar about his face, and for one horrible moment I found myself thinking I was looking at David, my young brother. It was only a fleeting impression, but the resemblance had been startling – the same intensely fair colouring and clear-cut features, and the way his whole face was creasing with laughter as David's often did – though not, thank God, for the same deadly reason.

I felt sick. How could anyone do such a thing? What possible satisfaction could there be in machine-gunning a solitary girl on a bicycle unless you were totally evil? I wasn't even wearing uniform. I was just a harmless civilian as far as my attacker knew, yet obviously he felt no more compunction in shooting me than he would a rabbit or a pheasant, or for that matter, I suppose, anyone who might get in his way. And yet that young German pilot must have been born, like any other child, into an 'estate of innocence' before, as the poet Thomas Traherne put it, he learnt the 'dirty devices of this world'.

As I lay there, blinded by dust thrown up from the road and deafened by the sinister rat-tat of machine-gun fire, I was shaking uncontrollably. Suppose he came back – took more careful aim? If I stayed there I wouldn't have a chance. I had to get away – but where to? If I made for the camp I could still get caught. I waited for a few minutes, crouching beneath the sparse hedge that lined the ditch, then, as the sound of the aircraft faded into the distance, decided to risk it and scrambled up, rubbing my bruised shoulder which had taken the full brunt of my fall, and wrapping my handkerchief round a nasty graze on my right knee. My bicycle, lying all anyhow, looked a wreck with the seat askew and the front wheel decidedly bent. There was no hope of riding it back to camp, and I half pushed, half dragged it to the gates in feverish haste, where Fred, on sentry duty at the guard house looked it over critically before transferring his gaze to me.

"You all right?" he enquired.

"I think so," I replied rather doubtfully. "I wasn't hit, anyway."

Fred muttered imprecations under his breath. "Wish he'd've come over this way. I'd have given him something to think about! ... You leave your bike here, Roxane – put it round the side, and I'll have a look at it for you when I go off duty."

"Thanks, Fred, you're a dear," I said. "But I don't know whether anything much can be done with it. It's pretty ancient."

Fred smiled. "Never you mind. I'll see to it. You get

along now. You look all shook up."

I did as he told me. I was rather more shaken than I'd realised, and was glad of a few minutes in a hot bath before having to go on duty.

September 5th 1940   *RNAS St Merryn*
We'd just learnt that the factory which had been working overtime to supply us with our uniforms had once again succumbed to a direct hit, and that consequently there would be no immediate expectation of the arrival of a further consignment. This information reached us by way of an Admiralty signal which became a famous collectors' item throughout ship and shore establishments, something to the effect that 'WRNS clothing will be held up until the needs of the Navy are satisfied.' This must have been greeted with incredulous delight in every mess and wardroom into which copies found their way, and one can only imagine the bewilderment of visiting foreign allies at this example of the incomprehensible British sense of humour.

I had visions of Their Lordships discussing in all seriousness the destruction of our uniforms, allocating the actual composition and despatch of the Admiralty Fleet Order to a more junior officer, obviously an unsuspected maverick in the fold, gleefully anticipating the effect of its double entendre. We all thought this must be the only possible explanation, for surely Their Lordships themselves *couldn't* have been so unsophisticated – could never have intended—! Or could they? An unworthy suspicion, and perhaps we maligned them, though I'd often thought I detected a certain gleam behind even the most exalted naval officer's eye. Anyway, whoever was responsible, I suppose it wasn't a bad idea now and again to let loose a shaft of humour to lighten the gloom of the situation we were all in, and everyone certainly seemed to have had a good laugh over it.

So, against a background of ever increasing air attacks,

we continued to perform our various duties wearing our light summer clothes, and the sailors got so used to seeing us on the parade ground that they stopped laughing. Our frequent dashes down to the shelters gave us all something else to think about. Nerves were on the stretch, everyone on the alert. You had to be, for the suddenness of the attacks left you no time to complete whatever you were doing, however necessary or important. The only thing that mattered was your own survival. Imperative not to be caught in the open.

September 6th 1940   *RNAS St Merryn*
We were all getting very tired with so many interrupted nights. I found myself making silly mistakes on watch, feeling only half awake, and even Chief Yeoman was beginning to get short-tempered. Everything seemed an effort, and people were swearing instead of laughing over small mishaps they'd normally hardly notice.

   Maybe Celia and I were more exhausted than usual during the air raid just after one o'clock the next morning. The normal routine for the dash from Bruce Hut to the air raid shelter was that everyone should leap out of bed to the *right* so as not to clash with anyone else. But Celia's bed, being at the end of the row, was next to the wall on her right, so she had to get out of bed to the *left*, which, of course, was the same side as me. Usually we'd got this manoeuvre to a fine art, arranging for Celia to grab her glasses and tin hat a few seconds before I reached for mine, but that night we must have responded rather more slowly to the familiar distant crump of the bombs, with the result that both our tin hats met with a resounding clash that left us stunned and half deafened. For a moment we were both immobile, half in and half out of bed, hardly aware of the usual commotion in the rest of the dimly lit hut. When I had recovered a little I heard Celia suddenly cry out in a high, sharp voice utterly unlike her own, and saw her leaning over the side of her bed, her hand scrabbling wildly across the floor.

"What – what is it? What on earth are you doing?" I asked her shakily, as I reached out for my glasses.

"My glasses, you idiot! What else?" she snapped. "I can't find the damned things! For God's sake, help me! It's too bloody dark – I can't see where—!"

I grabbed my torch and shone it around on the floor till suddenly she gave a cry of triumph.

"Ah! Here they are, not bust, thank God!" And hastily putting them on she managed to find her tin hat which had fallen off and rolled beneath her bed. "Sorry to panic like that," she added, replacing it on her head.

Relieved, I began to look for my shoes, suddenly aware that the sound of bombs dropping seemed to be getting much closer.

"Hurry up, Celia!" I urged her. "We'd better get out of here. Everyone's gone."

She turned her head and stared at me. I gazed back at her. Neither of us spoke. It was such an incongruous situation, with both of us in nothing but nightdresses, glasses and tin hats, two distracted looking females who might well have qualified for forceful admission to a loony bin. Suddenly this struck me as irresistibly funny, and I began to laugh. After a moment Celia joined in, just as another bomb landed frighteningly close by and the walls shook. Both of us instinctively dived under our beds, and lay there in the empty hut, helpless with laughter during one of the most serious raids St Merryn had so far experienced.

We never felt quite the same again about night time raids. We had been amazingly lucky that time; our number hadn't been on it. Perhaps this was a good omen.

As the Battle of Britain raged on I was thankful my parents were up in Cheshire. Their letters were fairly reassuring. Tony, still with an Officer Cadet Unit at Aldershot in Hampshire, seemed to be putting up with all the discomfort of air raids, though David, down at the Royal Naval College at Dartmouth, appeared to have had the worst of enemy action. Devon had taken a pounding, particularly at Plymouth and the naval dockyard at Devonport, but he assured us that he was all right and enjoying the training, so we all just had to keep our fingers crossed and trust to luck as so many others were doing.

Our periods on watch now became fraught with tension, and one evening we were brought up to date with the war situation with a vengeance.

Arriving at ten o'clock for the night watch Liz, Georgie Whitlock the teleprinter operator and I were surprised to see two sentries on duty outside the SDO instead of the usual one. That night it was Bill who challenged us, and after we'd responded I asked him what was going on.

"I dunno," he answered briefly. "Better ask them inside."

There was an undercurrent of excitement as Joy, Peggy and Celia greeted us.

"There's something happening," Celia told us. "They've rung through several times from Plymouth with an Amber alert – they're all in a bit of a froth."

"We *would* be going off duty just when something exciting is about to happen!" Joy grumbled.

"Bruce is duty officer tonight," said Peggy. "He's sent for Chiefy to come up."

After the usual handover the three of them left. I had the feeling that for two pins they'd have volunteered to stay on duty to see what it was all about, but just then Lieutenant Commander Bruce put his head round our door.

"Chief Yeoman will be up here shortly," he said. "I'm just going to see everything's in order outside. One of you, by the way, had better go round and check the blackout thoroughly. Make sure no cracks of light are showing anywhere." He glanced round at each of us in turn. "No need to get worried. You all know the drill. Just keep on your toes. I'll be back soon." As he disappeared outside, Liz took her place at the telephone switchboard, while Georgie and I went quickly through the building, checking doors and windows. As we returned to the SDO Georgie paused on her way into the teleprinter room and looked back at me uneasily. "You don't think this – this could be *invasion*, do you?" she asked, her face whitening.

A sudden chill struck at the pit of my stomach. "I've a nasty feeling we may be going to find out before we go off watch," I answered.

"Invasion!" Georgie whispered, half to herself. "It doesn't seem possible – not here, I mean – in England—." She broke off, then after a moment added more loudly, "I can't believe this is happening."

I didn't suppose any of us could. After all, when was the last time? Julius Caesar, the Vikings, then 1066 and all that with William the Conqueror. Long enough ago. No wonder we all thought ourselves so safe from invasion.

As we re-entered the telephone exchange Liz was talking into her voice tube, then she rang off and turned to us. "I've just been speaking to Sheila Hunt at Plymouth. They don't know for certain yet, but she says there's a lot of activity going on there."

"In that case, I'd better go and make the cocoa now," I said, "in case there's no time to drink it later on."

I'd never really liked cocoa, but on night duty it could be a life saver, thick and sweet and searingly hot, very strengthening when you were beginning to flag at three in the morning, the witching hour. I was just about to make another mug for Lieutenant Commander Bruce when he re-entered the SDO. His eyes lit up when I held the mug out to him.

"Thanks, Roxane," he said. "Now, are you girls all right? There may be something brewing, we don't know yet – but don't panic, we'll be informed as soon as anyone knows what it is. The Captain will be here shortly. Just tell me the minute anything definite comes through from Plymouth. I'll be in my cabin."

We assured him we would, and after a quick look round the room he smiled briefly at us all, and we heard his jaunty step going along the corridor.

We smiled at each other after he'd gone. I always thought he was like some impetuous, red-haired Peter Pan, though with a touch of arrogance and determination about him at odds with his rather cherubic expression. It was reassuring to know he was in the building with us just then.

Half an hour later a red warning came through from Plymouth, and we all stiffened and sprang into action. As Georgie set the siren going, Liz was already ringing through to Lieutenant Commander Bruce, while I stood wondering why there was no sound of enemy aircraft or of bombs dropping. Apart from the wail of the siren it was quite quiet, and this in itself was disturbing.

Then ten minutes later another light flickered on the switchboard, and Liz answered the call.

"Now it's a *double* red!" she said over her shoulder, and for the next quarter of an hour the switchboard flashed and clicked as if it were alive, but she remained calmly efficient.

Captain Farquhar had arrived from his house in Padstow and now rang through from his Day Cabin at the far end of the building. When Liz had dealt with this call she closed off the line as usual and spoke to us very quietly, her voice puzzled:

"The Captain's ringing his wife. I wonder why. He sounded in a great hurry – as if it were something really urgent."

"I wish we knew what was going on," said Georgie, unhappily. "Why doesn't someone tell us?"

We looked uneasily at each other, the same unspoken thought in our minds.

I voiced it. "I suppose we couldn't—" I began, then stopped. It was strictly forbidden to listen in to any calls, but surely, I argued to myself, this was different. Apparently Liz thought so too, for she quietly opened the line again, motioning us to silence, and we heard the phone still ringing at the Captain's house.

"Can't be asleep," she murmured, as we waited. Then we heard the Captain's wife answering, and froze, praying that no one would come in and find us out.

The Captain's voice was quietly controlled. "I'm afraid this is really it, my dear. It's invasion. Now you know what to do, just in case they're using gas. Have your masks ready, and check every window and door is properly sealed...."

We heard nothing after that fatal word. Gas! And we hadn't even been issued yet with gas masks!

After the Captain's call had ended other calls came through, and Liz was kept very busy, but Georgie and I had nothing to do but sit and wait, a prey to every horrid stretch of imagination. I found myself straining my ears for the sound of heavy steps outside, the sudden crack of the roughly opened door, and then the air invaded by the unfamiliar scent of alien presence....

Footsteps came, and as we all stiffened, hearts pounding, there was a knock at the door, followed by the appearance of an armed sentry.

"Oh, Fred! Thank goodness!" Georgie said faintly, as we subsided in relief.

Fred grinned. "You all look like you've seen a ghost," he remarked, then added, "The Germans won't bother to knock, you know."

Feeling rather foolish I said, "We thought you—." My voice tailed off, then I pulled myself together and asked, "What's happening outside? Do you know?"

"Oh, a right old flap – guards doubled everywhere.

Anyway, I'll be just outside this door. I've just changed over from Jim, and Bill's round at the other end of the building. Be seeing you." And out he went, as cheerful and unconcerned as ever. I envied him his detachment.

The next moment we heard more footsteps outside, then Fred giving the challenge, and our nerves jumped again, but the voice that answered was familiar and reassuring. As Chief Yeoman stepped into the room, large and calm as always, his presence dispelled fear, and when the Captain himself came in to see us a little later, we all managed to reply quite calmly to his questions. He was looking drawn and worried, which was hardly surprising given his responsibility in such a hopeless situation. There were so few of us on the camp, I supposed no more than three or four hundred or so to repel a far more powerful enemy. And of those few hundred a sizeable number were women.

Some minutes later Lieutenant Commander Bruce came into the telephone exchange, carrying a Tommy gun. We stared at him, fascinated.

"Nothing new come through, Elizabeth?" he asked, pulling up a chair nearer to the table.

"No, sir, not yet," Liz answered.

"Right. Well, this is where we sit and wait," he said calmly, and sat there, his cap pulled further down over his eyes, his feet in their flying boots crossed high above the table and his Tommy gun clasped to his chest. The rakish angle of his cap and his nonchalant attitude presented a false image, masking his own special qualities of force and determination. Beneath his cap we could just see his eyes, ice blue and watchful, as hard and cold as marbles. His gaze travelled constantly round the room, and his body, though relaxed in his chair was, I knew, ready to swing into action at the first hint of danger.

It was now past one o'clock, and we waited – and waited throughout the strangest night I'd ever known, all of us as silent and still as statues, but inwardly alert, nerves as taut as violin strings; Chief Yeoman like a looming statue in one corner of the room, a revolver never far from his hand, Liz firmly attached to her switchboard, Georgie sitting by the open door of the teleprinter room, myself in the doorway to the SDO, and in the centre of us all Lieutenant Commander Bruce with his Tommy gun, the focal point of our defence .... .

I never realised how tiring absolute inaction could be, with bodies held tensely in check but minds running loose in all directions, expecting the unexpected, bracing ourselves to face the unbelievable.

But nothing happened. Absolutely nothing. The loudest sound was of our own breathing, or the occasional footsteps of Fred outside and his reassuring "All quiet" as he passed our doorway. And still we waited .... .

And when the call finally came through from Plymouth at about seven thirty and Georgie had set the All Clear siren going, there was an air of utter disbelief. The anti-climax was complete.

Lieutenant Commander Bruce muttered, "What the devil—?" beneath his breath, and stood up, yawning and stretching, while we relaxed our tense limbs and opened windows and doors to let in the sweet, fresh air of early morning.

And when Liz, Georgie and I finally went outside at eight o'clock we just stood there for a moment, in silence, gazing round us, not quite believing what we saw. The summer haze was already dispersing, and the hills and fields of Cornwall seemed as quiet and peaceful as ever, undisturbed by any hated grey uniforms or guttural commands of triumphant invaders. Instead, the sun rising over the cornfields was already tinting them with gold and glinting on the roofs and runways of the station. Incredibly, we could see people moving unhurriedly about, opening hangar doors to bring out the aircraft, everything normal, no sign of panic anywhere.

A lump came into my throat and for a moment tears stung my eyes. Such an escape seemed miraculous. Could the threat of invasion really be over, or was this only a reprieve?

Nobody seemed to know, although there were rumours everywhere. Our curiosity was overwhelming. What had really happened last night? Had it been a sort of mock invasion – what the pilots usually referred to as a 'dummy-run' – or had our coastal defences and air protection been too fierce for the enemy, causing their final withdrawal? Would we ever find out?

September 18th 1940   *RNAS St Merryn*
As we went into the mess for supper after a long, much-needed daytime sleep, we were greeted with the appalling news of the callous sinking of the *City of Benares*, the ship which had been taking nearly a hundred children to safety in Canada, under the Children's Overseas Reception Scheme. Seventy-seven of them had been lost, apart from seven of their escorts and many other passengers and crew.

We sat at our table, stunned. It was unbelievable. We'd just had the most fortunate reprieve from invasion, then to be met with this!

"Nothing stays good for long, does it?" said Peggy sadly.

The food suddenly tasted like ashes in my mouth, and I turned away from the table. I couldn't stop thinking of all those poor little children. It was bad enough to be torn from their families and sent away from their homes in vulnerable areas, labelled like so many parcels, confused and upset. But to be lost like this, torpedoed over six hundred miles from land by a German U-boat in the middle of the night, in freezing, tempestuous seas that gave very little hope of survival! It didn't bear thinking of. What must their parents be suffering? A terrible mixture of anger, guilt and hopelessness.

I think this was the first time I began to feel over-whelming hatred against our enemies. A helpless kind of fury was building up inside me at the thought that our poor little evacuees, Billy and Susie from Bootle, might also have been aboard that unlucky ship. If only their stupid mother hadn't taken them back to Liverpool just because she found the country too quiet, and was afraid that her husband, on his own at home, might be having too good a time with other women in the pub!

They could easily have remained safely with my parents for the time being, away from the bombing that was plaguing the cities or the threat of evacuation abroad. I found myself saying a silent prayer for their safety.

September 20th 1940   *RNAS St Merryn*

Still as mystified as ever about our strange night watch, we had cautiously questioned all our friends among the pilots, until we heard a curious story that was circulating round the officers' mess. It had originated from one of Liz's friends, Johnny Hallam, who'd apparently been talking to a newly arrived officer, a very experienced pilot who'd mentioned having seen the corpses of German soldiers washed ashore at various points along the English coast, their bodies burnt and covered with a sort of green oil.

"He swore it was true," Liz told us. "He wasn't the only one who saw them, either. The others in his squadron did too. There must have been at least forty or fifty bodies, they reckoned. They think the Germans had been practising for the invasion, and some of their barges must have been sunk by our bombers who'd been attacking them all along the French coast for several weeks."

"For several weeks?" I echoed. "Then – if that was only a rehearsal, the panic stations that other night could have been for the real thing!"

"Well, *someone* high up must have thought so, or we wouldn't have been put on maximum alert like that," said Celia.

"But nothing happened," Georgie interposed, frowning.

"Well, *something* stopped them," I said. "I mean, we'd surely have heard gunfire or planes coming over if they'd really got as far as our coast. Could that mean they'd started out and been ordered back at the last minute? It doesn't seem to make sense."

We didn't like to ask Lieutenant Commander Bruce in case it was all top secret, and we as Wren ratings didn't qualify for such information. All I knew was that it had been a terrifying night I'd never forget.

September 24th 1940   *RNAS St Merryn*
As if to make up for the invasion that did not take place, the number and ferocity of air raids and machine-gun attacks on the station increased dramatically. It was thought that we were being mistaken for the RAF Bomber Station of Coastal Command over at St Eval, and it was lucky for us that we were now so quick to recognise the sound of German aircraft.

September 25th 1940   *RNAS St Merryn*
On this dreadful morning we heard that nineteen WAAF personnel at St Eval had been killed or wounded, shot in the back while seated in a row at breakfast by a German pilot who had machine-gunned them through the open windows of their mess. We were all sickened. No one at St Merryn had yet been killed, very few even wounded during the raids, but now our vigilance was increased. No sitting about on the grass outside our huts, enjoying the sunshine, unless there was a means of escape nearby through an open doorway; and bicycle rides through the countryside were becoming really dangerous.

September 28th 1940   *RNAS St Merryn*

It was generally expected that the Wrens would be able to
supply some necessary morale-boosting relief by organising
concerts and other forms of entertainment on the camp,
since there was no distraction arranged for the personnel,
no dances, cinema shows or visiting comics, so anyone who
had hidden talents in singing, dancing or acting was
immediately enrolled. I had already sung at one or two
earlier concerts accompanied by Margaret Blackwell, an
excellent pianist, but now Celia, acting as producer, decided
we should try something more ambitious, and assembled a
large and varied cast for a show in which one of the scenes
was based on a Victorian wedding.

It was not going to be easy. We only had the recreation
hut to work in, no stage, no curtains, no costumes, no
equipment, nothing except determination and enthusiasm.
Amazing what you could do when really up against it. The
word soon got around, and in no time at all electricians,
carpenters and painters appeared with suggestions, advice
and offers of help, while we concentrated on rehearsals and
making the costumes. The compulsory Wednesday afternoon sessions of 'Make and Mend' for all naval ratings had
surely never produced such ingenious and inspired results!
The most unlikely girls showed remarkable initiative. My
dress for my solo numbers was made of butter muslin
bought from a little shop in Padstow, which I sewed
together all anyhow, and someone lent me, most
surprisingly, an enormous fan made entirely of white
feathers. The girl told me it had been left her by an aunt,
but I didn't have the nerve to ask her if her aunt had been
a fan-dancer. A funny thing to take to war, but it certainly
looked impressive and gave the butter muslin a more
glamorous appearance.

The Victorian wedding was a comic number, in which,
for my sins, I was cast as the forlorn bridesmaid who had to
sing the sad little ditty 'Why am I always the bridesmaid,

never the blushing bride?' For this I wore my glasses, an appalling white straw hat garlanded with black ribbon, a dark blouse and a pillow stuffed up the back of my ankle-length skirt like a bustle, perfect for the part.

Well, the show was a great success, the first half anyway. The Captain and all the off-duty officers came to the first performance, which we repeated several times to accommodate all the other ranks, who were a most appreciative and extremely rowdy audience.

But there was one snag, a big one. I don't think Hitler can have been happy with my singing so was determined to spoil it, for at each performance, as I reached the halfway stage of my comic song, the familiar crump-crump of bombs drove the entire cast and audience precipitately down into the various shelters. Our language got bluer, but we always managed eventually to finish the show, though some of the fizz faded a little after such a long interval.

October 3rd 1940   *RNAS St Merryn*
It was my twenty-first birthday, and an astonishing opening to the day. I had come off duty at midnight and was still deeply asleep when the sharp whine of an aircraft approaching in a steep dive tore through the air, and the sudden rattle of machine-gun fire shook us all awake. We lay rigidly in our beds, paralysed with shock as a stream of bullets began to fly through the thin, temporary roof (part of the original one having been blown off in a raid two nights ago), pursuing its spiteful, spitting route across the floor between our two rows of beds, before finally landing with a vicious smack against the inner door by the foot of Celia's bed.

No time for a frenzied roll beneath our beds, no time to reach even for a tin hat, no time for anything but complete disbelief as we waited, hardly daring to breathe.

Suddenly the noise stopped, and we lay in terrified silence in case the aircraft came round again. But after a short while, when the sound of the engine began to die away, we dared to raise our heads and have a cautious look round. It was six o'clock. What if it had been seven o'clock instead, when most of us would have been up and moving about between the two rows of beds, easy targets for any stray bullets? The sound still hung in the air like an audible partition down the hut, and now there was only the line of bullet holes in the floor and the rash of bullets lodged in the wooden door like a malignant disease to convince us that we hadn't been caught up in an appalling nightmare, that it had really happened.

October 18th 1940   *RNAS St Merryn*
We were now in uniform! The news of its arrival had got round like wildfire, and we all rushed over to naval stores. An unexpected consignment had just been delivered, and the poor Wrens in charge had a tough time of it, with so many of us demanding the right size, length of skirt or fit over the shoulders. I didn't know who designed these outfits, but had the feeling they'd all followed what they considered to be a standard shape and length, and the results were hilarious. Any of us who could sew were able to alter some of the really serious discrepancies, but those who could afford it took matters into their own hands, and either sent their uniforms to tailoring firms they knew, or searched wildly for a local dressmaker. The only thing that was impossible to alter was the Wren rating's hat, a wilting, gaberdine monstrosity. We, of course, had already had some warning of what was in store for us, since the WRNS personnel who had been sent ahead to St Merryn to prepare for our arrival were actually wearing these appalling excrescences. But it was still a shock to see these on our own heads, and most of us were in fits of laughter. Was there an official way to wear this shapeless horror? Was the brim to be turned down or up, or didn't it make the slightest difference to the depressing end result?

"This is an offence to womanhood!" someone behind me declared, when she saw herself for the first time in the mirror. "I'm going to talk to my father about this. Something's got to be done! No one will ever take us seriously!"

Since her father was a vice-admiral we dared to hope he would agree with her, but for the moment we'd just have to put up with our dreadful headgear.

There was, however, one good thing about wearing uniform. We may not have been exactly satisfied with some of it, but it made an enormous difference to the poorer girls in Bruce Hut. Suddenly the gulf between our backgrounds became less noticeable.

They began to take a pride in their appearance, becoming smart, well groomed, all at once more efficient with an air of confidence that was new to them, even Ada daring to speak to us or voice a timid opinion. It was as if they'd begun to feel they were someone who mattered, with a sense of belonging to a great and powerful institution, a Royal service in which they too could play a part, however insignificant. And most important of all, we all had to wear the same deplorable hat!

With the arrival of our uniform new rules crept in. Hair and nails had to be kept short, only colourless nail varnish was allowed. No jewellery could be worn except wedding or engagement rings, and no scent, except very discreetly when going out in the evening, particularly when wearing uniform. Wren ratings had to wear the thick, black woollen stockings, and all of us, even officers, wore the standard black, laced-up flat shoes on all occasions. Also, now that we were in uniform, carrying our handbags was naturally not permitted, and this presented a real difficulty. The sailors had their 'ditty-boxes', but Chaucer's 'bag of needments', as far as we were concerned, was ignored. So we all, without exception, with the ingenuity of the desperate, surreptitiously stuffed our bits and pieces into our newly delivered gas mask cases, not caring if anyone in authority noticed the suspicious rattling inside. (It took Their Lordships at the Admiralty almost a year before they realised that members of the WRNS had no pockets in their uniform jackets big enough to store these indispensable 'needments', and finally bowed to the urgent entreaties of the WRNS hierarchy to supply us with smart, compact, navy blue shoulder bags.) And a little later our awful hats were replaced by saucy little round affairs more like the sailors' headgear. By then, many of us had become officers so never had a chance to wear them, but that didn't matter since the WRNS officers' tricorne hat was extremely smart and attractive, fortunately unlike the hideous versions of the male officers' caps favoured by the ATS and WAAF.

October 19th 1940   *RNAS St Merryn*
Not a nice day. It was decreed that all personnel, officers and ratings alike, should be able to recognize poison gas if ever it should be used against us, and we were all ordered to assemble in small groups outside a sealed hut some way from the main parts of the camp, and to wear our gas masks. Then one at a time, we had to walk into the hut, remove our gas masks and take a quick sniff of the gas before making a dash for the exit. The officers went first, but their reactions did nothing to reassure us. All of them looked rather sick as they walked quickly out into the fresh air. This, we were told, was mustard gas, and it lived up to its name, even the tiniest sniff seared our noses and throats. It was enough to fill one with horror at the thought of it ever being used against an unsuspecting population. An unpleasant and frightening experience, and we were aghast at being told there would be a further opportunity to learn the smell and effect of another gas known as Lewisite. Heaven hope neither of these noxious substances would ever be used against us!

October 21st 1940   *RNAS St Merryn*

Even with so much going on, with such a lot to learn, it was inevitable that boyfriends occupied a great deal of everyone's spare time. Joy became very friendly with a daring young pilot, Liz, of course, was always the centre of an admiring circle from whom she could take her choice, while several others in Bruce Hut suddenly announced their engagements. There was a disturbing sense of urgency everywhere, as if time was not on our side, and there could be no guarantee of present happiness extending into an unclear future.

I wondered if they realised what they might be letting themselves in for. St Merryn was a training station, and it was inevitable that accidents might and did occur, with inexperienced pilots learning to fly in strange aircraft till able to handle them in all circumstances, particularly the highly dangerous business of take-offs and landings on the heaving deck of an aircraft carrier. There were occasions when pilots overshot the landing area and plunged into the sea.

Fortunately there had been no fatalities, at least so far, but it was not surprising that such an undercurrent of anxiety should exist among the girls whose friendships had developed into serious attachments.

I was glad I hadn't become involved with anyone. Somehow I found it impossible to think beyond the end of the war, or to wonder what was to become of us after it was all over – if we won the struggle, that is. If we didn't, there was no point in speculating. Our future would be all too clear. So how could anyone make future plans? The present was all that mattered. In any case I could never have imagined myself going back to the sort of life I'd led with my parents. Before getting married, if I ever did, there would be my training at the Royal Academy of Music for three years, prior to embarking on the solo singing career which was my main ambition. The last thing in the world I'd ever envisaged for myself was to be in charge of a large country house, chained to domesticity and a boring and pointless social whirl. But that, of course, might not be a viable option, as that kind of life could well have gone for ever. Who could tell? No, I decided, come what may I was going to see this conflict through to the bitter end. I had an idea that Celia thought like this, too, as well as a few of the others. Ordinary life seemed to have been put on hold.

And then, without warning, one of my friends, a very likeable RNVR lieutenant with a Morris Cowley car, took me to the cinema in Newquay, and in the middle of a rather turgid John Steinbeck film, proposed to me. I hardly knew what to say. He was several years older than me, serious minded, forthright and responsible. I liked and admired him very much, but could see that he was not the kind of man who'd want a full-time professional singer for a wife. I did my best to make him understand my commitment to music, but didn't think I succeeded. Nor did he quite understand why I should be so keen to stay in the WRNS; the war, he added, might go on for years. But I knew in my heart that this was not the moment to opt out. I was sure we hadn't begun to see the worst of it yet, and heaven only knew what might be facing us. If we survived we'd surely find many changes. Nothing might ever be the same again. But it was hard to explain, and the last thing I wanted was to hurt him.

October 25th 1940   *RNAS St Merryn*
Surprisingly, I was soon to become the temporary owner of that sturdy Morris Cowley car. The nice lieutenant had been drafted to the new aircraft carrier HMS *Formidable*, and would be leaving St Merryn shortly. He didn't quite know what to do about the car, since he had no time to sell it, so he asked me if I would like to have it until I went on leave. Knowing that I lived in Cheshire and his home was in Liverpool, would I like to drive it up to my home from where he could arrange for someone from his family to

come over and fetch it? Of course I said yes, I'd be delighted. He had let me drive his car before, and knew I was a safe driver. I had passed my test in Chester on my seventeenth birthday, after Tony had been teaching me for almost a year. We had a narrow, circular drive outside the front of our house, and he'd made me practise driving round and round it, both forwards and backwards without touching the sides until I felt I could almost do it blindfold. And with luck I wouldn't be going home alone. I mentioned this to Joy, Liz and Celia in case their leaves should coincide with mine, and they all said they'd like to come with me. Celia's home was somewhere en route, and I could drop her off first, then carry on to Cheshire. Joy lived quite close to us there, and I'd invited Liz to spend her leave with us. Her home being in Devon, at Bideford, it had been easier for her to see her family more often than we could see ours. They agreed, so that was settled.

October 31st 1940   *RNAS St Merryn*

My friend the lieutenant had left the previous day after I'd promised faithfully to look after his car, and see it safely to Cheshire, but he had second thoughts about my own safety.

"I don't know whether I should let you do this," he said eventually, his voice suddenly anxious. "You won't try and go on your own, will you? Can you get some others, preferably experienced drivers, to go with you?"

"I'll be all right," I reassured him. "There are bound to be other people who'd like a lift, and I've asked Liz Welburn to spend her leave at home with us, so there'll be two of us going anyway."

"You'll take care, won't you, driving all that way," he said, not sounding entirely convinced. "Promise me you'll look after yourself."

"I promise," I said, then added, "and *you* look after yourself too, wherever you're going."

"I will," he said with a smile. "Here's my address. Write

and let me know when you've arrived home safely. And maybe—" he added rather hesitantly, "we might meet again some time."

And he turned and walked quickly away towards the officers' mess. As he disappeared round the corner of the buildings I silently wished him luck, genuinely sorry to see him go.

November 18th 1940   *RNAS St Merryn*

Life had gone on much as before, still with unexpected raids and machine-gunning of the camp. The German pilots seemed to have discovered that many of our buildings had long open-ended corridors, and they became adept at braving the anti-aircraft fire from the few scattered batteries in the vicinity of our area, and going into a steep dive to fire down into the exposed entrance. If caught in one of these, the only way to avoid their fire was to rush from the corridor into one of the side turnings into the various huts or offices.

On that murky afternoon Liz and I were walking back to Bruce Hut when the familiar throb of a German aircraft engine sounded in the distance, and moments later the plane dived towards us and began firing. The long corridor of our block was fortunately near by and we turned and fled down it and into the first side turning that led through to the recreation hut. We were almost too late, but managed to throw ourselves down, landing in a tangled heap on top of Petty Officer Jones who was just coming out of it. The poor girl had the breath completely knocked out of her, and we all lay there helplessly as the bullets sped along the narrow corridor behind us, fortunately not catching anyone in their line of fire. We waited till the sound of the aircraft faded into the distance, then sorted ourselves out while apologising profusely to Petty Officer Jones, who luckily had a sense of humour. It was only when we'd dusted ourselves off before going through into Bruce Hut that she caught Liz's arm and turned her round.

"Oh my goodness!" she exclaimed. "Just look at your coat! There, at the back. There's a bullet hole in it."

Sure enough there was, and from its jagged edges a faint smell of singed material reached us.

"It must have missed you by inches," I said, feeling rather shaken.

Liz had turned pale, but now this changed to anger as she removed her overcoat, holding it up for a closer look. I'd never seen Liz lose her temper over anything, certainly not heard her swear with such fury. When she finally paused for breath, there were tears of rage in her eyes. "Well, I hope someone bloody well puts a bullet into *him* – and I don't mean only in his coat!"

After a moment Petty Officer Jones turned to us. "Well, I don't know about you two," she said calmly, bending to pick up several scattered files she'd been carrying, "but I could use a cup of tea, and you two look as if you need one too. Come along."

She led us into the nearby kitchen where we discovered broken plates all over the floor, Ada having dropped them in panic as the bullets flew past the kitchen entrance.

She began rather incoherently to apologise, but Petty Officer Jones patted her on the shoulder and said kindly: "Never mind, Ada, just sweep up the bits, then you can have a cup of tea, too."

"In fact," she added, noticing the shaken expressions of the rest of the kitchen staff, "we'll all have one."

My God! What *would* we do without tea?

January 6th 1941   *RNAS St Merryn*

Christmas came and went in a flurry of snow and icy conditions which severely curtailed the flying, but in spite of the appalling cold there was a sort of holiday atmosphere in the camp. There also seemed to have been a kind of armistice elsewhere over the festive season, unless it was the weather which kept the German aircraft away. In any case there was a great deal of jollification and celebrating, and several of the younger Wrens, unused to any form of alcohol, had to be rescued from the sailors' riotous party in the petty officers' mess and brought back to their various quarters to be restored to sobriety. Their monster hangovers next morning were a dire warning to us all!

January 15th 1941   *RNAS St Merryn*
Great news! We had just learnt that some of us were to be promoted to third officer rank in the spring, when we'd be given ten days leave before going to London for an Officers' Training Course at the Royal Naval College at Greenwich. Celia, Joy and Liz with one or two others from Bruce Hut were also going, but none of us had any idea where we were likely to be sent after that.

"Mark my words!" Celia prophesied caustically. "We're going to be taught how to be ladylike, and how not to eat peas off our knives! What a bloody silly waste of time!"

February 20th 1941   *RNAS St Merryn*
The news seemed to be getting worse everywhere. So many of our big towns were being reduced to rubble with enormous casualties, and the losses of our merchant shipping were mounting dangerously. At home, people were showing incredible courage and endurance in spite of German claims that those in cities were near breaking point. The deep Tube stations were being used as shelters for thousands of Londoners, who slept as much as possible in such overcrowded conditions, and still managed to get up early enough to go to work. In a way, despite our raids I thought we really had the best of it down in Cornwall. There was fresh sea air on tap, and although now it was bitingly cold we at least hadn't yet been bombed out of our living quarters. What it would have been like to find one's own home no longer standing after returning late from work I just couldn't imagine.

Our departure was fixed for the following week, so we had many preparations to make. We had no idea how long our journey would take, especially if we had to stop because of air raids or drive slowly without lights in dangerous areas.

The first thing to do was to buy maps to plan our route, and Celia constituted herself as chief map reader, so would sit beside me to guide me. The only drawback to my driving was a complete lack of any sense of direction. I would cheerfully drive south when I should be going north, and often failed to notice obvious landmarks I'd already passed earlier by mistake. I could read a map, though always had to mark my route very carefully before driving some distance alone.

It was obvious that although it would undoubtedly be quicker to keep to the main roads, these would certainly take us close to vulnerable sites such as Filton aerodrome near Bristol. It might be safer to avoid the bigger towns altogether, if possible, and stick to little known cross-country roads, even though we might get hopelessly lost in the dark. After much discussion we finally decided to drive overnight and hope there wouldn't be too bright a moon to show us up.

"Well, we'll just have to play it by ear," said Celia. "And we'd better take something to eat and drink en route in case we get stuck anywhere." I agreed, and said if she'd like to organise that, I'd take the car down to the Padstow garage which usually serviced it, and get it all checked up.

"What time shall we leave?" Joy asked.

"I should think about eight o'clock," I replied, then noticed that Liz was frowning slightly.

"I suppose," she said rather uncertainly, "it really is safer to drive at night?"

"Of course it is," said Celia positively. "You can't hide a car in daylight. We'd be an easy target. It'd be far more difficult to see us if we were driving without lights in the dark. And as for finding our way, it doesn't make any difference day or night since all the signposts have been removed for security reasons."

"At least we shan't have to rely on my sense of direction," I said with relief.

"Well, if ships could navigate by the stars or the moon, it should be easier for us on land. There must be some landmarks we can recognise," said Joy.

So eight o'clock it was. No more argument. After all, the whole venture was a calculated risk, we might never reach our destination; but then, was living and working on an exposed and almost unprotected naval air station in the wilds of Cornwall any less of a risk? We'd already had to endure all forms of sudden attack any second of the day or night, so this car journey would not be so very different, and at least we wouldn't be the most important target.

We spent the afternoon packing up all our belongings, collecting our pay and travel warrants, having previously said goodbye to our First Officer WRNS in charge, and to everyone else in the SDO, including Lieutenant Commander Bruce who wished us good luck. Chief Yeoman seemed really sorry to see us leave, and Fred, on sentry duty outside, put down his rifle and shook our hands, wished us luck, and called out as we were walking away, "Drive carefully, girls! See you again some time."

I would miss Fred, though I was sure there'd always be many other Freds wherever we got sent. People like him were the salt of the earth, straight, kind and reliable.

It was an odd feeling as I drove away from St Merryn for the last time, an unexpected wrench leaving all the other occupants of Bruce Hut after living at such close quarters for nearly ten months. Petty Officer Jones seemed really sorry we were going, and Ada was close to tears as she thanked us once again for helping her at a bad time. But at last the goodbyes were over, and as we drove out through the station gates Stan, on duty at the guardhouse, saluted us smartly, with a friendly grin.

III

CRESCENDO

The start of our journey through Cornwall was remarkably uneventful, the roads almost empty, lit by a brilliant sunset, fading from flame to pink to pearl grey. The peaceful countryside seemed to be settling down for a quiet night, and we were well away by the time it grew really dark. Our only worry was the gradual appearance of a full moon. I put my foot down hard on the accelerator and drove as fast as I dared. The car was behaving beautifully and we covered the miles with ease.

It was only then that I realised how tired I was. It was a sort of long-term weariness after living so long on the knife-edge of danger, and although we were not likely to be very much safer on this marathon drive, I felt somehow that we could all relax. The thought of going home produced varied emotions. We'd be back among our families, once again in familiar surroundings that reminded us of earlier comfort and safety, and the thought of a whole night's uninterrupted sleep was wonderfully inviting.

Above all, my young brother David would be there too, on leave before joining the cruiser HMS *Neptune*. It only needed Tony to be at home as well for all of us to be once again a united family.

It was some hours later that my pleasurable dream of anticipation was rudely shattered. We were approaching the outskirts of Bristol, and our peaceful home run was at an end.

A sudden blaring of sirens and the familiar thrumming of German aircraft heralded violent anti-aircraft fire, which seemed to be blazing away all round and above us. Immediately afterwards we heard the thunderous vibration of exploding bombs which seemed literally to shake the earth, and realised with dismay how dangerously close we were to Filton aerodrome. As the crow flew it was hardly any distance from the road we were on, which was now clearly outlined by both moon and the fearsomely lit night sky.

"Quick! Douse the lights!" Celia shouted at me over the din. I obeyed hurriedly, but not before one of the attacking aircraft swept overhead, guns firing indiscriminately above us towards the aerodrome.

"We'd better get out," I said urgently, switching off the ignition and opening my door. "They're getting too close."

As the others scrambled out of the car Joy said, "There's a ditch – look! Over there, by that hedge."

"No! It's too near!" I warned her. "If they go for the car we'll get it too. Better run back down the road – somewhere further away!"

They all saw the force of this, and we made a dash for it, heads low, keeping to the lee of the hedge until we were several hundred yards from the car. Even that didn't seem far enough, but there was no more shelter beyond where we were crouching beside the road.

Then there was a sudden short lull, and Celia nudged me. "Let's go back," she said. "You can drive without lights easily enough, and if we go quickly there's bound to be some kind of side turning away from this road. No good staying here. We're much too close to Filton. We'll just have to risk getting lost."

The others nodded and we fled back to the car. Sure enough, a little further on, there was a tree-lined side turning to the right, away from the direction of Filton, and it was fairly easy to drive along it. It led to what eventually narrowed into a lane which wound its way from left to right, and get lost we did. At least the sound of the air raid behind us had become fainter, and I was able to put my lights on again and drive at speed. Around the next corner we saw what looked like a small Army truck parked at the side of the lane, whose driver appeared to be asleep. At our approach he stirred and turned round to look at us.

I opened my window and called out, "Sorry to disturb you, but we're lost."

"It's OK," he said sleepily, his voice husky. "I was just having a bit of a kip. I've been on the go for the last five hours."

Then he leaned out of his window and peered more closely at us.

"What's the Navy doing here?" he asked. "Lost your ship?"

We explained our predicament, and he smiled, obviously thinking us a little mad. "Cheshire!" he exclaimed. "That's some way. Did you get caught in that raid back there?"

"We thought it better to turn off the main road," I said.

"What's your route?" he asked, and we all got out of the car and showed him our map which he spread over our bonnet and shone a torch over it. Before long, Liz had unpacked the mound of sandwiches we'd brought with us, while Joy unscrewed the tops of the thermoses and poured out mugs of scalding hot coffee.

Our companion, who said his name was Phil, was impressed and most appreciative. "This is a bit of luck," he said after his third sandwich. "I've only had a slice of corned beef and a stale roll since I left." He peered down at the map. "Now, let's see."

By the end of ten minutes, he had not only shown us our best and easiest route, but also insisted on giving us two cans of petrol which he emptied into our fuel tank after casting a knowledgeable eye over the engine.

"Don't worry, girls," he said. "I can always get more where I'm going." He put the empty cans back into his truck, then turned to us. "Well, if you're all OK, let's get moving. You'd better drive without lights when we reach the main road. This moon's pretty bright. You can follow me till we come to your next turn off. And thanks for the coffee and sandwiches. Saved my life, you have."

We thanked him profusely as he climbed back into his truck and we set off. He guided us for a good way, and when we finally had to part company he drove off with a friendly wave. I was immensely encouraged, and knew we'd be all right. We'd found another Fred.

April 28th/29th 1941   *en route for Cheshire*
I don't think any of us will ever forget that hair-raising trip. It seemed to go on for ever. It was a mixture of driving with or without lights, at recklessly fast or agonisingly slow speeds, occasionally having to stop altogether and take cover where we could find any, and perpetually having to keep our ears cocked for the sound of enemy planes. It needed all my driving skill and alert attention, both of which were becoming less and less easy to exert.

Twice we stopped at some small hotel off a main road to have a much-needed short rest and be given cups of tea by a sympathetic night porter, who seemed to think we were on some urgent naval assignment. One of these kind gentlemen, an elderly, rather frail-looking man, was really concerned for our safety.

"They should never have sent you off on such a journey at night," he said severely. "If you'd been any of my daughters I'd never have let you go out with all these raids going on. What would your mother say?"

I didn't like to explain that all my mother and father knew was roughly the time of my arrival home, and that I'd be travelling with friends. I'd certainly made no mention of my driving a car myself all that way, or anything about the raids en route. I didn't want to worry them.

We dropped Celia off eventually at her home, and Joy took over the map reading office. It felt odd saying goodbye to someone I'd got to know so well, and with whom I'd had so much in common – short sight and an indelible memory of a certain night time air raid when we lay laughing helplessly under our beds in Bruce Hut after everyone else had rushed down to the shelter.

Hours later we reached Hartford, and to our surprise and disgust were greeted by the familiar sound of German aircraft. What on earth were they doing over Hartford? I doused the lights again and we crept along the road to Joy's home, afterwards cautiously making our way to the entrance to Oaklands. As I turned into our circular drive I gave a discreet toot on the horn before stopping at the front door. We had begun unloading our suitcases from the boot when the door opened and my parents stood there in pitch darkness in the hallway, my father shading his torch with his hand. Both were in night clothes with heavy overcoats on over them, and greeted Liz and I with relief and concerned questions about our journey.

The sound of aircraft grew louder and my father hustled us downstairs to the cellar. "The Germans are jettisoning their spare bombs on their way back from Liverpool," he told us. "They've been doing this for weeks."

So much for the safety and comfort of home! My poor parents, far from enjoying a quiet life, were almost as much in the firing line as we had been. After about half an hour in the cellar the All Clear sounded, and by the time we'd carried our cases upstairs it was well after four o'clock and beginning to get light. We were so worn out by then that we decided to let news and explanations wait till later, and hot and grubby as we were, fell into our beds to enjoy the deep, dreamless sleep of the totally exhausted.

April 30th 1941   *Oaklands, Hartford, Cheshire*
Something was tickling my toes, and I dragged myself slowly out of the warmth and comfort of oblivion and opened my eyes. There he was, sitting on the end of my bed, smiling mischievously at me, still in his cadet's uniform, David, my young brother. I sat up and hugged him, realising how much I had been missing him. We'd always been on the same wavelength. It was only nine months or so, but it seemed much longer now that I saw him again. He'd just turned eighteen on March 30th, but in his smart uniform looked older. It was lovely to see him again. He was so much a part of my happy childhood, the golden boy of our family, adored by all of us. Although with his very blonde hair, fair complexion and candid grey eyes he had often looked younger than his actual age, there was now a certain air of sophistication and assurance about him, no doubt acquired from his naval training. Girls had always found him attractive, even some who were at least two years his senior. Although Tony and I always knew he was really our parents' favourite we were never jealous of him. Perhaps it was because he'd never been the least aware of this, so never grew spoilt or conceited. Being the central core of attention seemed to us to be his rightful place in life and we contributed enthusiastically to keeping him there. He had a sort of inner radiance about him, a luminous quality that seemed to brighten all our lives and, I believe, those of everyone who knew him. Never oppressed by adverse circumstance, he could rise easily

above it, letting his own buoyant spirit overcome it.

We enjoyed that leave in spite of the occasional bomb dropping somewhere in our vicinity while we spent time in the cellar. My father thought the Germans were still trying to destroy the ICI works at nearby Northwich, but luckily they never managed to find the exact location. During the daytime David hauled the lawn mower out of the garage and mowed the unkempt tennis court, our old gardener having retired, and rang round to see which of our friends were available to come and play. Joy and her twin sister Peggy, plus boyfriend, came over, and, as word of David's return home got around via the grapevine, they were very soon followed by several of his one time girlfriends. Last of all, one of his special friends, Donald Thompson, roared up the drive in the sleek, three-wheeler Morgan car which he and David had bought a year or so earlier in a thoroughly dilapidated state, and worked on continuously whenever they had time during holidays. They were inordinately proud of it now that it had the ability to go at ninety miles an hour, and took it in turns to give all our guests a hair-raising drive along the Davenham by-pass to show off its paces. Even our mother agreed to go with David, though father declined, saying he didn't think he could fit comfortably into such a narrow seat. I found it incredibly exciting, rather like being in a racing car, it was built so low to the ground.

One evening Donald invited David to go out to dinner somewhere, and they drove off with an impressive roar of the engine, which we soon heard accelerating up the main road. By midnight they had still not returned, slightly to my parents' uneasiness.

"I hope they've not gone anywhere near Liverpool," my father said.

They hadn't told us where they were going, but I thought it unlikely they'd go in that direction. By one thirty they still hadn't shown up, so we all decided to go to bed. After all both David and Donald were eighteen and knew what they were doing. They'd hardly be pleased to find a reception committee anxiously waiting for them on their return, however late it might be. Donald was staying the night, so his parents wouldn't be expecting him.

It wasn't until halfway through breakfast that the reassuring growl of the Morgan's engine heralded its audacious sweep up the drive, and two blackened and bedraggled figures climbed stiffly out of it.

"Sorry we're a bit late," was all David said, his voice strangely hoarse. "Hold some breakfast for us, will you? We must clean up a little first."

I looked at them curiously. Their clothes were absolutely filthy and reeked of smoke, their voices rough with exhaustion. It must have been Liverpool then. Whatever had made them take such an unnecessary risk? Surely there were many other unavoidable risks we could be facing.

Later, they both reappeared somewhat cleaner, but obviously exhausted, and told us, over a large breakfast, that they'd gone to have dinner at the famous Adelphi Hotel in Liverpool, but towards the end of it a raid started, and everyone went down to the hotel cellars, where they spent over two hours.

"After the All Clear," David went on, "we went outside to see what damage had been done – and you wouldn't believe it! Worse than anything I've seen, even in Devon. A bomb had landed nearby – there was absolute chaos everywhere – so much smoke you could hardly see anything. Half the street had gone, it was just rubble – and everyone was screaming and shouting, digging with their bare hands trying to get people out. Then a woman came rushing up to us, begging us to rescue her children. They'd been buried under their house."

He paused, his expression suddenly stark. I'd never seen him look like that. Then Donald put down his coffee cup and said slowly, "It was sickening – seeing it at such close quarters. Of course, we went along to try to help, but no one we pulled out was alive. There's not much hope after a direct hit . . . ."

"That's the worst of it," David added. "Nothing anyone could do – except keep digging. The police and the firemen – everyone – were marvellous, they never stopped for a second. So of course we stayed on there . . . ." He sighed and glanced round at our parents. "I'm sorry if we worried you."

We were all horrified, to put it mildly, but deeply thankful they'd managed to get back without harm. I thought how lucky we'd been down at St Merryn during the raids. There but for the grace of God . . . !

May 2nd 1941   *Oaklands*

Meanwhile there were practical considerations like the ordering of our new officers' uniforms. We'd learnt that the form was for us to be measured up for these as soon as possible, so that, in the event of our successfully passing the cypher course at Greenwich, we'd be able to shed our ratings' uniforms (including hat!) and present our-selves at our new postings in correct officers' attire.

It never crossed our minds that any of us would fail. The thought of having to wear that hat for the rest of the war was a potent incentive to pass with honours.

So Liz, Joy and I set out very early one morning for a well-known tailor's in Chester. I drove my father's Vauxhall car (lent to me with firm instructions to bring it back intact, and ourselves with it, of course), and we spent the morning trying on or being specially measured for our new uniforms with the attractive tricorne hat and the single blue stripe of our rank as Third Officer WRNS on our sleeves.

After that, we blew a lot of our precious hard-earned cash on a splendid lunch at one of my parents' favourite restaurants, and followed this with a positive orgy of shopping for all the necessary things we'd been unable to purchase in Padstow. Chester seemed not to have changed at all since that day on my seventeenth birthday when I passed my driving test, though now there were sandbags dotted around certain buildings, and all the iron fences had been stripped away for war use, which gave an odd appearance here and there.

May 9th 1941   *Oaklands*

Liz, Joy and I were all packed and ready for our journey down to the Royal Naval College at Greenwich, this time travelling by train, since the Morris Cowley had been duly collected and driven back to Liverpool, and I'd written to its owner to thank him and let him know that it and all of us were still in one piece after our marathon journey.

Goodbyes had been said, and I promised to visit my parents again as soon as I could get leave. David had left to join his cruiser HMS *Neptune* as a midshipman, and although my parents were naturally sad and worried to see him go, they were slightly comforted by a kind letter from Captain O'Conor, which apparently he had written to all anxious parents of young midshipmen, welcoming these aboard, with the added reassurance of their future welfare under his command. We had all been very touched that a busy captain with all the responsibility of a great cruiser should have found the time to do this.

May 11th 1941   *Royal Naval College, Greenwich*

Well, here we were, learning to be ladylike and how not to eat peas off our knives (to quote Celia). I had the impression that there were few of us on this course who would have dreamed of eating peas or anything else for that matter off our knives, but still a rule was a rule, and the Navy was fond of rules. I tried to get used to putting on my deplorable WRNS hat whenever I even stuck my head out of a window for a breath of fresh air. However, the place was wonderful.

Originally designed and built by Christopher Wren and Hawksmoor as a Restoration palace for Charles II and his heirs, it was now listed as a world heritage site. The Painted Hall, where we all ate at a long, long table decorated with heavy silver candlesticks all down the centre of it, was one of the most beautiful halls I had ever seen, the designs and colours the mark of artistic genius. We were waited on like royalty by well-trained naval staff, and I quite saw that it would have been sacrilege for anyone to wield a knife in the wrong way. Our mentor was a charming but slightly terrifying lady of unimpeachable birth, breeding and good taste, who made us all feel that we were slightly out of place.

Most of us were going to be cypher officers, though there were other categories in technical or administrative sections. I was sorry I'd never have the chance to take part in anything active, such as boats' crew, because of my eyesight, but decyphering naval signals would be interesting and was all top secret. The training course was intensive, and we needed very retentive memories which I supposed would develop when we were all more used to the work. There was another form of cypher, something new, which all had to learn. We were told it might be very useful later on when we joined other cypher officers' watches.

May 22nd 1941   *en route for Liverpool*
We had all successfully passed the cypher course, and I was being sent to HMS Eaglet, Western Approaches, Liverpool, under the command of Admiral Sir Percy Noble. It was a particularly tiring journey. The train was packed, the corridors and third class compartments incredibly dirty, with most of their occupants weary and travel stained. We were due in at Lime Street Station at six o'clock, but I had my doubts that this poor, overworked engine would ever make it. It seemed too tired to pull us along even at the

slow pace we were going.

I was in the throes of anti–climax. I had always hated change, and after the colour and freshness of Cornwall the dingy towns we passed through were anything but uplifting. Little boys on walls and fences waved at us, but I was too low-spirited to wave back. It wasn't as if I was even going far away from home. I could easily get to Hartford from Liverpool for an off-duty period to see my parents, so why, I wondered, did I feel so depressed? It was sad that neither Joy, Liz nor Celia would be coming with me, but that was just the luck of the draw, and doubtless there'd be other kindred spirits in Liverpool.

I'd enjoyed being back at home with my parents, and most of all, of course, with David. Having Liz's company too had been fun, as well as seeing old friends. We'd had a good time, but despite this I found it hard to recapture that old safe childhood feeling. My parents, once so indomitable, suddenly seemed vulnerable and much older. They were alone, of course, except for local daily help, dear Nanna having finally left to get married, and life was not particularly easy for them. But their emotion on saying goodbye to us, and to David especially, made me feel that their strength and former support had somehow been withdrawn. I'd been away for only nine months, yet during that time had been plunged into the dangerous activity of the real world, and had learnt to take responsibility for myself. Now, in a subtle sort of way, I found myself taking responsibility for them.

Beside his extra duties in the Home Guard my father was overworking and didn't look well, while my mother seemed to be living in a state of perpetual anxiety, which perhaps wasn't surprising with three children taking an active part in the struggle against Hitler. But I thought the older generation, on the whole, was showing remarkable grit and courage while getting on, against all odds, with the difficult job of keeping the home fires burning.

May 23rd 1941   *Western Approaches, Liverpool,*
                                                   HMS Eaglet

I'd never been very impressed by Liverpool. Not my
favourite city, and the sight of Lime Street Station did
nothing to raise my spirits as our poor old train trundled
wearily in at its last gasp. We were only an hour late, which
I suppose was quite good going.

They'd certainly had a bad time here. Everyone looked
so tired and grey-faced as if they hadn't slept for weeks. I
managed to pick up a cab to take me to the WRNS
officers' quarters which were some way out of the centre of
the town, so had a good opportunity to see the damage
done to streets and buildings.

The girls on my watch seemed a pleasant lot and after
making me welcome showed me around. We slept only
four to a room, which was more restful after seventeen
others as in Bruce Hut. It was odd being saluted and
addressed as 'Ma'am' by other ranks, but I supposed I would
get used to it in time.

May 24th 1941   *Liverpool*

I should have been familiar with raids after St Merryn, but
this was somehow different, so much more concentrated by
so many more waves of enemy aircraft. This was not a case
of bombing a naval air station in mistake for the Bomber
Command station at St Eval, but a deliberate and well-
planned assault on a particular target, easy to see and hugely
vulnerable.

Our quarters were some way out of the centre of
Liverpool and reasonably comfortable, and despite the
raids, the city had far more to offer in the way of
entertainment than Padstow. Here there were hotels,
restaurants, theatres, cinemas, and shops of every
description which all managed to keep going. Towering
over all these was the Liver Building with its two impassive
Liver birds haughtily overlooking the drab and battered

buildings. During the day a permanent mist hung over the huge, smoke-laden city, a penetrating wall of dust filling the air which tasted gritty and unpleasant after the wonderfully clear fresh atmosphere of Cornwall. I had often been to Liverpool with my mother, either for shopping or visiting the dentist, but somehow had never noticed the funnels and masts of ships showing over the tops of the low buildings down by the water. Now the whole place was inundated with hordes of troops and seamen who came and went, drunk or sober, having spent a few short hours or days ashore before re-embarking in their various ships.

I kept wondering how our evacuee mother and her two children were, whether they were still safe. I'd have to try to go and see them sometime, if my mother hadn't lost their address.

May 25th 1941   *Liverpool*

It was something of a shock to discover where our cypher offices were situated. Our head of watch, Second Officer Martin, led us through an unobtrusive side entrance to the impressive building called Derby House, and along a narrow corridor till we came, surprisingly, to an armed sentry standing on a large trapdoor. He saluted, and opened this to let us clamber through. As the last one of us stepped down on to the winding staircase below there was a thunderous clang above our heads as the trapdoor was slammed shut. We were then led through a long corridor with open doorways on either side, from which emanated a much magnified, but totally familiar noise – the racket of teleprinters, those infernal machines which could drive one so easily to fury and despair. Shades of Chiefy!

A muted buzz of conversation greeted us when we entered a large room full of tables and chairs, and met the watch we had come to relieve. There was a stuffy atmosphere of stale air and dust about the place, and the room seemed overcrowded and too warm. I've never suffered from claustrophobia before, but perhaps, I thought, there was always a first time – and there was an awful lot of heavy building above us.

This, however, was nothing to what followed. We were shown another big room lit only by a faint blue central light overhead, and filled with double-decker beds, overcrowding with a vengeance, and told that, after eating in the canteen, we might sleep there during the intervening hours between our afternoon and midnight watches. My heart sank. Supposing someone were to turn off that light? I'd always been a real coward in total darkness, and panicked if I couldn't see a chink of light anywhere. The first time I obediently followed the others and managed to find a bed on the lower level, the other girls wanted to turn the light off. Fortunately I'd taken the precaution of bringing a small torch with me which I surreptitiously turned on when the pall of darkness became too oppressive. I found myself thinking back to Bruce Hut almost with affection, with its separate beds and curtained windows, and the faint blue light permanently turned on so that the girls coming off night watch could see to get to bed.

Fortunately another member of my watch, Doris Morton, felt as I did, and occasionally we bent the rules and went out for dinner in the evening. After all, we reasoned, we were technically off duty from six till midnight, and anything was better than trying to sleep in that Black Hole of Calcutta after the revolting meal served up in the canteen. Doris said firmly that the only place to dine was the Adelphi Hotel which so far had never been hit. The dining room was almost full, and there was an air of luxury we'd almost forgotten could exist. We dined expensively and well, and even when an air raid warning sounded we joined the other reckless spirits in refusing to go down to the cellars until the sounds of enemy activity became too close to be ignored. Until then we sat there in comfort, sipping our fragrant Nuits St George, thinking of all the others suffocating in their darkened prison below ground, deeply thankful not to be with them.

Of course, once back on duty, we paid for these occasional rash excursions by having to fight the overpowering need to sleep. And although, when it was our turn to share the four a.m. break, we managed to force ourselves to drink the muddy coffee to help keep awake, no power on earth could make us view the ersatz saffron cakes, limp sandwiches or tired soya sausages drowning in a sauce of doubtful origin with anything but distaste bordering on nausea. Serve us right, but oh it was worth it!

These outings inevitably became less frequent as the raids increased, and there were occasions when the relief transport was unable to get to Derby House over the wasteland of collapsed buildings or because of an ongoing raid. This meant that we were sometimes forced to remain on duty for a double shift, as someone had to be there to cope with the ever-increasing stream of urgent signals from ships under attack.

It was strangely disturbing to be in such close contact, as it were, with distant naval engagements, and in many cases acutely distressing. It was almost as though we were actually there with the convoys, and on one occasion we became involved in a way that upset us all deeply. We were immensely busy, working at full stretch deciphering the top secret messages pouring in, when there was a sudden stifled cry from Ruth, one of the girls sitting almost opposite me. She was on her feet, her face deathly white as she gazed down in horror at the deciphered signal on her table.

We all stopped working and looked at her in concern. I thought she was going to faint, but instead she snatched up the signal as if to read it again, and in a high-pitched voice of such agony I'll never forget it, cried out, "Oh God! No! It can't be Derek's ship! It can't—!"

We sat there, stunned and silent, till she turned to us all, holding out the signal in one shaking hand, and half whispered: "Tell me it's not true! It's a mistake. It must be—!"

Second Officer Martin moved quickly towards her and took her by the arm, gently leading her out of the room. She had dropped the signal and someone bent down to pick it up and read it.

It was only too true. The ship had been struck by several mines and blown up.

I felt quite sick. Ruth had been married for only three weeks after a honeymoon of three days, when her husband had to join his ship, and had always been rather quiet and pale, growing more haggard with anxiety each time she came on duty. I was really concerned for her, and wondered how long she'd be able to stand the sort of work we were doing. It was bad enough to feel totally helpless as ships struggled to guard their convoys under constant attack from U-boats, but we were not personally involved – at least, I thought, with a sudden lurch of my heart, not so far. David was still out there somewhere, a torpedo midshipman on board HMS *Neptune*, with hundreds of men on board. Would I, one bright morning, decypher shattering news of that lovely ship, that wonderful cruiser?

I thought how we all cheered when a German battleship was successfully sunk with the loss of almost two thousand men. And we congratulated ourselves on a great victory! How could we? What was the war doing to us?

May 27th 1941   *Liverpool*

I was beginning to feel more like a mole than a human being, working down in the depths of Derby House, not knowing what was going on above me. We could tell to a certain extent what the noise was we were hearing, but being underground it sounded muffled and far off. It usually started with the relentless throbbing of the swarms of German aircraft which gradually got louder, then this was followed by energetic anti-aircraft fire from the dozens of our guns in and around Liverpool. One could imagine the whole of the Mersey lit up like a firework display, and when finally the bombs came screaming down it must have been like Dante's Inferno above us. The worst was when a bomb landed somewhere close to us. The reverberation hit the eardrums like a blow from a hammer, and for a moment or two we were all deafened and stupefied. The walls of our office shuddered almost visibly, and I found myself glancing nervously up at the ceiling to see if it was still holding firm. The whole place seemed to give itself a shake, and then settled down again into its former pattern of construction. Fortunately we were so busy we regarded this as just a momentary, unwelcome interruption, before once more dipping our heads on to the half-decyphered signal on the table before us. A convoy was somewhere out there, at the mercy of a savage horde of U-boats waiting for its victims to come within close range of their torpedoes, and in a strange way we felt responsible for its safety. There was very little time to feel frightened, though there were moments when we undoubtedly did. Then the teleprinters would rattle ferociously again and we were once more inundated with pages of cypher. I had begun to memorise a huge number of everyday words and their corresponding cypher numbers, which saved a lot of time by not having to look them up in the cypher book. It was almost like learning a foreign language and very satisfying when you found you could suddenly recognize what you were looking at. I was also teaching some of my colleagues the new cypher we had learnt on the Greenwich training course, but it was difficult to find the time when on duty, so I was usually given the signals in the new cypher to cope with.

By now, there were no opportunities for dinner at the Adelphi Hotel. It would have been dangerous to leave our underground offices between the watches, with no guarantee of being able to get back in time to Derby House during a raid. It also might have been impossible to negotiate the collapsed buildings and unrecognisable roads. But at least the blue light in the sleeping area was being left on for security reasons in case we had to vacate it in a hurry, and my panic faded.

May 28th 1941   *Liverpool*

There was a convoy going to Gibraltar in a couple of days, and fourteen WRNS cypher officers would be sailing in one of the ships. In the meantime, hearing how frantically busy we were, they volunteered while waiting to embark, to join our watches and give us a hand. Since they were all very experienced in the new as well as the original cypher we were immensely grateful. A very friendly third officer named Isobel joined me at my table, and we sped through the mound of incoming signals with remarkable ease. Speed was essential in our situation as lives might depend on it.

She and her companions left to go on board two days later, and I envied them going to the Mediterranean, although I knew their journey might prove rather hazardous. I could imagine their ship sliding silently from its berth to rendezvous with the rest of the convoy, and for a moment a faint chill crept over me, an uneasy premonition that was horribly justified during my next watch on duty. I had half been expecting the convoy to run into trouble, as U-boats were often active along that route, and guarding a large convoy of ships of all sizes and speeds was no easy task for their escorts.

It was later that evening that we began to decypher urgent signals from the Admiralty warning the convoy of a sizeable U-boat presence in their immediate vicinity, and despite my efforts to remain calm and concentrated I found myself thinking of Isobel and those thirteen other girls, wondering how they felt.

It wasn't long before consistent news of casualties began to pour in, and from then on all of us were joined in the sickening need to fight a battle secondhand, while sitting in warmth and comparative safety within the four walls of our room. News was coming in of hard-pressed escorts dashing to the aid of badly-damaged stragglers with very little chance of getting through the ambush, and as the convoy's frequent signals told of desperate evasive action being taken, all we could do was to concentrate on the race to get the stricken ships once more together and in line with their escorting destroyers.

A sudden smothered gasp from the next table brought all our heads round from our work, and it didn't need the muttered "Oh God!" to tell us the horrifying news we had all been hoping not to hear.

The ship had gone, torpedoed. No news of survivors, though other ships were frantically searching. I dropped my pencil, my hand trembling so much I couldn't use it for the moment. What a waste! What an appalling, unnecessary waste! And suddenly I had a dreadful picture of Isobel alone in that thunderous darkness, in the heaving water, choking in the icy blackness, desperate not to drown, yet even as she struggled, knowing there would be very little hope of being picked up in the tumultuous chaos.

Overcome, I bowed my head, but watchful for such weakness Second Officer Martin, though as shocked and distressed as we were, told us all to keep going as there were other ships in similar straits, and somehow we managed very shakily to pull ourselves together.

June 25th 1941   *Liverpool*

I woke up earlier than usual, feeling rather odd, with a deep-seated headache and my skin burning. A glance in the mirror was enough to send me quickly along to sick bay where Sister Jennings, after one knowledgeable look in my direction, rose to her feet and pushed me into a nearby chair.

"Oh dear," she said in a resigned tone, "another one.

You're the fourth so far."

I sank thankfully down, "The fourth what?" I asked, puzzled.

"Measles," replied Sister Jennings in a matter-of-fact voice. "You must get to bed immediately."

I was stunned. "*Measles?* But how—? I thought you only got that when you were a child."

She looked amused. "Oh no. It can hit you at almost any age."

I felt almost indignant. Measles! At *my* age! How degrading! Here was I, assigned to an important, top secret job, in the fight against Hitler, and all I could do was to succumb to a revolting, childish disease I should have caught years ago when it didn't matter. And now, I had probably infected most of my watch.

"Never mind, dear," said Sister Jennings, with only the slightest irony in her voice. "We'll just have to win the war without you."

The worst part about Sister Jennings was that she always seemed to know exactly what one was thinking, and I relaxed suddenly, and laughed.

More degradation was to follow. I had to go to the isolation ward to join the other sufferers, but not on foot. Two disgustingly healthy looking medical assistants put me firmly on to a stretcher, covered me in a thick and itchy red blanket, and bore their infectious burden head first down the narrow staircase, negotiating the bend with practised ease while encouraging me with cheerful remarks about being better soon. Why are men so insensitive, I thought bitterly, so impervious to one's obvious shame and embarrassment?

There followed almost three weeks of misery, lying in a shaded ward, covered from head to toe in a painful rash, and regularly attended by a naval doctor who, to my affronted gaze, obviously thought himself God's gift to womankind, even to one like me who felt far too ill to respond to anyone. Doctors in white hospital attire are bad enough in this respect, but get one in smart naval uniform and bedside manner to match—!

July 16th 1941   *Liverpool*
During my stay in sick bay I learnt that my promotion to third officer had been confirmed on June 26th, which was encouraging, and I eventually recovered both health and spirits, and once again presented myself, though shakily, on duty. It was salutary to be made aware of real suffering out at sea in contrast to my overblown concern for myself in what was after all less than the merest hiccup in the serious pattern of events.

August 30th 1941   *Oaklands*
Unexpectedly home again, having been given ten days compassionate leave to look after my father while my poor mother had to go into hospital for a rather serious operation. It was a nerve-racking time. Not only was my father deeply worried over her condition, but the German aircraft seemed once again to have turned their attention to destroying the ICI works at Northwich, not far from the hospital, and we began to endure several highly dangerous raids. We were especially alarmed but reassured when we heard that immediately after the operation, when my mother was in the intensive care ward, a very courageous young VAD nurse, instead of going down to the shelter during one particularly ferocious raid, had thrown herself across my mother's bed to protect her from falling glass or possible collapse of part of the ceiling.

Fortunately, neither the salt flats nor the ICI works were ever hit, and after my ten days leave had passed, my aunt Nancy, my mother's younger sister, volunteered to come and stay until things had settled down. My mother duly recovered, and the running of the house became comparatively easy and efficient.

October 3rd 1941   *Liverpool*

My birthday once more, my second in the WRNS. But how different from the last one at St Merryn. I could still hear in my mind the terrifying sound of bullets hurtling along the floor between our two lines of beds in Bruce Hut, and the horrid spattering noise as they were finally lodged in our wooden door. I wondered how everyone was getting on there. It seemed so long ago and far away, like one of Vera Lynn's poignant songs. Whatever she sang the forces' sweetheart touched a chord in all of us, though here the context had been very different. No romantic allusion like in the song, only a memory of a very narrow escape.

November 7th 1941   *Liverpool*

Panic stations! I was being posted to a Royal Naval Air Station called Machrihanish up in Scotland, as an urgently needed replacement for a cypher officer with appendicitis. Apparently there were only two cypher officers coping with twenty-four hour watches. So, no time to waste. Get going!

Where was Machrihanish? The admin officer, new to her job, obviously didn't know, and answered flippantly, "Oh, just get to Glasgow and ask. There's a bus service from there, I believe."

Bus service? Where on earth *was* this place?

"You'd better spend the night in the Central Hotel. I'll book you a room," she said finally. "They'll know all about buses from there. Better start packing. Oh, and get yourself a map of Scotland. You can show me exactly where Machrihanish is when you come to collect your travel warrant. I might as well know too, in case anyone else gets sent there."

"But why *me*?" I asked. "Why not one of the others?"

"Well, you've been quite ill, haven't you? Measles in an adult is no joke. And you've been here over six months. You could probably do with a change. Couldn't we all?" she added rather wistfully. "I've only been here a few weeks, but I'd be ready to go to Scotland tomorrow if it were possible."

A quick call to my family brought slight indignation at the speed of events. I would find it such an effort, they said, to have to pack and get on a train with all my luggage in such a rush, and go somewhere nobody seemed to have heard of. Did I really have to go?

I explained the circumstances, adding that as a mobile Wren I was always at twenty-four hours notice to up sticks and go wherever I was sent, so there we were. Anyway, perhaps Scotland might be more peaceful than Liverpool.

My parents sighed and agreed, then added that they'd just had another letter from David, who was now enjoying life at sea as a full blown midshipman. The crew were a pleasant lot, very helpful apparently, and did not look down on young 'middies' as they termed his rank. No sign of any Captain Blighs aboard either.

November 8th 1941   *en route for Scotland*
I don't quite know how I managed it, but was once again in a crowded train, this time on my way to Glasgow and beyond. On the whole I had no regrets at all on leaving Liverpool. The permanent all-pervading dust and grime of the city had begun to get me down. There was so much sadness and exhaustion, in spite of the courage and true grit of its inhabitants. It amazed me how they managed to carry on regardless of the nightly horrors of the raids or injury or loss of loved ones. It struck me also that so many seemed to have little more to lose than their lives. The poverty and squalor I had seen there had shaken me more than I would have believed possible. One couldn't ignore it. I had had the chance to get away now and then to see my family, and now would be going away altogether, but most of those poor people in Liverpool had no choice but to stay and face whatever was coming to them.

I wondered what Machrihanish would be like. Being a naval air station it might be more on the lines of St Merryn, certainly with fresher air to breathe and quieter nights to sleep through than in Liverpool. No more mole holes to work in, or a black hole of Calcutta in which to try and sleep between watches. And now, in a way, I felt I was going home, being half Scottish myself. My mother was a McGregor and my father an Irishman so, as a Celt, I would surely find Scotland congenial. Perhaps this was why I had developed a restless side to my character, always wanting to look over the rim of the moon to see what lay beyond. How far away in time as well as location my home in Cheshire seemed, how distant and foreign my former style of living. I couldn't imagine ever going back to that.

The train finally reached Glasgow Central Station at nine in the evening, and the passengers poured out on to the platform in a storm of pushing and shoving in their haste to get through the ticket gate. This was Liverpool's Lime Street Station all over again, but with a difference. Except for the travellers there was not much sign of war weariness. Everyone seemed full of energy and super-charged aggression, and I stood beside my carriage to let them pass by while I got my breath after having lugged my heavy suitcase, gas mask and other belongings out on to the platform.

A few minutes later a tall young sailor approached and saluted me politely. "Anything we can do for you, Ma'am?" he asked in a pleasant baritone voice. "You seem to have quite a bit of luggage there. Where are you making for?"

I turned and smiled at him. "To the Central Hotel. I was going to look for a taxi."

"Oh, you won't need that," he said cheerfully. "It's quite close by. Wait just a moment." And he turned and strode away amongst the crowd, returning with three other young sailors, who all nodded politely to me, and collected my belongings, the first sailor tossing my suitcase effortlessly up on to his shoulder.

"Now, Ma'am," he said, "we'll walk you there. Mind you stay in the middle of us. Things get a bit hot here on a Saturday night, and you don't want to spoil your nice hat."

As I took up my station in their midst I thought with an inward smile that here was yet another Fred; not, I realised a moment or two later, that this one would ever be called Fred. No. It would have to be Frederick at the very least! He gave me the distinct impression that he was surely destined to become a rear admiral one day. His manner was neatly balanced between request and command, and I had no intention of disobeying him. It was the same feeling we all had at St Merryn when Lieutenant Commander Merlin Bruce strode on to the scene, issuing his orders far and wide.

It was only a short journey, but I was very glad of my escort. Saturday night was in full swing, men and girls alike shouting and swearing at each other, their accents incomprehensible to me; some, particularly a group of girls who couldn't have been a day more than thirteen, slinging broken bottles at a gang of young boys, who retaliated with fearsome Scottish war cries while chasing them all up the street. The yells and screams grew louder, the crowds more dense the further we moved from the station, but my four stalwart companions strode through them all like a knife through butter, and deposited me safely in the foyer of the Central Hotel.

I turned to thank them all, holding out my hand, which the future rear admiral shook, then with a very attractive smile, saluted and said, "Happy to assist you, Ma'am," before nodding to the others, who also smiled rather shyly as they saluted and followed their leader to the doorway.

"Now, there's the Navy for you!" I thought, relieved and encouraged, then suddenly realised I'd never even asked him his name.

After I'd been signed in and given my room key I

enquired about Machrihanish. The receptionist, a large, smiling woman, put me right on all counts.

"Och, Machrihanish, is it?" she said. "A bonny place, a wee bit from Campbeltown down on the Mull of Kintyre. You'll be taking the MacBrayne bus. I'll book you a seat. It leaves at eight o'clock tomorrow morning. You'll enjoy the journey. It'll take four and a half to five hours. I have a map for you here," she added, opening a drawer in her desk. "You'll stop at—"And here she reeled off a string of names that meant nothing to me, but which were so musical and pleasant on her tongue I nearly asked her to repeat them.

"And you'll be wanting your dinner," she added. "You'll just be in time."

I realised how hungry I was and went down to the dining room as quickly as I could. The dinner was good, but not of course up to the standard of the Adelphi in Liverpool, though it was pleasant to be able to sit and eat in peace without worrying about air raid alarms going off. There were several senior naval officers also dining there, who glanced rather curiously at me, but no one approached, so I left as soon as I'd drunk my coffee, and went up to bed for a wonderfully quiet night's sleep.

November 9th 1941   en route for RNAS Machrihanish,
Mull of Kintyre, Scotland (HMS Landrail)
The MacBrayne bus was a single-decker vehicle with spacious seating which was surprisingly well upholstered and comfortable, and whose driver was courteous and friendly. On this quiet Sunday morning there were not many passengers, a few naval and army officers, four or five businesslike civilians who were either studying their files or writing on large foolscap-sized paper, and a sprinkling of what I imagined to be local people returning home after a visit to the big city. As we began our sleepy crawl through the now almost empty streets of Glasgow it was obvious that the noisy and aggressive revellers of the night before

had given up and disappeared into their various habitats to sleep off the effects or attend to their wounds. I yawned and settled back into my seat. It was wonderful to relax and breathe in the soft autumn air which even now still held a faint hint of late summer, wonderful not to feel one's throat contract against the choking dust of Liverpool.

I had been too exhausted the previous night to study the map given me by the kindly receptionist, but now there was plenty of opportunity to recognize the colourful names of the places along our route down the Mull of Kintyre. As we left the outer environs of Glasgow the bus began to weave its leisurely way through some of the most beautiful countryside I'd ever seen. The view through my window was startling, so different from what I'd become accustomed to seeing during the last six months. Here there was a wonderful atmosphere of space, serenity and silence, and I sat entranced, my tired body soaking it all up.

Everywhere I looked there were low hills and high jutting crags tumbled beside shining lochs that were surrounded by graceful trees leaning over almost to the water's edge, casting a delicate pattern on the still surface. There wasn't a breath of wind anywhere. Everything was extraordinarily quiet after the endless bustle and tension of life in a bombed and vulnerable city. Whatever disturbances of war or local conflict – and there had been much bitter fighting between the clans of Scotland – these lowering mountains had remained locked in the imperturbable calm of centuries, oblivious to puny mortal upheavals going on around them.

Our destination lay deep into the Mull of Kintyre, and I had nothing to do but enjoy the various stops in the peaceful little villages on the way. Their names flowed past me in a colourful stream – Luss, Arrochar, Inveraray, Lochgilphead, Ardrishaig, Tarbert – so many I forgot some of them – though it was not possible to forget the impressive nine-hundred-foot summit of the pass between

Glen Croe and Glen Kinglas.This was known by the quaint name of 'Rest and be thankful', so called after an army general back in 1740 had led his exhausted troops up to the pass and allowed them to take a much needed breather there.

November 10th 1941   RNAS Machrihanish, Mull of Kintyre
(HMS Landrail)

We arrived finally at Campbeltown on the east coast, where three of us got off the bus. An attractive young Wren driver was waiting beside what looked like a small, eight-seater bus with a large amount of space at the back for luggage.

"Third Officer Houston?" she asked, as she approached and saluted me.

I nodded, returning her salute, then she transferred her glance to my two companions.

"Lieutenant Walton?" The young naval officer acknowledged her salute with a smile, and we watched a little curiously as she turned and smiled brightly at the rather older Army major standing behind me.

"Major Harris. Nice to see you again, sir," she said, saluting once more.

"Hello, Sally," he replied, smiling down at her. "Haven't seen you for some time. How are you?"

They were obviously old acquaintances, and Lieutenant Walton and I left them chatting while we loaded up all the luggage into the back of the vehicle.

The Major, turning his head, saw this and thanked us profusely. The Wren driver smiled at us and climbed into her seat. By tacit agreement, in respect for the Major's seniority in age and rank, we stood by to allow him to choose his seat among those in the back, but he settled himself in the front seat beside her, and we were left to choose our places behind them.

After a while the Major turned to us and enquired what we were coming to Machrihanish to do. When he heard why I was there he laughed suddenly and said: "Oh, you're the cypher officer relief, are you? You'll be very popular. Things have been a bit difficult since poor Janet was taken off to hospital. You've certainly arrived in good time." He paused, then turned to Lieutenant Walton. "And you – what are you here for?"

"I'm a met officer, sir," my companion replied. "I've just been on a course at Arbroath."

We didn't quite like to ask the Major what he did, so conversation lapsed between us.

It was a comparatively short drive to Machrihanish on the opposite coast from Campbeltown, and eventually we came to a narrow road, passing several smallish houses on the left of it, until we stopped outside a rather rundown-looking hotel.

As we all got out the Major said cheerfully: "Well, here we are. All the comforts of home. This is where we're all billeted at present."

As we unloaded our cases he continued, "This place was once a very well known golf course, you know, and all the players – quite famous, many of them – used to stay here." He paused, then added with a sigh, "I've always liked the old Ugadale Arms, though it's gone to seed a bit these days. But it's still fairly comfortable on the whole."

That was certainly true. My bedroom was a good size, with only three beds in it. And the view from the window of Machrihanish Bay was breathtaking, with its huge, wide sweep of beach and rolling dunes alongside the hangars and runways of the air station, which were now almost obliterating any signs of a golf course. I could tell the Major was rather nostalgic about it.

November 14th 1941   *RNAS Machrihanish*
That first day allowed me very little time for reflection or recovery from my previous exhaustion. Although the cold Atlantic air was invigorating I felt tired and rather

confused, having to be on call during a twenty-four hour shift of duty. Machrihanish was a naval air training station like St Merryn, and run more or less on the same lines, but there the similarity ended.

It was strange living and working in a hotel. Our cypher office was situated in one of the back bedrooms on the top floor, with no stunning view of the Atlantic to distract us. This room was never left unlocked on account of the top secret work that went on there. The signals distribution office was somewhere on the ground floor, with another bluff Chief Yeoman of Signals in charge, and the usual quota of Wrens manning the telephone exchange and teleprinter.

Nancy Macdonald, known as Red because of her magnificent flaming hair, led me up to the top floor and showed me around.

"We eat our meals in the dining room as and when," she explained in a pleasant voice faintly tinged with an attractive Scots intonation, "unless an Immediate signal comes in, then of course we have to decypher that at once and deal with it. But you can lie down on the bed and get some rest during the night if things are quiet. It's not exactly the Ritz," she added, seeing my rather doubtful look at the narrow bed in one corner of the room, "but better than having to sit up all night."

"Do we ever get really busy?" I asked.

"You mean if we have to work non-stop? No, not at the moment. But when the station really gets going and we have many more aircraft coming in, things may get a bit tricky with only the two of us." She smiled suddenly. "If that happens, of course, they'll just have to allocate two more cypher officers to work with us unless they want to have us both carried off gibbering."

"Oh well," I said, amused, "one can't have everything, I suppose. And at least we shan't have to cope with air raids here. Liverpool was ghastly."

"You'll soon get used to this," she said, reassuringly, and of course, after my second shift of duty I began to see daylight.

A few minutes before eight o'clock I was due to take over from Red, but since she had left me no urgent signals to work on, she suggested we might join all the others for breakfast.

On the way downstairs to the dining room she remarked, "The most difficult thing is to get enough sleep when you're off duty. People are always coming and going, you know, and they don't always realise some of us need peace and quiet. It can get very tiring if you skimp on your sleep."

She certainly looked rather weary, and I wondered if she'd been working extra hours before I arrived to replace the girl with appendicitis.

I was lucky in the two girls who shared my room. (One couldn't call it a cabin here.) Anne and Joanna were administrative officers, so worked the usual daytime hours, never blundering noisily into the room when they knew I might be sleeping there, and I was duly grateful. Inconsiderate colleagues would have been disastrous. There was also an added bonus in our officer in charge.

First Officer Lovell Caddy was a charming, sophisticated woman in her thirties, with a wonderful sense of humour, who presided over us rather like a hostess at a party or a garden fête. There were rules, but these were never thrust down our throats, and she was always totally understanding regarding the situation in our odd working hours.

Our meals were served in the spacious restaurant reserved for the hotel inmates – eight WRNS officers with others of all ranks and services, as well as various civilians who came and went on unspecified duties. I was surprised at the lack of protocol regarding our places at table. Everyone sat where they could find a vacant seat. There was a pleasantly relaxed atmosphere, and I found myself talking to all sorts of interesting people.

The food was good, and my only doubts about it arose from a visit late that night to the kitchen on my way up to the cypher office, in search of a hot sustaining drink during my shift.

As I was heating up a saucepan of cocoa, there was a strange skittering noise from below, and looking down I saw to my horror that the floor was crawling with cockroaches, which appeared to be engaged in a spirited Scottish reel around my feet. The half heated cocoa shot into my mug, and closing my appalled mind I made a dash for the door, and didn't stop running till I had reached my destination, where I set down the mug and locked the door with a trembling hand. The sight and sound of those bright orange creatures had made my flesh creep. What on earth must it have been like to work in such a kitchen?

I drank the cocoa and thought, what an idiot! I'd survived God knows what horrors, yet I'd gone to pieces at the sight of a few cockroaches! Why shouldn't the poor things enjoy a few night-time revels after the kitchen staff had gone to bed? Probably cockroaches liked old buildings with old kitchens. Why shouldn't they? Live and let live! And yet – oh well, I told myself, we can't all have nerves of steel. When I told Red about it next morning she laughed heartily and said, "Oh, I'm sorry, I forgot to warn you. Everyone's been trying to get rid of them for ages. Those poor cooks manage to keep the kitchens immaculate, but every now and then those wretched creatures escape and—"

"—present a sort of welcoming committee for unsuspecting newcomers!" I said rather bitterly.

"You're tired," she said. "Were you very busy last night?"

"No, not too bad," I replied. "In fact I managed to sleep for quite a while."

"Well, go down and have some breakfast," she said. "You'll feel better when you've eaten something."

"As long as it's not cockroach on toast," I responded. She laughed, and after handing over to her I made my way downstairs to the dining room, and found myself sitting next to Major Harris, who greeted me like an old friend. I had by then discovered that he was some kind of liaison officer for the station, and even relaxed sufficiently to tell him the sorry saga of the cockroaches.

He threw back his head and laughed outright. "Don't blame you for running," he said, "I can't stand the little devils. Give me the creeps, they do. Don't know why, I've seen enough insect horrors in my time in all sorts of foreign climes, but there's something about a cockroach! Don't let's talk about them. Puts me off my breakfast."

He rose miles in my estimation. Not many tough Army officers would admit to being squeamish about cockroaches!

November 25th 1941   *RNAS Machrihanish*
Machrihanish was a sort of intermission away from the war. No bombing raids or machine-gunning, only an increasingly intense training for the pilots marking its contribution. Here, one woke only to the piercing cries of seagulls and occasional distant bleating of sheep, and death seemed on holiday, at least at first. My parents were immensely relieved to know I was no longer in such immediate danger as at Liverpool.

The one thing that was missing at Machrihanish was any form of organised entertainment. I was told that plans were in hand to build some kind of large recreation hall for dances, films and lectures, or even amateur dramatics. This would be ready in the spring. In the meantime all sorts of buildings had been springing up all over the station, a large officers' mess, offices and sleeping quarters for senior officers and pilots, a smaller mess for the WRNS officers with sleeping quarters and administration offices, and further away a vast kitchen complex serving the entire community. The WRNS ratings would have their own quarters and recreation hut nearby. Some way further along the low cliff, on a narrow path just above the beach, the new signals distribution and cypher office were practically completed. All in all, it seemed we wouldn't be staying at the Ugadale Arms much longer.

November 27th 1941   *RNAS Machrihanish*
In one respect we were lucky. One of the younger pilots, John Mayne, was a really gifted pianist who often used to play for us on the old upright piano in one of the smaller lounges of the hotel. He was particularly fond of Chopin, and his playing reminded me of my lessons with Walter Gieseking's old pupil at Lausanne. The haunting sadness of some of the pieces brought a stark comparison of the desperate plight of the Poles in Warsaw with the wanton killing and destruction in Liverpool. The same defiance and endurance on the part of the victims brought a lump into my throat, and I felt almost guilty at being so safe and far away from the battle.

In a lighter vein, I used to sing through some of the popular arias and songs I had brought with me, with John as a marvellous accompanist, and we began to spend many evenings during these impromptu concerts responding to requests for various items in our repertoire. I hadn't sung a note in Liverpool. It had been impossible under those conditions, so it was a special pleasure now to go through my collection to such an appreciative audience. A number of the younger pilots used to drift in occasionally, and sometimes the classics had to give way to requests for more popular numbers, strongly reminiscent of those I had sung and played on the tinny old piano at the Ring o' Bells at St Izzy in Cornwall.

December 7th 1941   *RNAS Machrihanish*
Awful news of the Japanese surprise attack on Pearl
Harbor. No one could talk of anything else.

"This'll bring the Yanks in," Major Harris said
confidently at dinner that evening. "And mark my words, I
think this will prove to be a great mistake by the Japs in the
long run. Roosevelt will never stand for this."

December 8th 1941   *RNAS Machrihanish*
The newspapers were full of it, showing the most horrible
pictures of damaged ships half sunk, with their crews
throwing themselves into the churning water, most of it
covered with burning oil. The shattered remains of aircraft,
closely parked together and therefore most vulnerable,
showed how complete the surprise had been on that
peaceful Sunday morning. I felt sick. Now we had another
warring monster beside Hitler to combat.

But there were also more photographs in the evening
papers of President Roosevelt signing the formal
declaration of war against Japan, and I think we were all
reassured by the thought of another such powerful ally,
though none of us could know how far throughout the
world the war would now spread. We still had so much on
our hands here in Europe.

I often wondered how everyone was getting on in the
Liverpool cypher office, and felt rather out of things here
in Scotland, since we only had the radio and newspapers to
let us know how serious the situation in the Atlantic was
becoming. The losses in merchant shipping were
enormous, and the reports of the sinking of several of our
great battleships deeply depressing.

We were only a training station here, but now, after Pearl
Harbor, there seemed to be a new urgency about our work
as increased numbers of aircraft and pilots began to arrive.
The spurious feeling of peace and safety faded. Here we
were only on the outer edge of the battlefield, but no one

doubted that that huge area of conflict beyond our immediate orbit would spread and annihilate us all if it were not checked.

December 20th 1941   *RNAS Machrihanish*
It was after breakfast on a cold bright morning, when I was being given a lift from the hotel across to the station by one of the senior officers. I had just come off duty and was feeling rather sleepy and longing for my bed. But before that, I had to check up on something with Lieutenant Walton at the met office, and was grateful for a lift. I could probably catch one of the transports on the way back.

As we approached the met office someone waved us to stop, and I saw it was Lieutenant Commander Mackinnon, the First Lieutenant of the station.

My companion opened his window and cheerfully said good morning. I saw at once that Lieutenant Commander Mackinnon's face was rather drawn and that he seemed upset. His voice, too, sounded strange. "Have you heard?" he asked, leaning forward into the window. "Last night Force K blundered into a minefield just off Tripoli. *Kandahar's* lost. My young nephew was aboard. Very few survivors ... ."

He paused, and my driver leant forward and put his hand on the First Lieutenant's arm.

"God! I'm sorry, Mac," he said. "No, I hadn't heard."

"It's not on the radio or in the papers," Lieutenant Mackinnon said. "Someone I know rang to tell me."

Something flashed through my mind. Force K. Where had I come across that name? Some time back in Liverpool. There had been a connection somewhere with what we had just learnt, something to do with HMS *Kandahar.*

"This bloody war!" my companion muttered as we drove on. "I knew that boy. Nice youngster – very bright. Let's hope he's been picked up."

By the time I got back to my bedroom and fell into exhausted sleep it was almost midday, and I did not wake until about four o'clock. I'd missed lunch, so made do with several cups of strong tea and a rock bun, which well deserved its name.

December 21st 1941   *RNAS Machrihanish*
It was getting busier on watch, and I had hardly stopped since I had gone on duty at eight o'clock that morning, after relieving Red of a mound of work. She must have slept for a long time during the day as I didn't see her until it was almost time for dinner. By then, things had quietened down sufficiently for me to have time to eat, and I was on my way down the wide staircase towards the dining room when First Officer Caddy saw me and approached, holding out a small envelope in her hand.

"Oh, there you are, Roxane," she said. "This telegram came for you a short while ago."

I thanked her and automatically opened the envelope, my mind still connected with the work I'd been doing so assiduously all day.

The first words literally sprang out at me: *Admiralty reports David missing believed killed.* 'Admiralty reports'. No mistake then. It must be true. Then the pathetic remainder of the message from my father: "Can you find out anything about survivors?" Just that. Signed 'Dad'.

Through a sudden blackened mist I felt blindly for the banister and clung to it, unable to speak for a moment. Then I half whispered, "My young brother's missing. He was in *Neptune*."

"Oh, poor child!" Lovell Caddy's voice was deeply compassionate. I could hardly think for the shock, but managed to gasp out, "May I have permission to phone Liverpool, Ma'am? One of my watch, Bobbie Stocker, has a nephew on board. She might be able to give me some news."

Permission granted, I rushed upstairs into the office, locking the door behind me as usual, and grabbing the telephone in desperate haste. I was lucky to find Bobbie on duty, and in an unsteady voice asked her how her nephew was.

Her reply was shattering. "Not good," she said quietly. "Not good at all, I'm afraid. But I'll let you know the second I get any more news. It's been an awful disaster. They went into an unsuspected minefield. I don't know how it happened .... " Her voice suddenly tailed off, and I put down the receiver and sat at my desk, my head in my hands, suddenly realising why Force K had stuck in my memory.

HMS *Kandahar* was one of the ships in Force K, and among the others there was also the cruiser HMS *Neptune*. *Kandahar* was one of the first to be hit. God knew how many more from Force K had been lost or damaged since then. The signals must have been coming in thick and fast to the Liverpool cypher office, but since the disaster might still be ongoing it had not yet been publicly reported.

Now I had to find the courage to ring my father. What could I tell him? My mother must be going out of her mind with worry.

My father's voice was strange, a mixture of eagerness and alarm.

"Hello? Hello? Roxy, is that you? Have you been able to get any news?"

"Not yet," I answered, trying to keep my voice from breaking. "I'll let you know, Dad, as soon as I hear anything from Liverpool. They'll ring me when they hear any more." And then, as tears thickened my throat, I added: "Dad darling, I'll come home as soon as I can! They'll give me compassionate leave—"

"No!" he interrupted, his voice suddenly louder and incisive. "No, don't do that! You're better placed where you are – to get news. You couldn't phone from here. No one would tell you anything."

I hardly dared ask the next question. "How's Mum? Is she—?"

His voice flattened, becoming unsteady and tremulous once more.

"She's — she's very upset, or course. Terribly upset. We all are. Let us know quickly, Roxy, if you can — if there's any more news — anything at all . . . ." His voice tailed off, and I heard him replace the receiver. Some things were too hard to say.

I sat there, thinking this was the worst moment of my life, one I'd never forget as long as I lived. That telegram from the Admiralty to my parents must have been the final blow to my mother. She had always told us how frightened she had been during the Great War, when my father had been in the Army, and when so many telegrams to friends and acquaintances had been received with their stark message. It must have been a dreadful time for her, and now that fear had materialised, this time concerning an eighteen and-a-half-year-old boy, not yet fully a grown man, one of her sons, David, so bright, so clever, so much loved by us all. Not only by us, it seemed. Those whom the gods love die young. What a horrible idea, and how unfair to deny a full life to someone as young and gifted as he was!

I wondered if the poor telegraph boy who delivered these telegrams ever thought of the mountains of grief and despair he was leaving behind him at each new address. Did he give this a thought, or had he become so hardened to being the messenger of death that he could thrust it all aside, and go cheerfully home to his tea?

There was a knock on my door, followed by First Officer's voice suggesting I go downstairs with her. "I don't think you should be alone," she added, and I obeyed, numbed, beyond tears, almost beyond coherent thought.

Someone approached as I reached the smaller lounge, and gently put a glass of red wine into my hand. It was one of the squadron leaders named Neil, a man of about twenty-eight, and he spoke quietly, "Come and sit down." And when I had sipped some of the wine, he added, "You mustn't despair. People do get picked up, you know."

I would never forget his unobtrusive kindness that evening, nor the unspoken sympathy, particularly of the pilots, which I felt surrounding me in waves. I sat in silence, unable to speak for the painful tightness of my throat, afraid of bursting into torrents of distraught weeping. It was not the time for that yet. That would come later. All I could try to do was to hold on to my control, and remind myself that these pilots risked their lives every day and night, and would doubtless face even more dangers when they joined their fighting squadrons out in the main aerial battlefields. I felt that they were in some way in brotherhood with David, understanding what he might be going through, and what they themselves might one day be suffering.

Red was particularly distressed for me, and offered to take over the rest of my night shift, but I assured her I would be able to cope, and that it might be a good thing for me to be busy and have to concentrate on something other than the appalling news about David. The other WRNS officers were also very shocked and concerned. Perhaps personal disaster hadn't yet touched any of them, but mine brought the war closer, made loss and sudden bereavement seem much more possible.

Later that night, having assured Lovell Caddy that I was capable of coping with night duty, I sat alone in the office, trying to concentrate on a rather complicated signal. By now my desolation was complete. Life without David was unthinkable, but then, it seemed, the unthinkable so often occurred. I couldn't even begin to imagine how my poor parents could live with never knowing what had actually happened to him. I supposed they must have told Tony. I would try to ring him tomorrow. Meantime, the war would go on, the loss and the suffering, and its survivors would have no option but to pick up the bits and fashion them into a new design for living.

December 23rd 1941   *RNAS Machrihanish*
And so we waited – and waited for better news, the ever present ache of bereavement darkening every waking moment. Shock was a strange thing. There was total disbelief. Nothing seemed real. I found myself doing everything without conscious thought, just going through the motions like an automaton. A hundred times a day I was thinking this couldn't be real. It hadn't happened. Sometimes I even wondered if we'd all loved David too much, far more than each other. Perhaps it was dangerous to love someone like that. It could be a recipe for bereavement and loneliness, particularly in time of war.

Christmas Eve, 1941   *RNAS Machrihanish*
Tony rang to say that he had suggested that his wife Margaret and their new baby Anne should go up to stay with our parents for some time, as this might help our poor mother who was in an extremis of despair. He had got a few days leave over Christmas, and could drive them up to Cheshire that day. A tiny baby in the house might just be the distraction our parents needed. I think deep down we'd all accepted by now the fact that the loss of personnel from HMS *Neptune* was probably total, though this was still not acknowledged openly between us.

Christmas Day, 1941   *RNAS Machrihanish*
I spoke to Bobbie Stocker again in Liverpool. All the members of the various watches had been alerted to let her know of any details about survivors, but it was so far reported that there had been only one, a leading seaman, sole survivor of the seven hundred and sixty-five officers and men aboard. Apart from this, the only news any of them had received had been of further disastrous losses. We

wished each other a bearable Christmas, if such a thing were possible, and sadly rang off.

January 6th 1942   *RNAS Machrihanish*
My father was still insisting that I remain in Scotland and in touch with Liverpool, just in case of better news. Margaret and the baby would be staying indefinitely at Oaklands where Tony would spend any leave he was given, and my aunt Nancy was a tower of strength, so I didn't argue. We all had to keep hoping.

Some people bear misfortune with calm and dignity, but somehow I couldn't. Inwardly I was seething with hatred and anger, and could cheerfully have strangled Hitler and Mussolini with my bare hands. Not a good feeling — wild and futile and unintelligent. What was the use of raging against fate? It was time to pull myself together or I'd go off the rails entirely.

First Officer Caddy kept an unobtrusive but com-passionate eye on me, occasionally calling me into her office for a chat. Hers was an unenviable task, since there were now others with that recognizable stricken look, who went about their duties quietly with dignity and restraint.

March 20th 1942   *RNAS Machrihanish*
1942 had begun badly after the debacle at Pearl Harbor, and now it seemed that morale was at its lowest ebb. War news was becoming gloomier every day, with reports of the Russians retreating, the Vichy French collaborating with the Germans, and shipping losses in the Atlantic ever higher, while the Japanese appeared to be overrunning south-east Asia and occupying many Pacific islands.

There were major changes in the offing. We were all due to move from the Ugadale Arms to our new quarters over on the main station, since these were now almost ready. In about ten days, we were told.

In the meantime we began to experience a new

phenomenon, the sudden creeping mist that rose without warning from the sea. It was known as a 'sea-fret', or by the old Norwegian name for it, the *haar*, and it could cover the entire area so thickly that it effectively blotted out all activity in the air, proving hazardous for any aircraft coming in to land from out at sea. The met office always kept a strict lookout for this, but it was not always possible to warn pilots very far in advance.

March 30th 1942   *RNAS Machrihanish*
Today would have been David's birthday, his nineteenth, and remembering other birthdays I said a fervent prayer that at least he might now be at peace, and that he would always live in our hearts. I wanted to ring them at home, since my father had told me a week or so ago that he was planning a church service to inaugurate a garden of remembrance for David in the grounds of Hartford Church, close to our house, and naturally wanted Tony and me to be there also.

But today of all days, it was impossible to ring him, since this was the day of our move from the hotel, a frenetic operation – there was no other word for it. Having to pack up heavy boxes of confidential books and carry them downstairs from our top floor office for loading into the naval transport outside the front entrance was back breaking, though fortunately two young naval officers were detailed to give us a hand.

Carpenters and electricians then moved in to restore our cypher office to its former bedroom status. Meanwhile, downstairs was a sort of organised mayhem, with all the furniture and equipment for the SDO, including telephone exchange and teleprinter, having to be dismantled ready for transferring and setting up again in the new SDO building. The SDO Wrens were untiring. Well organised and cheerful, they seemed to think it was a great joke as well as a challenge, and the rather harassed Chief Yeoman of

Signals even began to look amused as the naval ratings detailed to help were given no chance to slacken their efforts.

As I passed by I heard him say in a tone of resignation, "You girls are like a lot of queen bees, bossing everybody about!"

"Well, you must admit we'll get this done much quicker than if it was left to that lot!" one of the Leading Wrens, a small, bright-eyed bundle of energy, retorted with a saucy wink at the grinning sailors, and I laughed and said, "It's no good, Chief. You'd better leave them to it. Moving house is more of a woman's province, after all."

"Huh!" he almost snorted, "That's not always been my experience, Ma'am. They just make more noise about it. I feel I might just as well not be here. Discipline's flown out of the window."

Another of the Wrens looked sympathetically at him. "Never mind, Chief," she said, "I'll go and get you a cup of tea. The kitchen's still working here."

He smiled at me, then turned to the Wren. "You'd better bring one for Third Officer Houston too, while you're about it." And I was never more grateful.

I felt rather sorry for Chief Yeoman. The ground seemed to have been snatched from under his feet. But I recognised the feeling. Who did that young Leading Wren remind me of? Of course! She was the spiritual sister of that future rear admiral who had so gallantly escorted me safely from Glasgow Central Station to the nearby hotel, even perhaps a distant cousin of Lieutenant Commander Merlin Bruce at St Merryn. Here was the same forceful character, the same self-confidence and determination – a Chief Officer WRNS in embryo if the war continued long enough, but even if it didn't I thought she'd very soon be wearing a tricorne hat and blue stripes on her sleeves. Funny, I thought, how young this type of personality manifested itself. She couldn't have been more than nineteen, at the

Top: Family photograph on holiday in Aldeburgh, Suffolk, August 1938.
Bottom left: David Houston aged 12 at Oaklands, Hartford, Cheshire, 1935.
Bottom right: David aged 15, as a cadet at the Royal Naval College, Dartmouth, Devon, 1938.

Top left: Tony Houston,
Lieutenant Royal
Engineers, Aldershot,
1940.

Top right: Singing at a
concert, St Merryn,
1940.

Right: First trip in HMS
Neptune, 1940. David
aged 17 with Dick
Holloway at Capetown.

Top: November 1940. Roxane on far left. A group of WRNS ratings walking past a Blackburn Roc aircraft at the Royal Naval Air Station, St Merryn, North Cornwall. NB: There were military buildings on the right, which have been airbrushed by the censor.

Bottom: The cast of WRNS Tyrolean show, St Merryn, 1940. Standing first and second left, Joy Harper and Roxane Houston; centre, Celia Allen; third from right, Pat Adams; far right, Elizabeth Welburn. Seated far left, Peggy Caunt; second from right, Margaret Blackwell.

Top left: In the garden of Belleaire, Greenock, 1943.

Top right: Roxane with Doreen Hartley on the steps of Belleaire, 1943.

Bottom: Staff of SOASC, Hazelwood, 1943. Far left, Roxane; standing fifth at rear, Leslie Wintle; second from right, Admiral Warren.

Top: Staff of SOASC in the garden of Hazelwood, Greenock, 1943. Standing fourth from right, Admiral Warren; behind on his left, Lieutenant Commander Leslie Wintle; front row second from left, the author.

Bottom left: Yvonne de Méric in tropical uniform, Kandy, Ceylon, 1944.

Bottom right: Elizabeth Welburn, 1945.

Top: From left to right: Lieutenant Commander Tony Trew (Captain of HMS *Walker*), the author, Lieutenant Derek Napper, Isobel Cowie, Mr Baker, Lieutenant 'Sandy' Powell. Greenock, 1945.

Bottom: From left to right: Mr Baker, Derek Napper, Jane Price, Isobel Cowie, the author, 'Sandy' Powell. Greenock, 1945.

No.   **Admiralty**

10th April   19 46

This is to Certify that Roxane Mary HOUSTON has served in the
Women's Royal Naval Service from the 9th day of August 19 40,
to the 20th day of March 19 46, during which period she has
conducted herself entirely to my satisfaction.

An enthusiastic and efficient Cypher Officer who was
later transferred to the Secretarial Branch where she acted
as Assistant to the Staff Officer Landing Craft. Here she
had considerable experience of operational duties and showed
organizing ability and initiative. A clear-thinking, tactful
and pleasant personality.

Rank	From	To
3/0	26.6.41	31.12.44
2/0	1.1.45	20.3.46

Vera Laughton Matthews   Director W.R.N.S.

Top: The *Nea Hellas*, 1945.

Bottom: Roxane's certificate of service from the WRNS.

Above: Roxane and her brother Tony onboard the cruise liner *Legend of the Seas* (in 2000).

Right: Roxane Houston as she is today.

most, and yet she probably had far more sense of leadership than I'd ever have, more certainty of knowing what to do in any situation, and that whatever she did would be right. Not much fear or doubt about her.

It was greatly to the credit of all concerned that the SDO was out of action for only a few hours. The Wrens on watch managed to get going as soon as the electricians had installed the telephone exchange and teleprinter lines in the new building, and calmly carried on as usual among all the disruption.

There was absolutely no question of any sleep either for Red or me. Although we would not be moving from our bedrooms until the next day, the noise of voices and general clatter around us was overwhelming and could be heard all over the building, so after a hasty lunch we went over to our new cypher office next to the SDO, and concentrated on unpacking and sorting out the contents of the huge pile of boxes.

The smell of fresh paint was overpowering even with all doors and windows wide open. First Officer Caddy looked in after a while to see how we were getting on, and was followed later by the First Lieutenant and the Captain, both of whom congratulated us on the speed of the changeover. They left finally, after hoping we were not too tired, realising that one of us should have been in bed and asleep. Of course we denied this, but a little later, about five o'clock, we were thankful to be bidden back to the hotel for the night, after being reassured that we'd be disturbed only if an Immediate signal came through from the SDO via the hotel telephone.

April 2nd 1942   *RNAS Machrihanish*
The move was finally completed, though not without a certain mild regret. Our new quarters were of the same construction as those at St Merryn, long, low concrete buildings situated in a rather exposed position up a gentle

incline on one side of the main station area with its hangars
and runways. The SDO, cypher and administration offices
were also of the same pattern, though closer to the sea and
easily accessible on foot or by bicycle. Red and I usually
went on our bikes, and I found it a real pleasure not to have
to fling myself off it because of being chased by a German
pilot enjoying a spot of machine-gunning.

One thing we noticed was that, as if galvanised by the
frequent bad news, the tempo of life on the station had
suddenly quickened and everyone seemed to be going
about their business with renewed vigour. This was
particularly noticeable in the SDO where the spate of
urgent signals for us to decypher greatly increased as more
pilots and aircraft began to arrive.

Since the WRNS officers' mess was no longer part of
the male officers' mess, we were not able to witness the
comings and goings of new personnel, and therefore my
surprise was complete when I was returning from watch
early one morning to our quarters and a voice behind me
called my name.

I turned quickly, and found myself looking up into a
familiar face – none other than my friend from St Merryn,
the owner of a battered Morris Cowley, that sturdy little car
capable of conveying as many as thirteen passengers to the
Ring o' Bells at St Izzy, and of surviving a hazardous drive
from Cornwall to Cheshire.

"Good heavens!" I said, "When did *you* arrive?"

He smiled. "Yesterday. I've been on leave."

I looked him over. More gold stripes on his sleeve. Now
a lieutenant commander with a couple of medals.
Promotion and decoration. How impressive!

I was about to congratulate him, but he added, "I'm in
charge of 766 Squadron. We'll be here for a time now.
There's a lot of work to do with them." Suddenly he looked
at me intently. "And how are you? If you don't mind my
saying so, you don't look as well as I remember you."

Briefly I told him about David, and he reached out and took my hand. "Oh God, I'm sorry," he said. "That must have been a terrible shock. I believe you told me he was about to go on board *Neptune*. I'd forgotten for the moment. It was that Force K disaster – off Tripoli, wasn't it?"

I nodded, finding it difficult to speak, but he understood, pressed my hand, and said, "Well, I'll see you around." Then he turned and strode away.

April 4th 1942   *RNAS Machrihanish*
After that unexpected meeting we all got used to the strange sight of a rather ancient looking Anson aircraft regularly taking off and landing on one of the longer runways. This led directly towards the hedge marking the end of it, with the beach and sea a short way beyond. I used to watch this in fascinated apprehension as the aircraft rumbled along the runway, gathering speed without showing any sign of becoming airborne as it sped towards the hedge.

"He'll never make it," I thought. "Who on earth is this madman?"

I must have spoken this thought aloud, for a young pilot who stood watching nearby said, "*He's* not mad. He'll make it all right. That's our new squadron leader, 766 Squadron. Got a hell of a nerve."

At that moment the Anson suddenly took off and roared up into the sky, clearing the hedge by what looked to me like no more than a few feet, and I breathed more easily.

The pilot smiled triumphantly at me. "There! What did I tell you? He was at Cape Matapan, you know. Got decorated too. DFC *and* DSO. A real hell of a guy. I wish I had his nerve."

"I might have guessed who it was," I thought with a smile, "but, please God, I'll never have to take off in that!"

April 5th 1942   *RNAS Machrihanish*

With the arrival of the new squadron the tempo of life on the station quickened imperceptibly. A sense of urgency seemed to take hold of us all, noticeably in the SDO which suddenly began to shower us with signals to decypher. Red and I had very little opportunity for occasional rest during our long night watches, while undisturbed sleep in the daytime became virtually impossible owing to the added noise of aircraft constantly overhead. The training of new young pilots was being intensified.

In a way, this was a help to me. We were so busy that there was little time to brood, and when coming off duty I was almost too tired to eat much breakfast before tumbling into bed and burying my head in my pillow.

The new pilots seemed to be enjoying themselves. When practising low flying out over the bay they had a mischievous habit of swooping down above the waterline whenever any of the WRNS personnel happened to be walking nearby, obviously amused to watch their victims throwing themselves down on the sand as they passed so closely overhead. An undoubtedly highly dangerous exploit under inexpert control which was quietly reported in the right quarter and a stern order went out forbidding any further reckless exhibitionism.

April 7th 1942   *RNAS Machrihanish*

For the last twenty-four hours there had been no flying. The met office had forecast an ominous *haar* rolling towards us from the sea. As I came out of the cypher office, intending to cycle down to our quarters for a quick lunch following a slight lull in the number of incoming signals, visibility still seemed fairly reasonable. I decided to risk it. Even if it grew any worse I was so familiar with the path up to the signals block I could almost have found my way there blindfold.

"You'd better hurry," someone said, as I finished my

lunch and left the table. "Look out of the window."

I did so, to be met by a thick swirling mist hovering a few feet above the ground, and I hurried outside, grabbing my bicycle. Visibility was practically down to zero, but at least I could just make out the hazy outlines of familiar buildings and didn't hesitate to mount. It was unnaturally quiet, all sound blanketed by the *haar*, and I cycled carefully in the uncanny silence until I reached the path leading to the SDO. Here everything seemed totally blotted out, and I dismounted and pushed my bike very slowly along the path.

At least, I thought, as the SDO building loomed up immediately ahead of me, no one could possibly be trying to fly anywhere in this, but no sooner had the thought crossed my mind than I became aware of a faint sound somewhere to my left, out to sea. At first I couldn't identify it, not because of its distance, but because I knew it couldn't possibly be what I felt I was hearing. The sound increased, and to my stunned amazement materialised unmistakably into an aircraft approaching from the sea.

It all happened so quickly there was no time to think. One incredulous glance upward and the mist parted to reveal a plane which seemed to be about to land on my head as the downwind blew my hat off. The pilot and I saw each other at the same horrifying moment, and as he wrenched the machine upwards I threw down my bike and pointed wildly with both outstretched arms towards the runway inland to my right. It was a purely instinctive action – I didn't even know if he saw it or not – then I dashed into the SDO and rang the control tower, asking for every landing light to be switched on. The duty officer must have responded instantly, for when I went outside again and peered anxiously through the mist I could still hear the aircraft's engine and just make out the vague blur of runway lights. Then, a few tense minutes later, to my overwhelming relief, I heard the telephone, and the Chief

Yeoman of Signals called out to me that the plane had landed safely. Weak with reaction I sank into a chair in the office and one of the Wrens brought me a much-needed cup of very strong, sweet tea.

That evening, at the station dance, a young sub-lieutenant came up to me and asked if I was Third Officer Houston, and when I turned and saw him I knew instinctively who he was. Apart from looking very pale and strained he seemed all right, but when he was thanking me and apologising for giving me such a fright (nothing, of course, to what he must have felt up there alone and lost in a dense fog) I was thinking how young he was, surely not many years older than my young brother. I grabbed hold of both his hands as if to reassure myself that he was really alive and well, and at the same time had the strangest feeling that this had been meant as a sort of compensation, that I had been given this chance to save a life in return for the loss of David's. Did this sort of thing happen, I wondered?

But that night I felt in no doubt, and for some reason wept as I hadn't when I had first heard the dreadful news about him. Perhaps, I thought, this might be a tiny seed of comfort if I told my parents about it. A life for a life. If only I had been able to give the same help to David when he so desperately needed it.

April 9th 1942   *RNAS Machrihanish*
The young sub-lieutenant had left to return to his station. After his aircraft had been checked and refuelled, and the necessary signals had been sent giving his ETA (estimated time of arrival) he called in at the cypher office to say goodbye and thank me once again for helping him to a safe landing. He looked much better now, the desperate drain on his self-confidence replaced by an almost jaunty air.

"My number wasn't on it," he said finally, as he shook my hand. "Lucky for me you were there."

"Any time," I answered lightly. "Mind you take care of yourself."

He smiled. "I'll try not to do it again," he said as he went to the door.

"Good luck!" I called after him, and later watched him take off and disappear into a clear blue sky, my good wishes following him.

July 17th 1942   *RNAS Machrihanish*
The news on so many fronts was uniformly bad, and Churchill's stirring speeches became more vigorous and aggressive as time went on. But in Scotland the summer passed uneventfully. It was surprisingly warm, with daylight lasting till late into the evening, ideal weather for flying. Now that the new squadron had settled down, the pilots under their energetic and forceful leader began to show greater confidence as they became more accustomed to their routine exercises.

After the initial activity involved in the arrival of large numbers of new personnel the volume of our work declined a little, and Red and I had an opportunity for social pastimes. There were invitations from local people who gave parties for us, and I even discovered some distant Scottish cousins who invited me for lunch in their gracious old house set in beautiful surroundings by a placid loch. It was some distance from Machrihanish and so quiet and peaceful I felt I had strayed into another world. All the same they took an avid interest in the activity at Machrihanish, and showered me with questions, some of which, of course, I couldn't answer for security reasons. But it was refreshing for once to be on the outside edge of things instead of being so closely and deeply involved in them.

Several of the station personnel possessed cars, and parties of us would be driven out of Machrihanish to explore the surrounding countryside and try out some of the simple fare provided by roadside cafés or pubs in the little outlying villages. As the long twilight faded into darkness the fragrant residue of a hot day still hung in the air, and as we sat outside talking time seemed to stand still.

It was incredibly peaceful after the constant vigilance needed in Liverpool or St Merryn. Even the occasional aircraft passing overhead posed no threat. Sometimes we didn't even trouble to look up at them, knowing them for friends.

These evenings went a long way towards reconciling Red and me to our punishing work schedule. Free time was precious, especially as so much of it had to be taken up with sleeping. With one of us always on duty we lived almost separate lives, never able to go out in the evenings at the same time, so we tended to have different friends.

August 4th 1942   *RNAS Machrihanish*
Another squadron had arrived with several foreign pilots who had escaped from various overrun countries in Europe and made their way to England, to join either the RAF or Fleet Air Arm. Five of these came from Poland, older and more experienced than most of our new young pilots, sad-faced men who had finally been forced to admit defeat, and were eager to find some more effective base from which to continue their desperate fight for their country. Their stories were horrific, though I didn't think they ever revealed the full gruesome picture of the horrors they had left behind.

The WRNS officers were often invited to the main officers' mess for informal parties, and towards the end of these pleasant occasions the Polish officers would gather in one corner of the large room, arms round each others' shoulders, heads bowed as they sang the sad, nostalgic songs of their homeland. I supposed they had drunk just enough to release their former control and dignified manners and could show their true feelings. Perhaps it was a relief for them, but it was painful to watch. There was so little any of us could do.

One of the pilots once told me that his entire family had perished in the battle for Warsaw, and I turned cold as I listened. What could one say? Nothing to give him any comfort, that was certain.

"To be an island," he added with a rather painful smile, "you are fortunate here in England. But we had no escape except to go somewhere where people could still continue to fight the Nazis. I could not stay in Poland. I am a good flyer and can be useful. That is all that is left for me now."

I began then to get a true idea of what it must have been like to have on their doorstep an enemy bent on total destruction who disregarded all the basic tenets of humanity. At least our enemy in St Merryn and Liverpool had been in the air above us, not face to face with us on the ground.

Red had become very friendly with an intrepid pilot from South Africa, while I had met another pilot, a Frenchman from Vichy France, with the unlikely name of Peter Bentley. He admitted to me that that wasn't his true name, and I sensed there had been some mystery behind his escape, so didn't question him any further. Apparently he had chosen his new name after having admired a Bentley car on his arrival in England. He was a charming person with a great sense of humour, and we became good friends. It was pleasant also to be able to talk French to him, though his English was surprisingly fluent.

As at St Merryn there were engagements announced by several of the Wrens. At Machrihanish there seemed to be time for personal life instead of the constant demands of duty which had previously been paramount.

Becoming engaged was still far from my mind, so I was all the more surprised when, returning from a late evening party with one of the station medical officers, he stopped the car just outside the station and rather tentatively asked me to marry him. I sat silent beside him, not having an idea what to say. He was a very nice man, extremely competent and everybody liked him, but I really didn't know him very well, and becoming a doctor's wife was certainly not on my agenda. I tried to explain about the Royal Academy of Music and my ambition to be a professional singer, and felt awful as he was so understanding about it. He said he'd had an idea of something like that after hearing me sing at an informal concert with John Mayne playing for me.

"If that's your serious ambition you must go for it," he said gently. "You've got a beautiful voice. You'd never be really happy if you let it all go. You'll meet somebody later who'll fit in with what you want to do."

No wonder he was such a good doctor! Not only had he recognized and understood my dilemma, but had dealt with it kindly and generously in spite of his personal disappointment.

"No reason why we shouldn't be friends, though," he added on parting, and I agreed wholeheartedly.

October 3rd 1942   *RNAS Machrihanish*
How quickly my birthday came around again! The year seemed to have disappeared without my realising it. Cards and presents came from my family, and my father wrote to say he had arranged a service to bless the garden of remembrance for David at Hartford Church. It had been disappointing that neither Tony nor I could get leave for it, but he thought it would be helpful for my mother not to delay it any longer.

It was a poignant day, dulled by the heartache and the unbearable thought that this time last year David had still been with us, a vibrant, living being, very much the central core of a loving family. But now, what? An empty shell from which his radiant spirit had long flown. Had it suffered a sea change into one of the myriad drops in the ocean, by now probably joined by many more after such heavy losses of valuable men and ships? We would never know what had happened to him, the only definite thing being his absence.

Christmas Day 1942   *RNAS Machrihanish*
It was a fine day, not too cold, and the church service was held outside on the parade ground. There were quite a few amongst us for whom it was particularly poignant, and when it came to that wonderful hymn 'Eternal Father strong to save', which was always sung at naval services, the last two lines 'Oh hear us when we call to Thee for those in peril on the sea' caught at my throat and I couldn't utter a sound. It was a relief when we were given the order to dismiss, and Red and I joined the other officers in the large mess for the Captain's party before lunch. The work had slackened off since the day before, so for once she and I could enjoy a drink together. It was a good party, the Captain a genial host, and by one o'clock everyone was well away and ready for lunch.

The kitchen staff had done us proud. There must have been some real professionals amongst them to have been able to serve up such a feast with all the trimmings. Later that evening the officers returned the compliment by helping to serve dinner to the naval and WRNS ratings, including the first draft of cooks and stewards who had been on duty at lunchtime. This became hilarious, as many of the officers, particularly the men, were anything but adept at offering food to everyone without spilling it, and the business of removing the empty plates and bowls afterwards caused even more merriment.

Shades of Villa Brillantmont, I thought, as I joined in this delicate operation. We'd all had to learn the difficult art of balancing two plates at a time on one hand, plus knives and forks, without allowing anything to slide off. I hated that part of my domestic education, and always felt a fool under the beady eye of the fearsome mademoiselle in charge, who made it plain she considered me utterly useless!

However, when it came to pouring wine and setting fire to the brandy on the Christmas puddings, here the men came into their own, achieving this with great panache. All of them, from the First Lieutenant downwards, excelled at this and were greeted with noisy approval. I noticed that Major Harris was in his element and the Wrens loved him.

March 19th 1943   *RNAS Machrihanish*

It was supposed to be spring, but all we saw were endless dreary grey skies with frequent sheets of fine rain that seemed to block out all available light. It was not particularly cold, but 'dreich', as the locals put it, a marvellously descriptive word that entirely mirrored our feelings. Even Red who had been born and lived all her life in Scotland, appeared to feel it too, and one morning when I arrived to relieve her from duty I found her sitting hunched over the table with her head in her hands. It was so unlike her that I was worried.

"Are you all right?" I asked, going over to her, and she glanced up at me. I'd never seen her look so pale and exhausted.

She sighed. "Oh God, I've never been so tired," she said. "I hope I'm not sickening for something."

I sat down on a nearby chair. "You know, I think this has been going on too long. Even if we're not actually working all through our twenty-four hours but just on call, we can't relax properly – not ever. I'm tired too. Everything's an effort. And my eyesight's not too good either. Perhaps I need new glasses."

"Maybe we ought to go and talk to First Officer," Red suggested. "We'll end up being completely useless if we go on like this."

I stood up and leafed through the sheaf of signals on her table.

"Yes, you're right. Look, you go off now, Red, and try to get some sleep. We'll talk about this when you're rested."

After she had left I sat and thought. This exhaustion had been creeping up on us for some time now, and the weather did little to help. Something had to be done and fairly quickly. I'd been worried about my eyes recently. They looked red rimmed, at times even bloodshot, and I had frequent bouts of headache.

March 20th 1943   *RNAS Machrihanish*
We went to see Lovell Caddy and explained our situation. She was not surprised, and said she'd been thinking about this for some time now.

"In fact, I've already applied for two more cypher officers," she added, then smiled at us. "You two have held the fort brilliantly up till now, but we're all so busy you really should be on proper watches with adequate rest in between."

That was good news. Then she looked more closely at me and said, "And you, Roxane, had better go up to Glasgow and see an eye specialist. I don't like the look of yours. I've met Commander Bradley before and he's very good. There's an Army draft going off from Campbeltown next week. I expect you could go in the transport with them."

Outside the door Red and I smiled triumphantly at each other.

"I must say," she remarked, "when the Navy thinks it's time to move, it moves mighty fast. I only hope the other cypher officers arrive before you go to Glasgow, as otherwise you won't get much rest fitting in a trip up there, plus seeing the specialist and then getting back here so late. You'll hardly be in your right mind to go on duty again at eight in the morning."

"As long as the wretched man doesn't say I must stop working," I said, feeling distinctly worried. "What'll happen then? Suppose he recommends my leaving the WRNS altogether? After all, the only use the Navy has for me is in the category of Writer. And that means close work like cyphering."

"Well, you'll just have to keep your fingers crossed," Red recommended. 'Tell him the long hours we've been working and that you're exhausted. He'll understand that, surely. And it'll be much easier later on with four of us."

March 27th 1943   *RNAS Machrihanish*

It was not exactly an easy journey. I was in the first of the convoy of four huge transports, perched up in front beside the driver in the most uncomfortable seat I'd ever sat in, with heaven only knew how many licentious soldiery packed in behind us. Red had relieved me half an hour earlier than usual so that I'd have time for a quick bath and breakfast before the Wren driver came to pick me up and take me over to Campbeltown. I just made it in time to board the transport at eight o'clock before the convoy lumbered out on to the winding road up the Mull of Kintyre. For most of the way I fought an overpowering urge to sleep, but the seat was not designed for that, and I was afraid I might slip off it at an awkward moment and upset the driver. He was a pleasant young man, but never thought (or was too embarrassed) to suggest we might stop somewhere for a few necessary moments en route with the result that by the time we reached the Argyll Arms things were a bit desperate, and I had to pull rank on him and ask him to stop and let me off. There were a few ribald comments from various points along the convoy as I climbed down, but I ignored these and quickly made for a suitable haven inside the hotel. As I came out again and clambered awkwardly up to my seat I thanked the driver and placated him by offering him two of the fresh bread rolls I had just bought, which he accepted with a sudden wide smile, and we munched away happily as the miles snailed by. I thought, beneath his shyness, he was another Fred at heart, and after a while he told me all about his family and where he lived, and we got on like a house on fire.

My appointment was for two thirty, and I only just got there in time, having been dropped some way from my destination and subsequently getting myself thoroughly lost. At the pace we'd been going our journey had taken well over five hours.

Commander Bradley was a naval surgeon commander based in Glasgow, a kindly man with thin greying hair and a quiet voice. After greeting me he put the usual drops into my eyes, and while waiting for these to take effect asked me how Lovell Caddy was. After a short chat he turned away and sat down at his desk to study a letter, then turned to me to ask a few questions about my work at Machrihanish.

"Mrs Caddy writes that you began working there in December 1941, and that you now seem to be having trouble with your eyes," he went on. "Had you done any cyphering before that?"

"Oh yes," I answered, "at Liverpool. I started there in May 1941, immediately after my training course at Greenwich."

"You were there during the blitz then?" he observed.

I nodded. "Yes, we were under Derby House. It was a very busy time, but at least we were on the usual watchkeeping schedule so had time off between working hours. But sometimes of course, because of the bomb damage, the others couldn't get over to Derby House to relieve us so we had to work a double shift."

"Hm," he said, frowning, "It must have been very tiring."

"It was," I said, "though being on duty for twenty-four hours at a stretch at Machrihanish was worse. At least, it wasn't so bad at the beginning," I added rather hastily. "I mean, we could sometimes sleep for a while during the night, but then we just got very busy suddenly, and it's been the same ever since – over a year now."

"Quite a time," he agreed, then after peering into my eyes for a moment he rose to his feet. "Let's have a look now."

It was one of the most thorough examinations I'd ever had, very calm and unhurried. Several times he stopped to note something down on a large pad on his desk while I waited in trepidation for the result. Finally, he turned round and smiled at me reassuringly. It was an attractive smile, slightly crooked.

"Well now," he said. "Tell me something. Was it very hot and dry working underground?"

"Yes," I answered, rather surprised at the question. "Almost claustrophobic. That was the worst of it really — except for—."

I paused and he looked at me with a sudden alert expression.

"Except for—?" he prompted.

"Well — we lost so many ships during those eight months," I explained, and went on to tell him about Ruth, the girl on my watch who'd actually decyphered the very signal about the sinking of her husband's ship. After that I suddenly found myself telling him what had happened to David just after I'd arrived at Machrihanish, and how I couldn't sleep properly for weeks afterwards for thinking of him.

There was a short silence, then he reached out and patted my hand.

"You've had a bad time," he said gently, and the sympathy in his voice almost broke my self-control. "But there's good news," he added. "I can see nothing specifically wrong with your eyes beyond your short sight and the fact that you're extremely tired. But you've been doing very close work day and night in unsuitable conditions first in Liverpool, then here in Scotland. Added to this you've had a great shock to cope with, and it's all got rather on top of you."

I swallowed convulsively and reached for my handkerchief.

"But now," he went on, "just relax for a few moments while I write a short note to Mrs Caddy. I'm going to suggest you do no more cyphering – ever! What you need is a quiet, steady sort of daytime job where you can leave at a definite time at the end of each day and get enough sleep at night. I don't want you tied to a typewriter or cypher book or any machine you have to peer at for long hours . . . ."

I hardly listened to any more. What joy to give up cyphering! In a surge of gratitude I realised he hadn't recommended that I be thrown out of the Navy as useless.

He finished writing the letter and handed it to me in a pale grey envelope. "You can take this yourself," he said. "It'll be quicker than relying on His Majesty's mail. Now here are some soothing drops for your eyes. They'll soon recover if you're sensible and get enough rest. Let me know how you get on."

On the way downstairs to the hall he added, "By the way, I've arranged a lift back for you with one of the officers who's going to Machrihanish today, Lieutenant Commander Bates, a friend of mine. I don't suppose you had time for any lunch, so he says he'll stop en route for you to eat something. Can't have you fainting with hunger on the way." He glanced at his watch. "He should be here about now. After you've eaten I'd sit in the back if I were you and sleep till you arrive."

As he carefully saw me down the steps outside the front door I was walking on air.

"Take care," he warned me, "I don't expect you'll see very clearly for a while after all those drops."

A car drew up beside us, an old but solid looking Rover slightly at variance with its owner, who at first glance looked anything but old or solid, though maybe 'rover' might have described him. It was too early to tell.

"She's been on duty all last night," Commander Bradley told him rather severely, and the Lieutenant Commander looked aghast.

"That's shocking," he said. "Never mind, I'll look after her."

Thanks and goodbyes followed, and almost before I realised it we were speeding away towards a 'nice little hotel' my driver knew outside Glasgow, with a menu 'to tempt even the most jaded palate'.

"That'd be lovely," I said gratefully.

And it was.

March 28th 1943　　　　　　　　　*RNAS Machrihanish*
The Navy certainly could work fast. Not only did two more WRNS cypher officers appear, all set and raring to go, but First Officer Caddy sent for me with some surprising news.

"I think we've found exactly the right job for you," she told me. "Daytime only, hours from eight till six. Secretarial work with Combined Operations. Assistant to Staff Officer Landing Craft at Largs, most of it top secret. You can guess what it will be for. How do you feel about that?"

"It sounds wonderful," I said. "Rather exciting. When do I leave?"

"In a few days, when you're a bit more rested," she said. "It won't do for you to arrive looking so exhausted. Catch up on some sleep, then you can give Red and the two new girls any help during the day if they need it until your own replacement arrives. She's due on the 30th. No more night watches for you. Commander Bradley was very firm about that."

I left her office, feeling breathless, my head in a whirl. There would be such a lot to organise.

March 30th 1943   *RNAS Machrihanish*
March 30th. David's twentieth birthday that should have
been. I wished so much I could have been home on leave,
but it just wasn't possible. I would have liked to have visited
his garden of remembrance at Hartford Church and added
some flowers. Instead, I telephoned home and spoke to
them all, my parents, my aunt and my sister-in-law, and
heard the baby Anne chortling in the background. Tony,
unfortunately, was also unable to get home, but he rang me
instead. We had heard some months ago that several of
David's friends from the naval college at Dartmouth had
also been lost. What thousands of unfulfilled achievements
lay on the seabed, while we who were left did our best to
fill the empty spaces.

But my watch informed me it was a quarter to eight,
and I was needed at the cypher office to relieve Red. No
time to dwell on the past. The inexorable present had
caught up with me.

March 31st 1943   *RNAS Machrihanish*
The two new cypher officers were settling in well, and now
there seemed little more for me to do. I realised how much
I'd miss Red. That was the worst of these assignments. They
were always changing just when I'd got used to and fond of
people around me. Luckily Red, like Liz Welburn, would
always be a long-term friend.

That evening I was walking back to our mess when I
received rather a surprise. My friend with the Morris
Cowley car suddenly materialised behind me and said, "I
was just coming to see you. What's this I hear about your
leaving for Largs?"

"It's quite true," I replied. "It's for a new job as assistant
to the Staff Officer Landing Craft. My eyes have rather
given out after all the cyphering and night watches, so I
have to do a daytime job."

"I'm sorry to hear that," he said sympathetically. "You

must take care. How are you getting to Largs, by the way?"

"I'm not sure yet," I answered. "I'm due to leave in about two days."

"I've a better idea," he said. "I'm taking a couple of my pilots over to Renfrew tomorrow afternoon. I could take you with me too. There's plenty of room. And your people could arrange for you to travel over to Largs from there. It's not all that far."

My mind flew back to the sight of that ancient Anson aircraft thundering towards the hedge marking the very end of the runway, and I said rather feebly, "That's very kind of you, but—."

He laughed suddenly. "Why do you look like that? Don't you trust me?"

Oh Lord, I thought, he's only one of the most decorated heroes of Matapan, and here am I letting him think I haven't the confidence to fly with him!

"Of course I do!" I assured him hastily. "It was just that I didn't expect you to suggest that. Of course I'd love to go with you."

He looked pleased. "You'll enjoy it," he said, as he walked briskly away.

Oh dear, you'll just have to pretend you're enjoying it, I told myself silently. How can you be such a coward?

April 1st 1943   *RNAS Machrihanish*
I was half hoping something might just happen to get in the way of his plan, but everything went smoothly, and at two thirty I met him by the control tower, and found two other pilots there also. They, of course, were thrilled to be going with him in the Anson, and were openly jealous when I was ordered firmly to sit in the cockpit beside him.

"So you'll have a better view," he said, making sure I was properly strapped in.

There was no getting out of it. I watched him covertly, seeing how calmly and competently he dealt with the controls as we taxied along to the take-off position, though my heart was thumping.

Then we were cleared for take-off, and he suddenly turned and smiled at me. "Don't you *dare* close your eyes," he said. "Half the fun is seeing how easily I can get over that hedge. Now for it, everybody."

And as I had heard so often before, those splendid old engines gave an ominous growl which increased to a thunderous roar, and we sped along the runway with the hedge getting ever nearer and us still anchored to terra firma. For a moment I was rigid with apprehension, blood running cold. Then suddenly I was caught up in his enthusiasm, an excitement I'd never felt before. After all, this was really *nothing* to compare with taking off from an aircraft carrier to attack the Italian fleet!

I glanced at him, saw his eyes fixed firmly ahead, his jaw set, revealing all his determination, and was lost in admiration. How could I ever have doubted him?

The two pilots in the rear of the plane were equally tense with excitement the nearer we got to the hedge, and when we finally just cleared it and headed out to sea, were loud in their awed approval.

"Piece of cake," my calm friend muttered out of the corner of his mouth, then turned his head to smile at me. "Tell me the truth now. *Did* you close your eyes?"

"Not once," I replied. "Honestly. It was so exciting."

"Well, you've certainly been honoured," he said, mock serious, "I don't invite many females to sit beside me when I fly this old kite."

After that it was indeed a piece of cake as we landed safely at Renfrew, where once again we said goodbye to each other.

Life at that moment seemed full of farewells.

IV

FORTISSIMO

April 2nd 1943   *Headquarters, Rear Admiral Landing Ships*
Unallocated (RALSU), Hollywood Hotel,
Largs, Scotland (HMS Monck)

What a fantastic place to work in! Hollywood Hotel was a hydro, a sort of health spa, situated on the road beside the winding Firth of Clyde. After the Ugadale Arms and our subsequent concrete mess and bedrooms on the station at Machrihanish, this was the height of luxury, all velvet and plush, thick carpets, cosy lounges with comfortable armchairs to sink into, and old fashioned, well polished furniture that might have graced a nineteenth century London club. Best of all, there were no vast dormitories with eighteen occupants, only quiet double bedrooms with wonderful views (at least from the front of the building) of shining water and a hazy glimpse beyond of Great Cumbrae Island.

I was shown to one of these bedrooms, and discovered that I was to be its only inhabitant, at least for the moment. That was a real bonus and my tired spirits rose.

A young Wren steward knocked at the door and asked if I'd be needing supper as it was growing rather late. She escorted me to an empty dining-room where I was offered hot soup, fresh rolls and an appetising fish pie encased in pastry almost of the standard of Villa Brillantmont. The sweet was fruit salad, but I couldn't manage that, and drank coffee instead.

Afterwards, feeling much restored, I explored the ground floor, passing unobtrusively by an open doorway which, judging by the sound of voices and laughter, obviously led to the main lounge and bar. After a while I finally came to one of the smaller lounges which seemed to have been turned into an office. It was so quiet I thought it was empty, but discovered a young sub-lieutenant there, busily scribbling on a large writing pad. He was facing a complicated looking map on the wall, and when he turned at my entrance I saw he looked harassed and uncertain.

"Goodness!" I exclaimed involuntarily. "Are you still working? It's after nine thirty."

He put his pencil down with a sigh. "I'll be here much later than this," he answered. "It's my turn to do the State for Lieutenant Church at the Admiralty."

"The State?" I queried. What on earth was he talking about?

"The number and state of all our landing craft," he explained. "Only it's such a business tracking them down, takes hours to locate them all. We have to do this every Friday."

"Oh," I said, taking a closer look at the wall.

He glanced at me with sudden interest. "I suppose you couldn't be the new officer we've been waiting for?" he asked hopefully. "Things are a bit of a shambles here. There's no proper system yet."

I could well believe it. "Can I give you a hand?" I asked.
"Yes, I'm supposed to be the assistant to the landing craft officer. That's not you, is it?"

"No, thank God!" he said fervently. "I'm only temporary. It's kind of you to offer, but you've only just arrived, haven't you? I'll be finished in another hour or so. This is the last State I'll have to do."

I left him to it, and since I didn't feel like facing everyone in the main lounge, made my way quietly up the stairs to unpack my things. Tomorrow was another day, and a good night's sleep was what I needed most.

April 3rd 1943   *HQ RALSU, Largs*
Breakfast was at seven o'clock when I met the entire staff, from Admiral Horan downwards. There were about twenty of them, all very pleasant and intent on making me welcome. Most of the WRNS officers were the same rank as I was, and as at the Ugadale Arms everyone sat wherever there was a vacant place. It struck me as a rather small contingent for what was surely destined to be part of the whole Combined Operations organisation, but I supposed there must have been many other similar groups dotted throughout Scotland, which was obviously an ideal venue for the training of landing ships and craft.

The Staff Officer Landing Craft, to give him his full title, was a tall, likeable lieutenant commander named Leslie Wintle, whose rather lugubrious expression masked an irrepressible, dry sense of humour.

He led me to the office and introduced me to an Army lieutenant named Baker who was working there temporarily, and a small, dark-haired young Wren whom he addressed as Wren Hens. No one mentioned her first name, and she seemed far too polite to invite anyone to call her by it. Her desk was in the far corner of the room, and she stood up with a shy smile as I shook hands with her, before sitting down again and putting more paper into her typewriter.

There were three other desks in the room, mine immediately to the left of the doorway, Lieutenant Commander Wintle's by the large front windows, and another desk to the right of this which was occupied for the moment by the Army officer until an RNVR lieutenant named John Norton arrived to replace him. It all seemed a bit makeshift and disorganised, obviously not having been in operation for long.

At ten o'clock Captain Henniker-Heaton came into the office and shook hands with me with a pleasant smile and a hope that I'd had a good journey. He told me that everything would be up and running very soon, and with a glance at the map on the wall added, "I'm going to send you over to Troon so that you can see how they manage things there. They seem to have a successful system. There'll be a boat for you at two tomorrow afternoon."

I thanked him and went to sit down at my desk as Wren Hens approached with a pile of papers and drawings for me to look at. She had been detailed to show me diagrams of all the types of landing craft our office dealt with. These were many and varied, all designated by odd initials and numbers. I was supposed to have some idea of the differences of design and operation, and even of what sort of landing ships would be carrying them. She talked knowledgeably of gantries and davits, and even started out on gaskets and other inner organs of landing craft which were likely to fail if not properly maintained. I began to wonder if she'd had training in marine engineering. It was very confusing, and having struggled seriously to take it all in I found that by four o'clock my concentration was definitely flagging.

Fortunately a welcome interruption came as someone entered the office, and a mellifluous voice murmured in my ear: "I've come to take you to tea. I'm sure you need it."

And looking round I recognized her as one of the WRNS officers I'd met that morning at breakfast. Her name was Yvonne de Méric, a very attractive girl with auburn hair and a great sense of humour. She seemed to be on the best of terms with Leslie Wintle, who said cheerfully: "Yes, take her away. She looks as if she could do with a break."

I followed her thankfully to the dining room where, over several cups of tea and some delicious sort of muffins, she regaled me with all that went on in RALSU.

"Of course, I've only been here for two weeks," she said. "We're quite a small outfit, but it's much nicer than having lots of admin officers in charge with never ending protocol. We really manage ourselves and everyone lets us get on with things as necessary. I work in the cypher office just across the hall from you. You're lucky in your office. They're a nice lot, and Leslie never loses his hair over anything."

That was nice to know. No bursts of temperament from anybody.

April 4th 1943   *HQ RALSU, Largs*

It was an invigorating spring day, the sea sparkling in the sunlight as the young sailor steered our boat competently past the various ships at anchor. I felt totally dwarfed by their great hulls which reared up out of the water like tall buildings, leaving long dark shadows rippling on the surface.

My boatman was a Scot, very young, and he called out the names of some of the places we passed, Great Cumbrae Island over on our right, then along the coast on our left, West Kilbride, Ardrossan, Saltcoats and Irvine, until we finally pulled in at Troon. There I was met and escorted to the Combined Operations offices where everything seemed highly organised.

It was much larger than our small hotel lounge, with a great map spread out over a huge table. A positive rash of coloured drawing pins and tiny flags were strewn about on the map, and my mind reeled. At the end of almost two hours I thought what an appalling strain on the eyes such a conglomeration of craft might give me. There was nothing really clear cut about the layout, though the WRNS officers there were proud to explain it all very thoroughly to me, realising they were instructing a complete novice at this sort of thing. I was entirely new to it, of course, but surely, I thought, there must be a simpler way to locate and identify so many landing craft. By the end of that confusing session I was certain of only one thing. I had to get out of having to copy the Troon example, though I hardly knew how. I'd have to be very tactful, of course. A new broom wasn't always appreciated.

On our way back to Largs, as we began to see the first ships anchored ahead of us, I was seized with an over-powering longing to steer our little boat myself. Glancing at my companion's intent face as he carefully avoided going too near them, I wondered if I could risk asking him to change places with me. There was probably a strict rule about allowing inexperienced passengers to take the wheel, but surely that couldn't be very different from driving a car, and there was plenty of room for me to navigate. I decided to try it, and after he'd recovered from his surprise he turned his head and smiled rather doubtfully. "Well, if you think you could, Ma'am," he said.

"I promise I'll be very careful," I assured him with what I hoped was a confident smile. "And if you stand next to me you'll be able to take over if necessary. It'll only be for a short while," I added, as he still hesitated.

He gave me an uncertain smile and changed places with me, watching me closely as I successfully negotiated the various obstacles in our way.

It was wonderfully exhilarating after being so long in that stuffy overcrowded office. The boat responded to the lightest touch of my hand on the wheel. What a pity I'd never be part of a WRNS boat's crew! And then just ahead,

I noticed the great, heavy anchor chain suspended high above us from the stern of an aircraft carrier. I had no idea what demon of recklessness prompted me just then, but without thinking I suddenly changed course and we shot beneath the chain, quite close to that towering hull, and came out on the far side of it before my scandalised boatman had recovered from his surprise to stop me. His face was a mixture of consternation and reproach, and I knew I shouldn't have done it. To make matters worse there was a shout from high above our heads as two seamen stared incredulously down at us from the main deck. The wheel was taken firmly from me, and we sped away at full throttle while I did my best to hide my face by looking away in another direction, hoping our spectators thought I was legitimate boat's crew, either losing control or just having a bit of fun.

"I'm really sorry," I said, trying to placate my disapproving companion. "I just couldn't resist it."

He gave me a polite half smile, and I hastily added that if he got into any trouble over what I'd done, I would of course admit to being the culprit.

"Oh, I don't expect there'll be any fuss," he replied rather stiffly. "I shan't say anything about it."

Then unexpectedly he relaxed and grinned, suddenly looking even younger. "You managed it very well, Ma'am, on the whole. As a matter of fact," he added, his grin widening, "I've often wanted to do that myself."

April 5th 1943   *HQ RALSU, Largs*

I had got back too late to discuss anything with the Captain, and managed to avoid him by breakfasting very early. It wasn't until ten o'clock that he came into our office and asked me pointedly what I thought of the system at Troon.

"It was very impressive, sir," I said, hoping I sounded enthusiastic. "They really showed me around and gave me a lot of ideas."

He smiled encouragingly at me, and I added quickly before I lost my nerve: "I just wondered, sir, if it's possible to give me a day or two to try out something a bit different for our office here. I think it might work rather well."

He looked surprised, but only said: "Well, if you like, by all means. As long as it works, have a go at it. I'll be in the day after tomorrow to see how you've got on."

I thanked him, and after he'd left drew a deep breath of relief.

"That was brave of you," Lieutenant Commander Wintle commented behind me. "Full marks for tact. What have you got in mind? If you can make the State on Friday nights easier and quicker to do we'll all be grateful."

"Well," I said, "to tell you the truth I found all those drawing pins on that map yesterday terribly confusing. The colours all blurred into each other, very difficult to see. I think we need something much easier to read. Where are all our landing craft actually based? I mean, who looks after them, keeps them in working order?"

"Ah," said Leslie Wintle. "You've hit the nail on the head. Some are at Port Glasgow and some at Dumbarton, and one engineer lieutenant, Jim Ewing RNR, is in charge of the lot. He's got a tremendous team there, though very few people seem to realise what valuable work they do. I think you should have a chat with him."

"I will," I said, then added rather hesitantly, "but first – I spent most of last night working out something to show you. Look." And I handed him the large sheet of paper I'd brought with me to the office. Lieutenant Baker and Wren Hens also came over to peer at it. "I thought something like this might be a bit clearer than huge maps."

Under two main headings of Port Glasgow and Dumbarton, I had drawn several long vertical lines indicating the various types of craft, each line headed by their initials, and identified by different coloured drawing pins. "That way," I explained, "we'll know exactly how many we have in working order, and where they're based."

There were murmurs of agreement, and encouraged I continued: "Then I suggest we leave room at the bottom of each line for any craft out of order and being repaired, and where. Then when it returns to base we just replace the drawing pin back into the main line of its type. The same goes for a craft being taken out somewhere for duty. These could both be indicated by separate headings such as 'under repair' and 'out on duty'. Any other details of these could be kept by me on a daily work list, so we'd know exactly what's going on."

There was a short silence while I glanced up at them. "What do you think of all this? Will it work?" I asked tentatively. There was a longer pause while everyone digested this with frowns and muttering. I left them to it and walked over to the large window to stare out at the peaceful water, and to wonder if I'd put my foot thoroughly into it. Supposing they thought it was no good, what would the Captain say?

After a while the others offered helpful suggestions, and one valid criticism came from Lieutenant Baker.

"It'd be tricky to count all down those long lines," he pointed out. "Why not put them all in groups of five? Much easier to see."

This was immediately accepted by everyone including myself. It was so obvious I'd missed it. The discussion lasted a good hour as we worked in and out and around every suggestion put forward, although my basic idea had obviously been accepted. Even Wren Hens, in her gentle voice, entered tactfully into the arguments for and against till we had thoroughly thrashed the whole matter out, and were ready for a break and some lunch. I could hardly wait to see how the finished article would look. It was going to be a long and busy afternoon.

By four o'clock Leslie Wintle had had a long talk with Jim Ewing, then introduced him to me. He said I might ring him any time if I needed information or help, and ended by giving us all the latest details regarding the numbers and types of craft currently at Port Glasgow and Dumbarton to add to our wall chart, till everyone was satisfied and no further amendments were needed. We just had to put the final neat chart tidily up on the wall with all the coloured drawing pins in their correct places. And all that was left after that, of course, was to convince Captain Henniker-Heaton.

April 6th 1943   *HQ RALSU, Largs*
It was with some trepidation that I greeted him when he called in to see what I'd prepared. He examined it closely at first in thoughtful silence, then asked a number of very pertinent questions. I was prepared for this and hastily showed him my proposed daily work list, giving the necessary updated details on any ongoing movements and temporary conditions of craft.

Towards the end of his careful inspection I thought he began to look impressed, and was very relieved when at last he turned to me with a smile.

"It's very clear and easy to understand," he commented. "It should work very well. That was a good idea of yours, and I congratulate you."

I hastened to say that all the others had contributed their ideas too, and he smiled round at us all then and remarked: "Well, I can see you're going to make an excellent team. Keep up the good work. It's going to be needed."

As he left we all relaxed and Leslie gave us the thumbs up sign.

April 8th 1943   *HQ RALSU, Largs*
The final member of our staff arrived, a very dark, good looking RNVR lieutenant named John Norton who had been working for a shipping firm in Portugal, and knew far more about the subject than any of us. Lieutenant Baker

had left, so the newcomer took over his desk. There were now only the four of us, and luckily we all got on well.

April 15th 1943   *HQ RALSU, Largs*
We were beginning to settle into our routine, and I found the work fascinating and learnt a lot about the peculiarities of landing craft. I would ring Lieutenant Ewing every morning on arrival in the office for an update on my daily work list, and with this valuable information the keeping track of so many landing craft became fairly simple. In fact, the Friday night State took just over an hour to be collated, typed and delivered to the teleprinter room for transmission to the Admiralty. Our contact there was a lieutenant named Ken Church, a rather quiet individual who was in charge of the whole section dealing with landing craft. He took his job very seriously indeed and was very competent, but never realised when either Leslie or John were pulling his leg. They teased me too, of course, but I could take it after all the ridicule we'd endured at St Merryn.

April 23rd 1943   *HQ RALSU, Largs*
It had been a hectic week. Apart from keeping track of the usual comings and goings of craft commandeered by FOIC (Flag Officer in Charge) and other senior officers, a completely new batch of landing craft had been sent down from Port Glasgow. Our job was to arrange for the dispersal and basic training of their crews with the landing ships which would be carrying them. As might be expected there were frequent occasions when minor disasters happened, and we, being in charge, had to arrange for replacements to be sent out and the damaged craft conveyed back up to Port Glasgow for repairs.

We worked the full seven days, often well past the designated six o'clock limit. No union or watchkeeping hours for us! Anything outstanding had to be cleared up before we could lock up and leave the office, and often when particularly busy we had to stagger our mealtimes. The odd thing about all this was that I never once felt tired. It was stimulating to be part of the preparation for the huge undertaking that was being planned, and encouraging to work alongside such friendly and intelligent colleagues who never allowed themselves to be put off by petty obstacles, and always dealt coolly and decisively with such disasters as came our way. I also discovered that some measure of the success of our team could be attributed to our indispensable Wren Hens. She was always polite and tactful, and in moments of stress would approach me to say in her quiet voice: "Excuse me, Ma'am, but what about…?" and put her finger exactly on the spot I'd missed. She was also unfailingly able to produce an errant paper or important signal that had become submerged beneath the scattered papers on Leslie's or John's desk, and would hold it out with the quietly spoken words: "Excuse me, sir, is this what you're looking for?"

As time went on we all became very fond of Wren Hens. She never grumbled if she had to work late during a crisis. In fact she would often offer to stay on without even being asked, and we made shameless use of her extra help. Leslie occasionally felt guilty about this, and would insist on her taking the odd afternoon off whenever things were fairly quiet. But her enjoyment of the work we were doing was not assumed. She was genuinely and very intelligently interested, every bit as much as we were, and we'd have missed her very much if she'd not been there. Even quite exalted visitors to our office had a pleasant greeting for her, though she never took advantage of that and would return as soon as possible to her chosen place in the background.

April 25th 1943   *HQ RALSU, Largs*
Lieutenant Ewing at last paid us a visit, and approved our wall chart. He was a grey-haired man of about forty-seven

or eight, sturdily built, slow of speech though very quick to grasp any new idea, and he reminded me forcibly of our Chief Yeoman of Signals at St Merryn. There was the same calm demeanour, and I was sure the same total unflappability in times of crisis. He looked a rock of a man, and we all took to him immediately. His was not an easy job, but I supposed his long experience in the Merchant Navy was a good preparation for it. He was in the right place at the right time, Leslie said to me afterwards.

I had never imagined that landing craft could have a reputation for being temperamental, even recalcitrant at times, but after Jim Ewing had told us about some of the crises caused by their behaviour I began to feel they might almost be human.

"Oh, they've got personalities all right," he added with a grim smile. "Either that, or they can be infected by gremlins – you ask some of my lads! There's one particular craft we've got—." And he told us that it only needed a really high-ranking officer to ask for its use, then it was a thousand to one it would either blow a gasket en route from Port Glasgow, or by refusing to start when tested would make it necessary for the whole team to work on it all night." And, of course," he went on with a resigned sigh, "we never get any thanks for it when we've finally managed to put the blasted thing right and get it out on time."

"It's a hard life," Leslie commented soothingly, taking him by the arm and leading him out of the office. "Come and have a drink. The bar'll be open by now, and I'll introduce you to our admiral. He's a nice old boy."

May 16th 1943   *HQ RALSU, Largs*
It was a glorious Sunday morning, and for some reason the work had slackened off a little so we were all able to join Admiral Horan for his usual after-church session in the main lounge. He was a pleasant, friendly man who liked to

get to know his entire staff, and made a point of having a few words with everyone there. When it came to my turn he was standing with his back to the large windows and I had a beautifully clear view over his shoulder of the glittering water beyond. Summer seemed just around the corner.

"Well, Roxane," he said. "I hear your new system seems to be working very well. How do you like being in Combined Ops? Better than cyphering, eh?"

I assured him that it was and that I enjoyed my present work, and was about to say more when my attention was distracted by the sight of an aircraft in the distance approaching Great Cumbrae Island. It was one of the amphibious flying boats, a Catalina, and looked as if it were about to make a descent on the water. It crossed my mind that it was rather an odd place to choose. Perhaps it was in trouble. I was trying to take in what the Admiral was now asking me, when to my horror I saw that the aircraft had not only reached water level but had taken a sudden dive right into the sea, sending up huge sprays on either side of it before disappearing totally from view.

I must have given a sudden gasp, for the Admiral whipped round and followed my gaze. "What is it?" he asked. "What's the matter?"

I pointed past him, hardly able to reply. "Over there – that Catalina – it's gone in – right under."

Others in the room had noticed it too, and there was a sudden exodus to telephone, someone shouting for a boat, others rushing to fetch binoculars, while the rest of us crowded helplessly against the windows. I felt sick, wondering how the crew and passengers could ever get out in time. The thought of them struggling to reach the air was horrifying. It was like watching a film, not quite real.

After what seemed an age we could see a boat frantically making for the opposite shore. It was quite a long way. Could they ever be in time?

Someone had handed some binoculars to the Admiral who suddenly gave a startled exclamation.

"Good God! There are people there – in the water! Can you see them? Look like swimmers."

Leslie also had binoculars trained on them. "Three girls," he said, his voice sharpening with excitement. "Look! They're dragging someone out onto the beach. It must be quite shallow there."

Another few moments passed, then someone else shouted: "Look! There are two more!"

I found I was clutching John's arm. "Do you think that's all of them? Supposing there were passengers."

"I hope to God not," he replied, staring intently out of the window.

Leslie was squinting through his binoculars, then turned his head to say: "I don't think there can be. None of the girls are going back into the water, perhaps there were only three on board."

A sudden cheer arose outside the hotel where a group of chattering sightseers had gathered, and the Admiral, red faced with excitement, cried out: "Well done! Oh, very well done!" and we all let our breath go in relief.

It wasn't until lunch had almost ended that we learnt the full story. The Admiral was called to the telephone and after a while returned with a beaming smile to make his announcement.

"I'm sure you're all anxious to know what actually happened," he said. "It appears that the aircraft had engine trouble, and the pilot tried to put it down as close in to the shore as possible. Instead, the plane went right under, fortunately not in very deep water, and three Wrens who'd been sunbathing there after a swim rushed in immediately and dived down to haul the pilot, navigator and one other out. They were all unconscious, and I gather the girls had quite a job getting them out of the aircraft and keeping their heads above water as they swam ashore with them.

The men are now on their way to hospital, and are expected to make a full recovery. But those three girls – if they hadn't been there, or hadn't been such strong swimmers, those poor chaps wouldn't have stood much of a chance. Real little heroines they were, those girls! Ought to be given a medal!"

He sat down to spontaneous applause from everyone, and I thought, after this no one can ever laugh at the Wrens again, even if we can't match the correct naval stride when marching!

May 26th 1943   *HQ RALSU, Largs*
We were in the fourth year of the war, and it had begun to seem interminable. In 1940 we'd all been geared up to withstand the imminent threat of invasion and the endless air attacks. But after the invasion threat had passed there was no improvement in the general situation. Although 1941 had brought encouragement with both Russia and later America entering the war as our allies, from 1942 onwards the endless sinkings by U-boats of our convoys in the Atlantic and other areas seemed unstoppable, bringing even more shortages to an increasingly exhausted civil population. Life in the services wasn't so bad. At least our food, though rationed as strictly as everywhere else in the country, was supplied regularly to us, and we had no need to stand in queues for bread or other commodities. My letters from home gave a weary account of the time spent on searching for even the smallest luxury, and even necessities were growing scarcer. A black market had grown up and was flourishing, although there were still people who resisted the temptation to use it except as a matter of urgency in cases of illness.

All this was bad enough for us on our island, but how much worse, how much more difficult and dangerous must everyday life have been for the stoical populations of the occupied countries, how frustrating for them to live perpetually in expectation of the hoped-for Allied invasion which was taking so long to plan and execute! As the numbers of our landing craft increased I found myself becoming impatient, and had the growing impression that this feeling was subtly shared by everyone in Combined Ops. What did it matter if our working hours increased week by week? Our only raison d'être was the constant supply and maintenance of those indispensable carriers of the liberating invaders of a shackled continent. And if we couldn't keep accurate track of all that then we were no use to anyone at all. If *we* were growing impatient, how much more so must those imprisoned populations be!

May 28th 1943   *HQ RALSU, Largs*
A letter came from Red at Machrihanish, the first since I'd been at Largs. Things were much easier now, she wrote, with four cypher officers and much shorter watches. I half expected her to tell me she was going to marry her nice pilot from South Africa, but there was no mention of him. Instead, she told me that the station medical officer who had once proposed to me was now engaged to one of the admin officers, and I was very glad for him. I had known her quite well, and thought how suitable a wife she would be for him, much better than a full time professional singer who'd long forgotten all she'd learnt of her domestic science training at Villa Brillantmont. The next news wasn't so good. Poor Peter Bentley, the Frenchman who'd escaped from Vichy France, had had to make an emergency landing while flying over Holland, and he and his crew had been captured, and were even now prisoners of war at some Oflag in Germany. "I've given you an address for him," she wrote, "in case you'd like to send him a parcel or something. It must be pretty dreary for him." She ended her letter on a rather wistful note, adding: "I sometimes think this war's never going to end. At least, in Combined Ops it must be exciting and important. You're so much

more in the centre of activities than we are here."

I supposed we were in a way, though we'd never actually see our little landing craft leave, attached by their davits to their parent landing ships. People like us were only some of the hardworking stage managers in the background. The main stars of the piece would always be performing in a production scheduled for a very different theatre. But still, I thought, the success of every production depended entirely on the planning and dedication of its stage management, didn't it?

"So, take heart, all you backroom thinkers and devisers, plotters and planners, givers and takers of orders, all you who turn thought into action – Dammit! We must fit into all this somehow!"

Needless to say, this two a.m. patch of purple prose, penned in bed in semi-darkness by the light of my torch after a long day and increasingly sleepless night, was not included in my reply to Red's letter. She'd only have laughed.

There was a PS to her letter. "I hope your eyes are better now that you're working much shorter hours during daytime."

Much shorter hours? During daytime? Eight a.m. till whenever? I smiled at that. Well, I supposed you could call it easier. Anyway, I was enjoying it and my eyes were fine, and for the moment that was the main thing.

June 23rd 1943   *HQ RALSU, Largs*

We were about to move, this time to Greenock under the direct aegis of FOIC. It seemed that the disseminated forces were being gathered into a coherent whole. There was a new air of energy as we packed the contents of our office into tidy files and boxes, and very carefully took down our wall chart, keeping it as flat as possible so as not to lose hundreds of coloured drawing pins.

"Though how the hell," said Leslie, "are we going to

transport the thing to Greenock? One false move and we've had it. Have to start all over again from scratch."

None of us could have borne to have faced that, and John and I stared up at it, frowning. Then a quiet voice spoke in the background, and Wren Hens supplied the final solution.

"Excuse me, sir," she suggested tentatively to Leslie, "would it be possible to lay it flat on the floor, and cover it with another piece of stiff paper or cardboard the same size? Then it could be fixed to our chart closely round the edges with sticky tape, and it wouldn't be so easy for all the drawing pins to fall out."

We all gazed at her, then began to smile.

"I might have known *you'd* think of something," said Leslie.

John was inspecting the outer edges of the chart. "I think that would work," he commented. "Hens, you're a marvel!"

But Hens only blushed and returned to her desk, while I hunted for a tape measure.

"Help me measure the exact size," I said to her, "then we'll go along to stores and see if they can match it with something stiff enough."

We took the measurement along with us, and presented the Wrens in naval stores with a real headache before they discovered something suitable. We had to compromise in the end with two separate pieces of thin cardboard. They hadn't anything big enough to fit the entire chart. Still, half a loaf, etc . . . .

Leslie, however, was doubtful, but we overruled him. "Leave it to us," I told him firmly. "Hens and I can fix it quite well. And we'll travel with it in the transport to make sure no one has the bright idea of trying to fold it up."

"OK, you're on," he said. "You girls are always better at this sort of thing than we are."

Lucky we were. It was not going to be an easy job.

June 25th 1943   *en route for Greenock*
0800 hours on a bright summer morning.

As I finally brought my suitcase and other belongings out of my room, I thought that the Hollywood Hotel could never have been in such chaos before. It was like seeing an elderly Victorian lady being subjected to all sorts of indignities, her lovingly arranged surroundings disturbed, all her guarded possessions scattered about with no one caring what happened to them. In the end I was quite glad when the time came to help Leslie, John and Wren Hens to remove our precious wall chart and carry it tenderly down the hotel steps and into the huge naval transport outside. We'd had quite a job to fix its protective covering securely and keep it flat, but somehow we managed to load it with the assistance of two sturdy sailors, who entered into the spirit of the thing with slightly alarming enthusiasm, offering advice and warnings in equal measure till I began to wonder if it wouldn't have been easier to have taken the whole thing to bits and put it all together again on arrival at our new office. But there was always the horrid possibility that it might not fit the available space on any of the walls. I quashed that defeatist thought firmly, and climbed into the transport with Wren Hens to sit one on each side of it to prevent any of the suitcases stacked up further inside the interior from falling on to it.

I think the sailors were secretly very impressed by our dedication, although I heard one of them say to his companion with a smothered laugh: "You'd think it was the Crown jewels!" and was tempted to tell him it was top secret and extremely fragile as well as highly important to the war effort. But then I thought better of it. He could think what he liked. What did it matter as long as we got it to Greenock in one undamaged piece?

Oh, the joys of moving house!

June 26th 1943   *HQ Senior Officer Assault Ships and*
                        Craft (SOASC) Greenock, Scotland
                        (HMS Warren)

Moving day had been one to forget, a hideous jumble of unloading our precious wall chart, luckily intact, in our new office in the rather insignificant house called Hazelwood, supervising the fixing of it on the only possible wall, deciding where to place our office furniture, checking telephones, unpacking files and other equipment, and consuming a snatched sandwich lunch and odd mugs of tea. All this after a rather nerve-wracking journey, since the sailor who drove us seemed to have no idea of the safest speed, but rumbled along with great dash and display, taking corners just too fast for comfort. I called out to him to slow down a bit which he did for a while, but this didn't last.

By the time we had more or less set up our new office it was nearly seven o'clock. We decided to call it a day and were given lifts to our new separate quarters. I was almost too tired to take in my surroundings, but somewhat cheered by the sight of the magnificent house set high up and back from the road, with a winding drive through banks of evergreens leading past a spacious lawn up to the imposing steps of the front entrance.

Friendly company, a strong gin and tonic, followed by a sustaining meal gave me just enough strength to unpack my overnight necessities before falling into a really comfortable bed and dreamless sleep.

As always when waking in a strange place to unaccustomed surroundings, it took me longer than usual to get up, but my companion in the bedroom said not to worry. She'd obviously come in after I'd gone to sleep and didn't disturb me.

"I'm sure you won't be expected in the office too early this morning," she said. "Not after yesterday. I work at the cypher office at FOIC, but I'll wait for you and take you over to Hazelwood. That's where your office is."

I thanked her, and went down to breakfast with her. Her name was Ruth Ward, and she was about my age with short curly hair framing a bright, smiling face and enormous candid grey eyes, altogether a very attractive personality.

During breakfast she explained about the house. "It's called Belleaire, 29 Newark Street, and belongs to a very rich ship owner. I don't know what he can think of having his home commandeered like this and filled with hundreds of strange women, but we're very lucky here. Wait till you see the double drawing room. It's almost like a ballroom, where we have dances. We use it as our mess at all other times."

"This dining room's fantastic," I remarked. "And what a view we have over the water, all those ships. You could almost lean out of your cabin window and touch them."

"Yes, both the Queens are in at the moment," Ruth said, staring out through the window.

"The Queens?" I queried.

Ruth looked back at me again and laughed. "Yes, you landlubber! The Queens *Mary* and *Elizabeth*. Those two enormous liners. They're troop carriers. The *New Amsterdam* was in last week, and before that the *Isle de France*. After all, this is the Fleet Anchorage. You'll have to learn to recognize the ships that come in."

"Well," I said, 'I do — quite a few, but in the Fleet Air Arm we knew more about recognizing aircraft. And in Combined Ops, of course, I can recognize any landing ship or craft at a glance. And that's not easy when they're mostly so small."

"I take it back," she said contritely. "After all, I'm only a cypher officer." She paused, then added, "By the way, I haven't been yet, but some of the cypher officers work on board the Queens going to and fro to the States, and they bring us back all sorts of goodies we can't buy here, Revlon lipsticks, and perfumes as well as nylons. Make out a short list and I'll give it to whoever is going on the next trip. You can give her some money, and if it's too much or not enough you can adjust it with her when she comes here again."

"What a wonderful idea!" I said. "I can see I'm going to enjoy being in Greenock. You know, I thought Hollywood Hotel in Largs was luxurious enough, but this is something else. I mean, look at the length of this table! It must be long enough to seat thirty people at least."

"The food's not bad either," Ruth said. "The cook in charge used to cook for some duchess or other, I forget who, but she can make anything out of almost nothing. We do pretty well here. I could get used to this," she added enviously.

Hazelwood was a rather sad contrast, with its narrow hall and distinctly poky rooms. Ruth almost commiserated with me. But it had a little garden at the back where we could occasionally drink our morning coffee if there was a lull.

On my arrival I found Leslie and John discussing the position of our desks, but obviously not agreeing, and they both turned to me with relief. Wren Hens was busy unpacking some files and pretending not to notice.

I saw at once where the desks should be. There wasn't much choice, we'd have to have electric lights on all the time anyway, the window was so small. Fortunately both of them meekly accepted my advice, and the rest of the morning was spent in rearranging everything to the satisfaction of all. At lunchtime we were bidden into the garden where we all met Admiral Warren who gave us a pleasant greeting and a short talk on what we were there for. Afterwards Yvonne had the bright idea of taking a photograph of all the staff, which John missed, being called to the telephone just at that moment.

The Admiral and several high ranking officers from FOIC Greenock called round to our office and studied our wall chart with interest and, thank goodness, approval. I had been afraid they might have suggested some amendments.

July 10th 1943   *SOASC Greenock*
I was not sure how we were going to fit it all in, but our social life suddenly took off at a stroke, and I found myself accepting invitations to go to parties on board destroyers, battleships, aircraft carriers, frigates, and even over at Gourock on a submarine. Although it was safely moored alongside the quay I could still imagine how claustrophobia might strike when actually under water. "Mind your head on those stairs – there's no room to swing a cat," the Captain, an RN lieutenant commander, said cheerfully, as he led me to the tiny wardroom area, and this was even truer when all his guests had arrived. It might have been imagination, but I felt the air getting thicker by the minute, and by the time we left was full of admiration for submariners. Theirs was the most dangerous and difficult of all naval services.

Having been attached to Royal Naval air stations I found I had particular friends on several aircraft carriers, which were much more to my taste than submarines, with lots of wide-open airy spaces on all parts of the vessel. I was frequently invited on board with any friends I cared to bring along with me and, of course, we returned the compliment by inviting officers from all these ships to our dances at Belleaire whenever they were in port, so a constant stream of visitors of varying nationalities came to enliven the scene.

The dances were held every alternate Sunday evening in the large drawing room, at one end of which was a small anteroom with a raised dais, on which excellent music was always provided by members of one of the resident Marine bands which the larger ships always carried. At the end of the evening the musicians were invited into the kitchen and given well deserved drinks and other refreshments by the Wrens on duty there before returning to their anchorage home.

There was another source of entertainment, known as Chief Officer's guest nights, to which I was always invited, almost commanded to attend, being a singer and expected to perform as part of the show, so to speak. Our Chief Officer WRNS was a rather strange lady named Pat Nye, an ex-actress, who would for these occasions always dress in full evening men's attire, complete with stiff white shirt, bow tie and small cigar which, with her Eton cropped hair, caused some confusion if you didn't know her well enough. I discovered that Belleaire had something of an ambivalent reputation, but being the unsophisticated character I was, I never really got the message until one evening when I happened to pass by the open doorway of one of the officers' cabins, and saw a very curious sight.

Ruth was in our cabin, and I entered it and quickly shut the door behind me. She was sitting on her bed, filing her nails, and glanced questioningly up at me. "What have you been up to?" she asked. "You look as though you've seen a ghost."

"You'll never believe it," I said. "I've just seen those two next door, Peggy what's-her-name is sitting on Rosemary's lap, and they're kissing – I mean *really* kissing!"

Ruth looked up at me with an odd expression on her face, half amusement, half disbelief, then she burst out laughing.

"Don't you *know*?" she demanded, her grey eyes opening to their fullest extent. "Do you mean to tell me you've been in the WRNS over three years and you *still* don't know? Honestly, Roxane, where have you been all that time? On another planet? I can't believe it."

"But I – well, I mean, I've never come across *that* before," I stammered, feeling every kind of fool. I sank down on my bed, then sat up again with a start. "So *that's* why he asked me – that man I was dancing with the other night!"

"What man?" Ruth asked.

"Oh, Mark something – rather a snake, I thought. He said: "'You're not one of *them*, are you?'"

"Oh God!" Ruth uttered. "And I suppose *you* said – looking the picture of innocence – 'one of *who*?' Now you listen to me! Your education's been sadly neglected, and you'd better know a thing or two for your own safety."

And she proceeded to bring me up to date on everything a smart girl of my age ought to have known, and ended by asking me if I'd ever read a book called *The Well of Loneliness*.

"No, of course you haven't," she answered her own question. "It was banned here, but of course everyone managed to get hold of a copy from somewhere. It's very enlightening."

I stared at her in amazement. Ruth, the girl who looked rather like a Botticelli angel with those huge innocent eyes and mellifluous voice, instructing me in some of the facts of life I'd never even heard of.

Oh well, we live and learn ... .

July 25th 1943   *SOASC Greenock*

The glorious summer weather continued, the light evenings stretching even later than at Machrihanish. I borrowed a bicycle and joined several others to go as far as Loch Lomond, cycling all round it and relaxing in the late evening's peace and quiet after an intensive day's work. Audrey Clarke, whom I had met on my cypher course at Greenwich and who had gone to St Merryn just after I'd left, had recently arrived at Belleaire. She had a sparkling personality and a cheerful and optimistic view of life. I had never known her to be depressed about anything and she joined in all the social activities that were offered her.

She and another girl, Doreen Hartley, also joined the cycling group and we explored much of the area. When we had time we went over to Helensburgh and Dunoon on the far side of the Firth of Clyde, and it was at Dunoon, in spite of my firm intention not to become seriously involved till the war was over that, rather surprisingly, I became engaged to a tall, very handsome RNVR lieutenant named John.

Leslie and John Norton, back in our office, behaved like Dutch uncles and demanded to meet him in order to give their approval. Both being married, I think they considered themselves good judges of character and reliable advisers. They seemed to have doubts when I told them that my fiancé might be going to a job in Africa after the war. What was I going to do about my singing training they'd heard so much about? There was no Royal Academy of Music in Africa. I don't say they influenced me in any way, but after a couple of months I exercised every woman's right to change her mind and broke off my engagement. It wasn't only because of the singing. There were other reasons, and both my Dutch uncles thought I'd done the right thing in the end.

"You can't really have been in love with him," John said, and Leslie added: "It's a long commitment, Roxane. Would you ever have been happy without your singing career?"

I sighed. They were right, of course. But what a difficult business love was, and what a weak-minded idiot I was becoming!

Other people had problems, of course. Nothing felt permanent as future plans seemed uncertain. The departure of ships was a daily occurrence. They were so near that if we leaned far enough out over our window sill we could almost recognise friends as their vessels, dressed over all, slipped away down the Firth of Clyde to the open sea, the larger ships with their resident marine bands playing them out. It was a familiar sight to us. The crews must also have been used to the white sheets being laboriously waved out of windows, giving the prearranged signal to those on board that someone on shore cared, a sad, nostalgic assurance which all too often was the only one given and received.

Fortunately, life wasn't without its funny side. We were now three in our cabin as Doreen Hartley had joined us there, and it was while we were all deeply asleep that something woke me to tingling consciousness. There was a brilliant full moon and because of the heat our curtains were not drawn over our open windows. I turned over in bed to face the door on my right, and could clearly see it was half open. As I stared at it I was astonished to see a head come round the door and a startled male face looked straight at me.

Fully awake by then I called out: "What the hell are you doing?" and the head disappeared with alacrity. I just had time to see the sailor's uniform and to notice that his hair was tousled, and in a flash realised he looked drunk.

There was a sudden noise outside on the landing, then hurried footsteps down the main stairs, whispered voices and barely smothered male laughter before the front door was slammed shut.

After a stunned moment I got out of bed and cautiously looked out on to the landing. Not a soul in sight. No one but me awake. When I returned to my bed the others hadn't even stirred, and I began to wonder if I'd dreamed it all.

But it was no dream. We heard at lunch time that several drunken sailors had got into Belleaire via a carelessly open window, snatched all our drying undies from the laundry, and had even had the nerve to look in some of the cabins and bathrooms. That was odd enough, but later on, reports came in from all over Greenock saying that women's undies were strewn around the town, and left hanging on any available support to float gently in the breeze, to the shocked embarrassment of the older inhabitants, and the obvious delight of the younger and less high-minded element.

I'm afraid I was one of these. In fact, most of us were, and I think the basis for our amusement lay in the thought of Chief Officer's bloomers gracing public monuments and buildings. I believe an acutely embarrassed Council official offered to have all the underwear laundered and returned to us, but somehow none of us were too keen. In the end a solution was found by Chief Officer herself. No one could deny that she had a fairly rumbustious sense of humour, and she suggested, quite seriously, that suitable items among the freshly laundered underwear might be donated to a local charity in aid of sailors' families.

Needless to say, there was quite a run on the underwear departments of the main Greenock shops, though we never heard if the sailors' charity had accepted her generous offer.

September 10th 1943   *SOASC Greenock*
It hadn't taken us long to get thoroughly re-settled into our usual busy routine. Our proximity to FOIC Headquarters gave us the feeling of being drawn into the central core of the great forces being assembled for a certain longed for event that might not be so far off, for all we knew then. At Largs we had been one of many widely dispersed smaller groups, but by now everything was merging into a single and vitally important aim. I felt the difference myself. When I thought how naive and uncertain I'd been only a few years ago it was hardly credible how confident I'd become now, not only knowing what needed to be done under any circumstances, but actually able to do it. Leslie and John, if for some reason both of them were temporarily absent, had no hesitation in leaving me in sole charge of the office (with, of course, the capable Wren Hens as my indispensable second in command).

I even had to deal one afternoon with an urgent request from a harassed officer at a naval base some distance away for a floating crane to rectify an accident to a landing craft that had fallen into the sea from its parent ship.

"We can get hold of a crane easily enough, but you'll have to get permission from FOIC," the distant voice went on. "He'll have to be the one to authorise it. Could you ring him up and ask him? We're in rather a state here. I thought it might be better if the request came from your office. My name's Randall – Lieutenant RN, by the way."

I was appalled. Ring up the flag officer in charge! No lower rank would do? A personal request from a mere Third Officer WRNS, assistant to the absent Staff Officer Landing Craft? Wouldn't it be better to ask Admiral Warren instead?

But then I remembered he was out somewhere and not expected back till much later, so summoning up my courage I rang through to the main FOIC switchboard, sounding as authoritative as I could as I identified myself, and asked to speak urgently to FOIC.

Fortunately, the Wren on the switchboard had often put calls through to us and knew me, and in a very few moments had connected me with his office. Surprisingly, he answered the call himself, and after I'd identified myself I outlined as clearly as I could all I knew of the situation requiring a floating crane.

He took it all in at once. "Yes, tell them to go ahead," he said crisply. "And afterwards I shall want a full report of what happened, and who was in charge." I thanked him gratefully, then rang Lieutenant Randall back and gave him the good news. He sounded very relieved.

"Good show!" he said warmly. "Ten minutes – that's what I call service! Many thanks. What did you say your name was?"

I told him, and added the message about a full report for FOIC.

"That's OK," said the lieutenant, quite cheerfully now. "It was nobody's fault really. Something just gave way. But it'll be all right now we can have that crane. Thanks again for your help."

As I rang off I smiled across at Wren Hens, understandably rather pleased with myself.

"Well, that's someone who's happy," I said, and she smiled back, obviously rather impressed, and suggested I might like some tea.

The only thing was, I thought, suddenly doubtful, would the floating crane be successful? Supposing something else went wrong? Oh, well, I did all I could. Now it was up to the people on the spot.

I wondered what Leslie and John would say when they got back.

October 6th 1943   *SOASC Greenock*

My birthday had passed almost unnoticed, except for family cards and presents, and a celebratory drink with Leslie and John and a few friends in the mess at Belleaire. It was odd, but I'd never felt so far away from my family and home. It seemed like another world. We were so taken up with the demanding present which took all our thought and energy. There never seemed to be enough minutes to a day.

Admiral Warren frequently called in at our office, always taking an intense interest in how our system was working. He was an affable man, easy to work for, always pleasant and informal in his approach to us all. He was entirely my idea of a seasoned sailor, with his bluff manner and wind-burnt complexion, and his far-seeing, alert blue eyes that had scanned many a distant horizon, someone who radiated energy, enthusiasm and confidence, on whom you could place entire reliance in any situation. We all liked him enormously. There was no fussy overseeing of what we were doing. He was confident that all of us under his command knew our jobs and left us to it, and as things got busier we took this in our stride and enjoyed it. For some

reason he could never get my name right, and in the end
settled for Roxalana, and I gave up trying to correct it.

December 10th 1943   SOASC *Greenock*
Christmas was approaching. Where had the time gone?
What with a steadily increasing workload and endless
parties on board countless different ships the days flew by.
More and more coloured drawing pins were added to our
lists on the wall chart, as the numbers of landing craft grew,
and our calls from the Admiralty in London grew daily
more frequent. There always seemed to be some kind of
confusion to be cleared up, and the inevitable solution
often seemed to be in our office. We were gaining a
reputation for quick answers. This was no reflection on the
serious, hardworking Lieutenant Ken Church who for
some obscure reason was teased mercilessly by both Leslie
and John, particularly John, whose sense of humour was
seldom understood or appreciated. I remonstrated with
them both about this when I thought things were getting
out of hand.

"You must be making his life hell," I protested. "The
poor man can't help not having your sense of humour. I
don't always get the joke myself. It's not fair. He's a nice
chap and very competent, and you shouldn't be so unkind
to him."

"We're too subtle," said John. "That's the trouble. It
needs a particularly subtle brain to appreciate us."

"I don't know about *subtle*," I countered, "I should have
said the word was *childish*."

"Oho!" said Leslie, looking up from a bulging file, "we
have an embryo Chief Officer in our midst!"

"Yes. Don't you go pulling rank on us," John added,
mock severely. "You'll need a few more stripes on your
sleeve before you can get away with that."

I subsided and smiled at them. I never gave a thought to
rank. They were like older brothers, and I was very fond of

both of them. You couldn't work together at such close quarters day in and day out without developing a certain relationship, one I knew I'd miss badly when we inevitably had to go our separate ways. But that wouldn't be just yet. We were only beginning to approach the final dénouement, though none of us knew when that was likely to be.

February 24th 1944   *SOASC Greenock*

Leslie had decided I needed a break, and one morning announced that I should travel to London early the following Friday, taking the updated State with me down to the Admiralty, so that I could make the acquaintance of some of our hitherto unseen colleagues including, of course, Lieutenant Ken Church. Then, on my way back, I could stop off at home for a few days rest.

"We don't want anyone getting stale," he added, "and it may be some time before any of us get the chance again. I'm sending Wren Hens off for a short break when you get back. I've a feeling we're going to be working flat out very soon."

I nodded. That much was daily growing more obvious, certainly from our point of view here at SOASC.

March 3rd 1944   *The Admiralty, London*

The train journey seemed interminable, and the nearer we got to London the more damaged and dilapidated the view outside the window became. Poor old London! What a lot that wonderful old city had had to endure in the past! Now it was exhausted, weary and dust-laden, having been too long in the front line of conflict, and it reminded me forcibly of Liverpool. At Paddington Station I saw lines of grey-faced people moving slowly about as if too tired to care if they ever reached their destinations.

I managed to share a taxi with two American GIs who were suitably shocked at what they saw. I was only going as far as the strange concrete building known as the Citadel, just inside the lower end of the Mall near the Admiralty Arches by Trafalgar Square. Below this building were the heavily guarded Admiralty headquarters, and there I said goodbye to the Americans who were going further on. I thought how smart and well-dressed they looked compared to our other ranks, and wondered where they were bound for.

After going through the identification routine at the underground entrance I was given instructions how to find Lieutenant Church's offices, and walked slowly along corridors past hurrying officers of all ranks until I eventually found the department I was looking for. How odd, I thought, here was I among many people I'd spoken to so often on the telephone, and nobody had the faintest idea who I was. Beyond an occasional glance no one took any notice of me at all. I was amused, thinking this must be what it was like to be invisible, and wondered what they would think when I handed the Friday State over to them so much earlier than usual.

Eventually I came to a large desk at the centre of the rear wall of an enormous busy office, and knew at once that the officer sitting there was Lieutenant Ken Church. He was intently studying some kind of report and did not look up as I approached. I quietly placed the large envelope I'd been so carefully guarding on to his desk, and enquired innocently: "Lieutenant Church?"

He raised his head quickly, staring up at me uncomprehendingly for a moment, then a sudden smile came and he rose to his feet.

"I know that voice," he said. "So you've arrived safely."

"I've brought you the State," I said, shaking his outstretched hand. "Leslie thought you might like to have it a bit earlier than usual."

"We would indeed," he said. "Many thanks. We're pretty busy here, as you know." I smiled back at him, and after a brief hesitation he added rather shyly: "It's very nice to meet you at last. Did you have a good journey?"

"Not too bad," I answered. "Horribly crowded, though."

By now the word had got round and there was a general surge towards me.

"Never tell me it's Roxy from Greenock!" said a voice I knew well, and I turned to see a tall, attractive second officer I'd spoken to many times over the last few months.

"You're Joanna," I said, smiling, and as I looked round at the rest of her colleagues I saw that most of them were gazing at me curiously as if at some strange animal in the zoo.

"You don't look a bit like your voice sounds," a small, plump third officer commented, looking me over rather critically.

"*You* do, exactly," I retorted, returning her look, thinking it was time to call a halt to odious comparisons, and there was a general laugh.

Ken Church had now put his papers neatly away in a drawer, locked it, and came round to the front of his desk. "I'm sure you must be hungry," he said. "Come and have some lunch in the canteen."

And he took me by the arm and led me out of the office and down several corridors till we reached the babble of voices and inviting odour of cooking. It was a funny business, this meeting up with the owners of intangible voices. Yet Lieutenant Church in person exactly fitted his voice. It was so familiar that I felt I'd known him for years. He looked to be in his mid-thirties, of medium height and build, with nothing remarkable about his features or colouring. His eyes were of an indeterminate hazel, yet there was something about his expression that was pleasant and reassuring. You might never notice him in a crowd, I thought, but you could never think him nondescript. He was undoubtedly the right man for the right job, and I would tell Leslie and John so. I wondered if I was a surprise to him, but as we talked and worked our way through a very adequate lunch I began to feel the same relationship between us that I felt for Leslie and John, an uncomplicated, pleasant exchange of thought and ideas against a background of mutual interest. There were no long silences, no creating idle conversation to fill them.

Afterwards, I went back with him to the office, and spent some time making friends with everyone there, till it was time to catch my train back up to Crewe Station, where I had to change to get to Hartford. Somebody actually arranged transport for me, and the Wren driver got me back to Paddington in plenty of time. Talk about VIP treatment!

March 10th 1944   *Oaklands, Hartford, Cheshire*
My short leave had passed far too quickly. My poor parents looked strained and unhappy, my mother appearing to be far away in another sphere, and my father not seeming at all well. He had a habit of breaking off a sentence in mid-flow as though what he was saying suddenly seemed unimportant or else forgotten. I found this very disconcerting, it was so unlike him. My sister-in-law Margaret with baby Anne had left to stay with her parents in Leatherhead, and my aunt Nancy was with her married daughter. But the neighbours were helpful and sympathetic, and my parents had now found reliable daily help in the house, so I didn't feel quite so guilty at having to leave home and return to duty.

March 20th 1944   *SOASC Greenock*
It was just as well that all of us in our office had managed to get a few days leave, although I had the distinct impression that the others, like me, had found it really hard to switch off from what we'd been so busily engaged in. The war had so taken us over that to shift our minds into another dimension centred basically on home affairs and

the interests of family (particularly a stricken family like mine) was very difficult, and I began to feel that I wasn't managing to answer their unspoken call for support. I'd mentioned this to Leslie and John, and they'd understood immediately. There was a limit, they told me, to the number of demands anyone could respond to all at one time, however much one might have wanted to do so, and I supposed I'd somehow set the thought of David a little to one side in order to be able to concentrate on the immediate task in hand. But as far as my family was concerned I still felt inadequate, and had a guilty sense of relief when back once more in our stressful but familiar war setting.

April 5th 1944   *SOASC Greenock*

Our life now appeared to be like a vast engine revving up into top gear. We seldom left the office till after ten o'clock, and on several occasions were still working till about two or three in the morning. None of us seemed to notice the time, though Leslie was firm about Wren Hens being escorted back to the Wrennery before nine o'clock. She always offered to stay on but he was adamant. Either he or John also escorted me afterwards back to quarters, as there had been reports of strange men lurking outside Hazelwood and near the entrance to the grounds of Belleaire.

No one had actually been attacked, but we couldn't afford to risk losing valuable trained personnel for whatever reason at this juncture.

May 2nd 1944   *SOASC Greenock*

There was only one telephone for social calls for the entire occupants of Belleaire, with the exception of Chief Officer and her immediate entourage. It was tucked away in the small cloakroom off the main hall, usually half covered with coats and other paraphernalia, so we had to rely on anyone who happened to be near enough to hear its frequently muffled ringing to answer the calls and shout for the person concerned to come at once. Since there were so many of us the telephone was in constant use, and long conversations were ruthlessly interrupted by anyone waiting to make a call. On that particular day I had just finished breakfast at seven thirty when one of the Wren stewards approached and said there was an urgent call for me. In sudden foreboding I picked up the receiver and heard the voice of Mrs Storey, our parents' immediate neighbour in Hartford. She told me very gently that my father had died suddenly during the night, and that my distraught mother, being alone in the house, had rushed round to her nearest neighbour. Mrs Storey told me that my father had recently had his bed moved downstairs to the morning room to make it easier to be looked after during the day, but during the night he had a little bell beside his bed in case he should need to call my mother from upstairs. Apparently, she had woken up thinking she heard him call out, and still only half asleep had gone downstairs to find my father lying with his hand outstretched towards the bell. She'd spoken to him but he never moved or tried to reply, and in panic she had rushed round next door for help.

"I didn't know he was so ill," I stammered, hardly able to take this in, "He just seemed rather tired, but was still sleeping upstairs when I was on leave recently."

"The doctor's been," said Mrs Storey, "but there was nothing anyone could do. Your poor father's heart just gave out."

I sat on the stool beside the telephone, feeling utterly shocked and helpless. What was happening to our family? I couldn't bear to think of my mother. Only three years ago David had gone, and now this. What would she do?

Endless telephone calls followed throughout that day. There was so much to be decided. Friends and neighbours rallied round wonderfully, and our doctor got someone to go and stay with my mother for a few nights until after the funeral, when other arrangements could be made. I finally got in touch with Tony who said he could probably get two days compassionate leave to attend the funeral, and Chief Officer Nye sanctioned the same for me. Leslie and John said they'd manage for two days without me, and Admiral Warren expressed genuine sympathy and insisted I must go home for at least two days. Ruth and Doreen promised to keep an eye on things in our cabin, helped me to pack and even organised a Wren driver to get me to the station in time to catch the overnight express as far as Crewe, where I'd have to change and wait for the early morning milk train at five thirty back up the line to Hartford.

I knew Crewe Station well, having had to change trains there whenever I'd travelled down from Machrihanish. There was always something peculiarly depressing about a station restaurant, if one could call it that, at that hour of the morning, and although there were usually other service personnel trying to kill time over undrinkable coffee and stale buns, there was an atmosphere of stalemate, as though we'd all taken root and would never move on anywhere again.

May 3rd 1944   *Oaklands, Hartford, Cheshire*
I hardly remembered the final lap of my journey to Hartford. Apart from being so tired, I was confused and incredulous that this should have happened so soon after I'd been home on leave. When eventually I entered the house at breakfast time the greatest shock was to see my mother, once so energetic and full of joie de vivre, lying on a sofa covered with a rug, holding out her trembling arms to me as I bent to kiss her. She seemed to be in deep shock, blaming herself for not having reached our father sooner after she thought she'd heard him call out, though I assured her that the doctor had told us there would have been

nothing she could have done. He had also ordered her very sternly not to attempt to attend the funeral, and although I offered to stay with her she begged me to go with Tony.

"There'd be no one else from our family now," she said pitifully, and since two of her closest friends were going to sit with her I didn't argue.

May 4th 1944   *Oaklands*
Although Tony and I were the only immediate family members, the church was packed throughout with friends and neighbours and many of my father's ICI colleagues, including one dear old tea lady who came up to Tony and me after the service, and told us in a tremulous voice that she would always remember Mr Houston as he treated her like a duchess. That was one of the nicest things about our father, his never-ending courtesy which won him many friends from all walks of life.

We had also arranged for a short service of blessing over David's garden of remembrance, and although our family had never been deeply religious I found myself hoping that somehow he and our father had met. It made David's death seem a little less lonely.

May 25th 1944   *SOASC Greenock*
It had taken a very short time after my return to get back into the swing of our busy routine, and as the hectic days passed we began to have a very good idea of a certain crucially important date approaching. Although Wren Hens did not have access to all top secret information it became obvious that any intelligent girl working so closely with us would be able to put two and two together. I imagined that the heads of the various Combined Ops and other groups had sworn in ratings like herself to strict secrecy, though I never had the slightest doubt of her complete integrity. We were all immensely careful not to talk about our work. "Walls have ears!" and "Careless talk costs lives" might have

been hammered on to our brains in letters of stone. Such a huge, pluperfect, over-the-top, top-secret secret and so many thousands to share it was a shattering thought!

June 1st 1944   *SOASC Greenock*

A great deal of our telephone conversations were dealt with on the 'scrambler', that invaluable telephonic invention that turned plain speech into gobbledygook, enabling highly secret discussions to take place in perfect safety, and we learnt about the possible delay of Overlord, (the code name for the invasion of Europe) due to sudden unsettled weather. Everyone was on tenterhooks, particularly poor Jim Ewing who became almost rattled over the uncertainty. Not the only one, I thought, my mind switching over to General Eisenhower and the other sea lords who must at this time have been on the cliff-edge of their endurance. How long could the secret hold if the poor weather caused protracted delays?

June 3rd 1944   *SOASC Greenock*

The weather had deteriorated ominously during the last week, but now seemed to have calmed down a little, though it was still far from being helpful. Towards the end of the afternoon Leslie drew me aside.

"I want to show you something," he said, "something none of us will ever have the chance to see again, at least I hope not. Get something to eat and then wait for me outside at about ten o'clock – I'll be in the car."

Curious, but obedient, I did as he asked, and duly found myself sitting beside him as he drove towards the cliffs further up the Firth of Clyde. He parked the car at a convenient spot, and led me over to the cliff edge to gaze down into the water. It was now about ten fifteen, not anywhere near darkness, but with that subtle lessening of light that heralded the end of a day.

"Look over there," he said, peering through his

binoculars and pointing. "Do you recognise some of those?"

And there they were, hundreds of our little landing craft looking absurdly small and vulnerable as they hung from their davits, riding the wind as they swayed against the sides of their numerous parent ships. These were the real life representations of the hundreds of different coloured drawing pins on our wall chart. And all round, dwarfing them, were much larger ships, an aircraft carrier, several destroyers, sleek and menacing, smaller frigates, corvettes and LSTs (Landing Ships Tank), all casting their various shapes of shadows behind them. There were so many that barely a clear patch of water could be seen. We were staring down at a great modern armada, a coldly determined gathering of men and ships and arms, the liberators poised to change the battered face of Europe, and rid its home soil of the deadly stain of Nazi pollution that had darkened it for so long.

Sudden emotion flooded over me, and I found myself silently crying out to all the imprisoned people across the Channel: "They're coming! You'll soon be free! Get ready!" How would they react, I wondered, to their first hearing of this momentous news? Would the conquered of Europe be rising in stealth, waking at last from their long enforced nightmare to answer the call to arms? I could imagine the underground resistance fighters and the well-organised Maquis checking their long thought out plans of action, the old soldier bringing out his hidden weapon, ancient from another war but kept well oiled and useful, the determined housewife reaching suddenly for her deadly sharpened carving knife, the young children pausing in their play to run out into the garden and gather up their best jagged stones to throw, all of them preparing a merciless retribution for their captors while they waited for the approaching forces of freedom.

"They'll be leaving soon," Leslie said, scanning the scene

below, "a few at a time. It'll take quite a while to get them all down south and ready for the off. I only wish this blasted weather would settle down a bit. It won't be easy landing if the sea's very rough."

A sudden chill ran through me. This armada seemed so powerful and would soon be joining hundreds of other forces, but I couldn't bear to think of what they would have to go through before it was all over.

I turned away, silently wishing them God speed, and beside me Leslie sighed deeply. "Well, that's that," he said quietly, "part of the first wave. Come on, we'd better get back."

He put his arm round my shoulders and led me back to the car. I shivered suddenly. Landing craft were no longer just coloured drawing pins on our wall chart. They and the men they carried were all too real.

As we drove off he glanced intently at me. "That's something you'll be able to tell your grandchildren, anyway," he said encouragingly, and I tried to smile. What a futile, grotesque and wasteful thing was war!

June 6th 1944   *SOASC Greenock*

It was five to eight and our small office was crowded as we waited to hear the morning news bulletin. Admiral Warren with his married daughter Lynette Heycock who was in the FANY (First Aid Nursing Yeomanry), and other members of staff had just joined us, and we all stood around in silence. There was an air of suppressed excitement about the Admiral, and as the pips sounded he stiffened. Nobody moved as the calm voice, totally devoid of any emotion, began the momentous announcement, telling us of the Allied forces' landing in Europe. We all leaned a little nearer to the radio so as not to miss anything, but the Admiral suddenly clenched his right fist into a ball, and struck the palm of his left hand with tremendous force, uttering loudly: "By Christ! They've done it! They've done it!" in a sort of rhythm, punctuated by the sound of his fists clashing together. He began to stride up and down in the limited space available as if he couldn't contain himself, and I noticed tears in his eyes.

At that moment I think all of us were there with the men in the various landing craft, as they were borne inexorably towards the shallows under furious gunfire to wade ashore onto dangerously exposed beaches.

As we listened everyone seemed stunned with a mixture of triumph, incredulity and exhaustion. So this was the beginning of the end which Churchill had once spoken of, the solid culmination to which all our scattered efforts had been aimed for so long. It had been an arduous and stressful time, and its cessation would be hard to realise, almost as though we'd temporarily stopped breathing.

An uneasy thought crept into my mind. My brother Tony in the Royal Engineers was probably somewhere in the forefront of the invasion forces, and my heart plunged suddenly. Oh God! Not Tony as well! Look after him, God! I prayed desperately. Take care of *him*!

June 7th 1944   *SOASC Greenock*
After the initial gripping excitement of that first assault wave we were as busy as ever. The long build-up to D-Day had been immensely tiring, but somehow we managed to find our second wind and continue along the same lines as before.

Our instructions were precise and urgent. Thousands more troops and their equipment had to be ferried across the Channel to reinforce the invasion army, and replace the dead and injured who would have to be collected and evacuated wherever possible by the doctors and nurses of the accompanying medical teams. These, together with an enormous amount of stores and repair equipment of every kind would have to be transported on D-Day plus one, so hundreds more landing craft were going to be needed. This would be an ongoing requirement, the Admiralty told us, for as long as necessary, and all the Combined Ops groups were going to be busy.

Throughout that day every free moment was spent in listening avidly to news of the Allied progress into France, knowing that so many of our families and friends were involved in the desperate battle for supremacy. The weather had picked up again, which was a blessing for the advancing Allied armies, though our main comfort lay in the knowledge that the entire indigenous populations must surely be ready and waiting for the chance to lend them their assistance.

But we managed somehow to keep pace with the stream of urgent requirements flowing into our office, and felt that we were doing our bit.

June 30th 1944   *SOASC Greenock*

Rather sad news, at least from my point of view. Yvonne de Méric, with whom I'd become very friendly at Largs and here at Greenock, was being posted to Mountbatten's Headquarters of South-East Asia Command (SEAC) at Kandy in Ceylon, and would be going on embarkation leave for a fortnight before leaving the country. I was really sorry to see her go, and we arranged to meet up as soon as possible after the war. I supposed we'd all be used to these goodbyes by the time peace came.

August 22nd 1944   *SOASC Greenock*

Two of His Majesty's Canadian ships, the *Prince Henry* and *Prince David* arrived in the Clyde yesterday for convoy duty, and lost no time in making their presence felt by inviting fifty WRNS officers, and as many WRNS ratings aboard the *Prince Henry* to a party which could only be described as splendiferous. Gin flowed like tap water, and the food was beyond anything we'd eaten since rationing came in. Huge joints of ham, chicken and turkey with every kind of adjunct in the way of salads were followed by rich chocolate mousse, meringues and a coffee cake to die for, all smothered in real cream, and it was no wonder everyone let good manners go by the board and tucked in as if we were starving inmates of a besieged city.

Our host was Commander Edward Watson, a very tall, thin man, not the least good looking with his bony features and determined long chin, but with an unexpected charm of manner that made him oddly attractive and approachable. But I was sure there was another side to him, a forceful, highly competent characteristic which ensured his orders would be obeyed immediately and without question.

During the evening various groups dispersed under escort around the ship. The crew were excellent hosts. Somewhere in the kaleidoscope of guests I caught sight now and again of Ruth, Audrey Clarke and Doreen Hartley among others, and even shy Wren Hens who seemed to be having everything explained to her by at least three sailors at once. Everyone appeared to be enjoying themselves hugely.

I was inspecting one of the gun emplacements and turned to find the Commander at my elbow.

"You interested in guns?" he enquired with a smile.

"Well – yes," I answered. "When *I'm* holding them, that is."

He laughed. "I take it you've had some weapons training? How's your eyesight?"

"Yes, I trained at St Merryn – the Royal Naval Air Station in Cornwall. None of us were any good with the .303 rifle. The kickback against our shoulders was too painful, and anyway we couldn't hold it steady to take aim. It was too heavy, so we had to lie on our stomachs supporting the rifle on our elbows, if you see what I mean. But we were much more successful with the .45 Webley Scott revolver," I added, as faint amusement appeared on his face. "I managed to hit a matchbox at twenty-five yards. I don't see so badly with glasses."

"Good for you," the Commander said.

"We never had to use it, thank goodness," I said. "But it must be very exciting to shoot with one of your guns."

"Let me show you around," he offered, and proceeded to do so very thoroughly. "By the way, we're going out on gunnery practice tomorrow," he added. "Perhaps you'd like to come out and watch it. Very noisy, but you're right, quite exciting."

I jumped at the chance. My Dutch uncles would *have* to give me time off for that!

August 23rd 1944   *on board HMCS* Prince Henry
Leslie had kindly given me the day off, though I think both he and John were rather envious of my good fortune of a trip out to sea. The weather was fine and warm, the sky completely clear, and I could see the aircraft approaching in the distance with the target drogue towed out some way behind it. I knew this was always used for firing practice but had never seen it in action.

When I arrived on board I was met by Commander Watson, who welcomed me, then added rather surprisingly as I saluted him: "No need for that. Call me Ed. And you told me last night I think, that your name is Roxane." To my astonishment he actually pronounced it correctly in the French way (as it should be, having come from the heroine of Edmond Rostand's play *Cyrano de Bergerac*. A pleasant change from Roxalana or the misspelt Roxanne).

"Now," he said, leading me some way behind the gun emplacements. "You're to stay here and not come any nearer, do you understand? You don't want to put the gunners off. If you find it too noisy you can always retreat into the wardroom."

"I don't mind the noise," I said. "In fact, I wish I could have a go at firing one of your guns myself."

"Not on your life!" he said sternly. "If I catch you trying to do that I'll have you thrown overboard!"

I laughed, and promised good behaviour, and he left me to go and talk to the gunnery officer. I had the impression that all the gunners were on their mettle in front of a spectator.

In a very few minutes the aircraft was much nearer, and the gunners braced themselves. I wondered how I'd feel if it had been an enemy out to bomb us, but there was no doubt how the men felt after their first shot at the drogue. I was aware of the sudden sharpening of their attention, how their hands gripped the guns as they took careful aim, and how their bodies were shaken with the vibration as they fired. The noise was terrific, but as the plane completed its first run the drogue was still intact and every gun followed its passage with ferocious determination. As we waited for the aircraft to complete the turn for its second approach I could feel the tension, and as the guns blazed away once more it was incredibly exciting, and I was suddenly seized with an almost insane desire to handle one of them myself. Mindful of Ed's dire warning I controlled myself. To give way to excitement was to lose concentration, and I had not been taught how to cope with that. Even these highly trained gunners obviously felt the thrill of the chase but could control it to their advantage.

It was not until the middle of the afternoon that one of the gunners managed to hit the drogue. We had had a break for lunch, with only orange or lime juice to drink. Just as well after last night. The gunners and anyone on duty today, of course, had not been at the party. I think some of the officers were rather surprised at my interest in gunnery practice, but I assured them I'd never been so thrilled by anything as I had been that day, and they seemed pleased. I thanked the gunnery officer and congratulated his team, and as I left the *Prince Henry*, Ed came to the top of the gangway to see me off. I thanked him warmly for a wonderful day.

"You're the first girl I've ever come across who'd enjoy spending a day being deafened by gunfire," he said, then paused and added: "And I didn't really mean I'd have you thrown overboard, whatever you did."

"I knew you weren't really serious," I said, and invited him and his officers to one of the Sunday dances at Belleaire whenever they were in harbour. "Just ring me at Belleaire or my office."

"Thank you, I will," he replied, and I gave him the telephone numbers, saluted finally, and made my way down to the waiting boat, while everyone on deck waved me goodbye.

October 1st 1944   *SOASC Greenock*

A letter from Yvonne de Méric arrived with unexpected good news. On her way out on board ship to Kandy in Ceylon she had been taken ill, but fortunately had met a charming young diplomat named Dudley Cheke, who had looked after her till she reached hospital in Colombo. After two weeks there she had quite recovered, and she and Dudley had been married up in Kandy, and were deliriously happy. She would be leaving the WRNS and going to Australia where Dudley was to be posted. She ended by saying she still had my Cheshire address, but could always trace me at WRNS headquarters in London if my family had moved. Meanwhile, she'd send me her Australian address when she knew where they'd be living. All very romantic, and I was immensely happy for her.

October 3rd 1944   *SOASC Greenock*

My twenty-fifth birthday. It seemed a long time since I'd felt really young and carefree, and yet I still enjoyed parties on board ship, still bicycled out into the evening glories of Loch Lomond and other enchanted localities during a late summer reluctant to give way to autumn, and still slept peacefully in my bed at night.

But it didn't seem right, somehow, while across a narrow channel of water one of the most hideous and desperate battles that had ever been fought against the forces of evil was still taking place, and on its victorious outcome depended the future safety and happiness of a great part of the world.

October 6th 1944   *SOASC Greenock*

I had recently become friendly with Jane Price, a second officer who worked in the Convoy Routing Office at nearby Gourock, dealing with merchant ships. She told me that the destroyer HMS *Walker* was in harbour, and that the brother of a close friend of hers was on board. He had naturally contacted Jane on arrival, and the result was an invitation from Lieutenant Commander Tony Trew, the captain, for her to bring a few of her friends on board for a small party one evening. Jane was a bright, attractive and very definite personality with a great sense of humour, and in no time at all she'd organised date, time and guests for the party. There were about six of us, Isobel Cowie, Audrey Clarke, myself and two other girls from Jane's office.

It was a great evening, full of laughter. Tony Trew was a charming host, Derek Napper, the brother of Jane's friend, showed us all over the ship, and Dacre Powell (usually called 'Sandy' Powell after a current popular comedian), a shy but attentive companion. We all got on very well, and Jane promptly arranged a reciprocal evening in the guest room at Belleaire. It was possible to book it in advance for dinner, and was an easy way to entertain privately.

October 20th 1944   *SOASC Greenock*

It was sad to see them leave. We knew they'd be going on the arduous run to Archangel, the port up in Murmansk in northern Russia, as part of the escort for a huge convoy of merchant ships, and sympathised with anyone having to brave the kind of weather they would be facing. Jane said she'd let us know when they'd be due back. She, Isobel and I had formed a pleasantly friendly trio with Tony, Derek and Sandy, and during their time at Greenock they had been as frequent guests at Belleaire as we had been on board HMS *Walker*. We got so accustomed to the ship it would have been easy for us to think ourselves part of the crew.

December 19th 1944   *SOASC Greenock*
HMS *Walker* was back, looking very unlike the svelte and elegant ship we'd known, which perhaps was not surprising given the battering she must have received on such a journey.

We decided, Jane and Isobel and I (that is, Jane decided and Isobel and I agreed) that since Christmas was so near, to give them a special Christmas dinner, candles, crackers, presents and all, to help them feel at home. We went to a great deal of trouble over buying gifts and arranging little delicacies as far as we could find them in the Greenock shops, and on the actual evening decided to wear 'civvies' to add a bit of glamour to the proceedings.

But we were not prepared for the sight of our guests. Three exhausted looking men whose uniforms were anything but trim and smart arrived on time, greeted us warmly, exclaiming at the decorations around the room and on the dining table, but giving us the impression all the time that although their bodies might be safely on shore, their minds were still elsewhere.

It was an extraordinary feeling to make conversation with someone who didn't seem to be there, and we hastened to give them some fairly stiff drinks in the hope that they'd relax a little.

By the time we'd finished dinner, we all sat around the glowing fire at the end of the room, smoking or cracking walnuts.

"Wonderful to sit near a fire," Tony remarked with a deep sigh, leaning back on the sofa.

"Wonderful to feel everything round us is still," Derek added, yawning.

"And dry!" Sandy said with relish, holding his hands out to the blaze.

They began to tell us something then of their experiences with the convoy.

The worst thing of all, they said, had been the relentless pitching and tossing of the ship, and having to grab hold of any kind of support each time a huge wave struck, so as not to be swept overboard. Sleep was almost an impossibility at times, as they frequently woke up to find themselves half out of their bunks or actually on the floor.

"It was quite a strain on the eyes, too," Tony went on. "The light was so bad, what with the storms and the fog, and we often lost sight of the convoy, especially if one of the ships had got out of line."

"And then we had to chase around to find the damn thing," Derek added. "Frankly, I often wondered if we'd ever get any of them to Archangel."

"I wouldn't have minded so much if it hadn't been so cold," said Sandy, stretching his long legs out in front of him. "It's a wonder we didn't get frostbite. I've only just begun to feel my toes again."

No wonder they looked so tired. Apart from having to be constantly on the alert against lurking U-boats, the endless physical discomfort of that bleak, frozen-misted demi-world and the biting sting of icy spume on their faces must have made it almost impossible to see far ahead. I could imagine the difficulty of having to search for ships that had strayed from their positions during a ferocious storm. The task was so urgent, the responsibility so heavy, and failure might have resulted in the loss of a ship loaded with much-needed stores of food and equipment for our Russian allies.

The contrast between this matter-of-fact account of their appalling hardship and the warmth and safety of our guest room at Belleaire was stark, to say the least, and we were pleased to see our three guests stretching themselves out comfortably against the cushions of the sofa and armchairs. Perhaps telling us about all this might have helped to distance it from their tired minds, and a quiet evening among friends was far more effective than the most elaborate of parties on board ship.

December 23rd 1944   *SOASC Greenock*

At a party with Leslie and John on board one of our cruisers we were told an amusing story. A joking signal had been sent from a nearby frigate to a gleaming, imposing American cruiser which had recently arrived in the fleet anchorage. The signal had read: "Can you spare us some of your ice cream, chum?" to which had come the following terse reply: "Sorry, brother, we're feeding the British already."

Fortunately, in the interests of Anglo-American relations, no comment from the frigate was forthcoming. David hadn't a chance against this Goliath, and there were times when silence was golden.

Christmas Day 1944   *SOASC Greenock*

Awful to think of the kind of Christmas the Allied forces must be spending over in Europe. Here we were, safe and well in Scotland, able to celebrate Christmas Day with the usual morning church service followed by drinks with Admiral Warren and the rest of the SOASC staff, and a Christmas lunch, almost as if we had been at peace. We missed our families, of course, but that was the only real disappointment. Nothing to compare with the carnage surrounding the troops fighting their way through the debris of ravaged towns and villages and the desolation of wasted countryside, uncertain if they would live to see another Christmas. It could not be safe to think of peace at such a time. Too much that was unthinkable lay in between, and the only necessity would be to keep moving forward step by step, and ignore the horror and devastation. Whoever spoke or wrote of the glory of war could never have truly experienced it!

January 1st 1945   *SOASC Greenock*
Notification of my immediate promotion to second officer arrived, and Leslie commented: "About time too. You should have been given your second stripe at least last year."

Oddly enough it had never occurred to me. I'd been so interested working in Combined Operations that the possibility of promotion and perhaps transfer to another job wouldn't have been an attractive proposition. There might not have been any firm guarantee of remaining in SOASC, and I'd very much wanted to see things through till Europe had been liberated, whenever that might have been.

"I expect they forgot all about me," I said.

"The poor girl's got no ambition," John remarked sadly.

"Well, it's not as though I was a regular in the Navy with aspirations for a top rank," I told him.

Leslie smiled. "Well, if promotion had meant your moving somewhere else I can only say I'm thankful it hasn't come through till now. Never mind, your next posting may carry the rank of first officer. You never know. Our job here will probably be coming to an end before very long, then we'll all be shunted off somewhere else." The thought chilled me a little. It had to happen, of course. One couldn't remain in the same outfit for ever, but I'd got so used to working with the same colleagues, and knew the routine from top to bottom that I couldn't imagine any other job could possibly be as crucial and exciting as my present one had been.

February 10th 1945   *SOASC Greenock*

The Superintendent WRNS at FOIC called me into her office and asked me if I'd like to go to Kandy in Ceylon, to work as assistant to a Colonel Powell in Mountbatten's Conference Secretariat. The job would probably carry promotion to first officer and be very interesting. I would be flying out early in April after a fortnight's embarkation leave followed by a week's special training at the War Cabinet Office with Lieutenant General Brian Kimmins. This would mean leaving Greenock in the middle of March.

It was not altogether a surprise since there had been rumours that the SOASC office might be closing some time in the near future, and that would mean that Leslie, John and Wren Hens would also be given new postings. I supposed the landing craft with necessary back-up of stores and equipment would henceforth be operating from further down south.

So – more goodbyes. It was inevitable, and much as I'd miss my colleagues the time had come to move on. The end of the war in Europe seemed to be getting closer, and at least we'd been a salient part of what might eventually be recorded as the greatest invasion in history.

March 13th 1945   *SOASC Greenock*

The last few weeks had been chaotic. There was so much to do, so much, also, to decide. My mother had bought a small country house called Garden Cottage, in the little village of Hook in Hampshire, and I had promised to help her with the move. Her friends up in Cheshire had been wonderfully supportive, and my Aunt Nancy would be staying with her over this period, so at least we could get the main business of the move over before I had to leave. Apart from this there was all my tropical uniform to be bought from Gieves, the service outfitters in London, as well as planning what to take to Ceylon with me.

One thing I was determined to do. My mother had been through such a dreadfully sad time, and I wanted her to have some pleasant memories before I left. My first cousin Terence Rattigan's play *Flare Path* had just reopened in London to rave reviews, and I rang him to ask if he could possibly get us two tickets, as these were so difficult to obtain. Originally written in 1942, it had run for over six hundred performances, followed by great success in America, and it looked as if it was certain to repeat its previous popularity.

"No," he replied firmly, "I've a better idea. I'm on leave for another week. You'll both come and see it with me. I have a box. It'll be much more comfortable for you. And then I'll take you out to dinner after the show."

That sounded wonderful and I thanked him profusely. I hadn't seen Terry for a good many years, but I remembered him with affection, particularly when, at the age of sixteen or so, he used to visit us in our house in Chelsea, and bully my brothers and me, as well as any young cousins or friends who were around, into performing his latest drama. He was author, director and producer all in one, and a stern commander who stood no nonsense. We were too young to argue. I was only eight, and even Tony at nearly eleven obeyed orders, something he didn't often do. Our Green Room (for the performing artists) was under our enormous grand piano, from which we crawled out in response to our cues. David, being only five, was only allowed to look angelic in a static role without any lines to learn. We enjoyed it all immensely, and performed with great panache in front of our long-suffering families. It was easy to see where Terry was going. Ideas seemed to flow into his mind without the slightest difficulty.

The next thing to do was to book my mother and me for three nights into the Basil Street Hotel in Knightsbridge, braving the horrific V2 rockets. Making our base here made shopping much easier. I didn't remember the hotel, but my mother had always told me that when I was three years old I'd attended Madame Vacani's dancing classes which were held in the huge ballroom there. The manager informed me that it was now the main restaurant, and added reassuringly that so far there had been no bomb damage near by.

He was to be proved wrong....

March 14th 1945   *SOASC Greenock*

A very cold, depressing day, the sky permanently overcast after heavy snow falls during the night. I'd always hated final goodbyes, particularly when there seemed little chance of future meetings, at least for some time, if at all. Once packed and ready, my desk emptied and tidy, there was nothing left to do except exchange addresses with friends and colleagues.

I went over to Hazelwood just before lunch to say goodbye to Admiral Warren and the rest of the staff. They all wished me luck, saying they were sorry to see me go. Wren Hens looked quite upset when I thanked her for being such a marvellous help and so nice to work with. Then Leslie and John took me out to lunch at a nearby restaurant, and we got almost maudlin over our wine. We'd been working together every day since April 1943 beginning at Largs, almost two years, and it was rather like saying goodbye to a second family. We swore to meet up again somehow, and in the meantime to take great care of ourselves.

They dropped me back at Belleaire in Leslie's car. It was snowing heavily again, and as I stood outside the front door on the top step, waving back at them till they disappeared through the main gateway, my heart plummeted downwards.

Oh dear! I'd never been very good at farewells ....

March 16th 1945   *London*

Terry met us in the foyer and escorted us to his special box, which had a wonderfully wide view of the stage. He had always been a great favourite of my parents, and his mother Vera was quite my favourite aunt. That night he had really done the honours, with champagne to start with before the curtain rose, and other refreshments brought to our box during the two intervals. The play was a winner from every angle. Set in a great country house commandeered by the RAF, with all the action taking place in the room set aside as the mess, it was about a young pilot who is thought lost over in Europe, eventually escaping and getting back to England. This sort of thing must have happened many times. Terry was always able to put his plays into a topical setting, and the timing and subject for this one touched a chord in many hearts.

Terry sat beside us, half hidden by the curtain of the box, and although I supposed many of the audience must have recognized him in the foyer, he did his best to be unobtrusive, and the restaurant he took us to afterwards was not one of the well known ones patronised by theatrical circles, so we were able to talk in peace.

We knew he was a gunner in the RAF and flew in Catalinas, the amphibious flying boats, and he told us how he had written *Flare Path* during that time, always taking the rough draft of his play with him. Having only one copy it never left his side, and the only way it could be lost, he added, would be if he also disappeared during a flight. It must have been very worrying for him, but at least he'd been successful and we'd just seen the finished product.

A fascinating evening, and my mother looked happier than I'd seen her for a long time.

March 17th 1945   *Basil Street Hotel, Knightsbridge,*
London

I had just finished shopping and was returning to the hotel when I came up the stairs to the entrance of Knightsbridge Tube station. Outside on the pavement there was an extraordinary atmosphere. People were just standing with their mouths open, staring up at the sky, some clutching at each other, obviously terrified.

I stared at them, puzzled, then a man nearby muttered: "Those bloody rockets! Never give you any warning. You never can tell where they're going to land. Must have come down only a few streets away."

I had heard nothing, but soon there was the sound of police sirens, and people began running as fire engines and ambulances roared by along the main street. I dived down the side alley leading to the hotel doorway, and quickly went upstairs to our room, hoping my mother wasn't too worried about me. So the manager hadn't been right after all about there being no bomb damage near by. By the sound of things just then it was serious.

Damn Hitler and all his works!

March 27th 1945   *Garden Cottage, Hook, Hants*
A hectic ten days. There was no time to think of anything but the impending move. It was a sad, nostalgic time for my mother, but she bore up remarkably well, and my Aunt Nancy was as usual a tower of strength. Friends and neighbours rallied round with offers of meals and help in clearing the accumulated belongings of my family. A special friend of my father's hired a large and comfortable car, and almost before we could take breath we found ourselves ensconced in our new home. It was hardly a cottage. It had three bedrooms and plenty of space elsewhere, with a well stocked garden. My mother had wanted to be by the sea, but this was not possible at the moment. I tried not to show my concern for her, but fortunately one of her closest

friends planned to go and stay with her until she was settled, so at least she would not be alone. My mother had a gallant spirit and would not give way easily under adversity.

March 29th 1945   *Crosby Hall, Chelsea, London*
During my week's training at the War Cabinet Office I was billeted in the WRNS officers' quarters in Crosby Hall, a picturesque old house once having been the home of Sir Thomas More, but now temporarily commandeered by the Navy. Lieutenant General Kimmins was a charming, friendly man and an excellent teacher. I knew nothing whatsoever about south-east Asia, but by the end of that week I felt fairly confident that I would remember at least three quarters of the mound of information he'd been drilling into me. I was not allowed to take notes since much of this was confidential, and I learnt instead the advantage of collating my thoughts just before going to sleep at night, and surprisingly finding them clear and fresh in my mind next morning.

April 6th 1945   *RAF Lyneham, Wiltshire*
Another goodbye was looming, not to a person this time, but to a country. Mine. But this was just unfinished business. Even after the war in Europe ended, hopefully fairly soon, there would still be the war against the Japanese in the Pacific.

I had been given a free day the day before leaving, used for final packing and the usual odds and ends of preparation for travel. The weather had been atrocious, though we were not as snowed under as up at Greenock. It was just steel grey skies and swirling sleet that stung my face, and just then the thought of warmth and blue skies was distinctly attractive.

At eight o'clock a car picked me up at Crosby Hall. The Wren driver was cheerful and efficient, and told me she'd often done this journey, so I leant back and relaxed. It was a pleasant change to have someone else at the helm, so to speak, instead of having always to be the driving force myself.

I must have fallen asleep, for it seemed no time at all before we approached the main entrance to RAF Lyneham, and were going through the usual identification parade before being allowed to continue towards the officers' mess.

It had stopped raining, and a pale sun was trying to break through the depressing clouds. My luggage was brought into the main hallway, and as I turned to thank the Wren driver a squadron leader approached me, asking if I was the officer due for Ceylon. After that my luggage was whisked away, and half an hour later I was led out of the building towards the York aircraft waiting on the runway.

There were only a few passengers besides myself. The pilot, Squadron Leader Eric Hilton, told me he'd be picking up others from Cairo, so this would be a comfortable trip. First stop Malta.

As the plane lifted off I took a last look at the receding ground, and wondered if Ceylon might be the final period of my war service. One never knew, of course .... .

V

DIMINUENDO

April 6th 1945   *Valletta, Malta*
How wonderful to see a clear blue sky again, to feel
surrounded by soft, warm air! I'd never been to the
Mediterranean, and the sight of the small island with its
brilliant cream buildings rising out of the sparkling sea was
breathtaking.

The flight had been calm and uneventful, the landing
feather light, and as Eric showed me to my quarters he said:
"You'll have plenty of time for a shower, then perhaps
you'd like a drink before dinner and I'll show you around
a bit afterwards. By the way, I think you're in the same
block Churchill had."

It was a large, comfortable room with a large,
comfortable bed, and a balcony with a magnificent view,
and as I looked round I wondered if I might even be
sleeping in the great man's bed! What a thought!

My main luggage, a large, green, naval type suitcase was not unloaded from the plane, since we would be taking off again very early next morning. I'd been warned about this, so had packed my hand luggage accordingly, thinking I wouldn't need my tropical uniform until we reached Cairo. As yet it wasn't uncomfortably hot, and anyway I could always remove my thick uniform jacket if necessary.

Dinner was excellent, and afterwards Eric took me outside to show me some of the sights which Malta had to offer. Despite the bomb damage it had endured not all its beauty and grace had been obliterated. We passed wonderful old temples and churches, through narrow winding alleys, and down broad stairways. Everywhere could be seen the many varying foreign influences which had gone to the present formation of that fascinating and colourful island. The people were charming and welcoming. Eric took me into a small taverna for a glass of wine, and we talked to many of the customers. They'd had a very bad time earlier on during the war, and told us horrific stories.

We were due for a fairly early start next morning, and at about ten thirty I finally fell into bed and slept dreamlessly until my alarm shrilled in my ear seven hours later.

April 7th 1945   *en route for Cairo*
We took off at seven o'clock into a cloudless blue sky, and for the first part of the trip flew mainly over the sparkling waters of the Mediterranean. Some time later, as we began to approach Egypt and the gold of the vast desert below us, Eric sent a message to ask me if I'd like to sit in the cockpit with him to get a clearer view. As I looked down through the window, I thought how easily anyone could get lost in those endless wide open spaces with so little protection from the heat of a blazing sun. We were flying low enough to see the occasional camel train and what I supposed to be oases with a few scanty trees. Then I caught my breath as

the Pyramids finally came into view through the heat mist, those three miraculous creations, two erected side by side with the third smaller one set slightly off line. I could see a small crowd of people already moving about near by, and wished with all my heart I could have been among them.

The outskirts of Cairo lay immediately ahead, and as we approached the airport there was a sudden ominous clonk somewhere beneath the plane, and Eric's grasp on the controls tightened as he gasped out: "Christ!" half under his breath, before ordering me peremptorily back to my seat.

I obeyed quickly, strapped myself in, and waited apprehensively. It said a great deal for his competence as a pilot that we finally made an uneven, bumpy but safe landing, and he told me afterwards that one of the landing wheels had somehow been damaged.

"I don't think we've a hope of going on for some time," he added. "We may have to find you another plane."

In the meantime, after a lot of fruitless searching, I discovered to my dismay that my suitcase had been mistakenly offloaded at Malta and would be sent on after me by the next available plane. This, though reassuring, meant that I'd have to continue wearing my winter uniform in the heat of Egypt, and this had already hit me as I disembarked from the plane. There was a smell of dust and sand everywhere, and the hot dry air encircled me, almost clinging to my face.

I was eventually settled into the WRNS officers' quarters, where I made another discovery, this time totally unexpected. I literally bumped into a great friend, Elizabeth McIntyre, from my old school, The Downs in Seaford, Sussex, whom I hadn't seen for several years, and we spent hours trying to catch up on news of our families and friends.

April 9th 1945   *Cairo*

Elizabeth had taken me over completely for the last two days while I waited for news of the resumption of my journey. I wasn't in any hurry, so she insisted I accompany her to swim at the Gazira Club, even lending me one of her attractive swimsuits. The heat was stifling, and it was an enormous relief to get out of my winter uniform and laze about in the cool water. When she was on duty various friends of hers, both male and female, looked after me, even helping me to make enquiries about my lost suitcase. But there was still no sign of its arrival, so I resigned myself to wearing warm clothes for at least the next part of my trip.

This turned out to be in a DC3 aircraft, the famous Dakota, with an Australian Air Force crew and passengers, about twenty of us altogether, though I was the only female on board. At first they looked a little askance at me. Not only a girl, but an officer in the British Navy! I could see the wary expressions on their faces, but when they heard the saga of my lost luggage and the damaged York aircraft they became very sympathetic, assuring me it would be cooler after we'd taken off.

The plane, unfortunately, had one great disadvantage. It would normally have been used for the evacuation of wounded, and had not been adapted for ordinary passengers. We had to sit sideways on to the cockpit, with great hooks sticking out from the fuselage into our backs. These hooks were for attaching the hammocks in which the wounded would lie, so as to be protected from the effects of any sudden air turbulence. This was bad enough, but I discovered that my feet were resting on a large, square trapdoor, and I didn't like to show my cowardly instincts by asking what lay beneath it. I had a nasty vision of it opening only on to thousands of feet of air. One of the Australian airmen noticed me surreptitiously testing it, and winked at me, offering to change places with me.

"You couldn't fall far through that," he added

reassuringly. "Only a few feet into the hold."

Relieved, I smiled and thanked him but refused his kind offer.

The usual facilities were not particularly private, being situated at one side towards the cramped rear of the interior, but I supposed one could get used to anything if necessary. It certainly wasn't going to be such a comfortable flight as in the York.

When we were finally cleared for take-off the pilot told us we'd be first landing at the RAF base at Lydda in Palestine, and then at Habbaniyah, near Baghdad in Iraq.

April 10th 1945   *en route for RAF Shaibah near*
                                            Basra, Iraq

It was rather like being on a bus with the short hops between landings. We always seemed to be beating the clock, being offered breakfast of eggs and bacon each time we stopped to refuel. It began to be really uncomfortable still wearing my thick uniform, and without my jacket the hook at my back was only too evident.

The RAF bases at Lydda and Habbaniyah consisted mainly of landing strip, control tower, mess and kitchen, maintenance workshop and rather basic accommodation. It must have been exhausting to be stationed at these arid ports of call, having to work on aircraft in the blazing sun with the sickening smell of fuel permeating everywhere. Most of the men were deeply sunburnt, and all wore wide brimmed sun hats. But they were a cheerful lot, and wished us good luck each time we took off again.

I was half asleep when one of the crew came up to me and asked if I'd like to go forward to the cockpit.

"Pete wondered if you'd like to see the view from there," he said. "It's quite something. I don't expect you'll have seen anything like it before."

I thanked him, and followed him to the cockpit where the pilot turned his head and smiled at me. He had an alert, craggy sort of face, and an unexpectedly deep voice. I was beginning to get used to the Australian accent. There was something friendly and casual about it.

"I thought a Sheila like you might like to have a go at flying this old bus," he said, and I looked back at him, rather puzzled. His suggestion must be a joke, but what on earth was a Sheila?

"My name's Roxane," I told him, and was surprised when he laughed.

"A Sheila's what we call a girl," he explained. "Like we'd call an English bloke a Pommy. But yours is a nice name," he added, as if afraid he might have been misunderstood. "Come and sit down."

I did so, and promptly had my breath taken away at the incredible view outside the window. We were passing over huge, rugged, sunbaked mountains rearing up from rolling desert, their jagged outlines casting broken lengths of shadows leading downwards to get lost in the sand. Overhead I was rather surprised to see occasional bunches of cloud.

"I expect you'd like to find out what it feels like to pilot a plane," Pete said suddenly. "I wasn't joking."

He seemed to take my agreement for granted, for he pointed to a small round knob in front of me.

"See that? That's what you'll have to twist if you want to avoid that cloud that's coming at us. Look. Like this." And he took hold of the knob and turned it very gently to the left, and the plane swerved equally gently in that direction.

I was appalled. The man's mad! I thought. He's asking me to fly this plane when I haven't the faintest clue about planes! I wouldn't have minded so much having a go at steering a landing craft, but *this* – even with the pilot sitting so near me there'd be no knowing what could happen if I turned that knob too far or too fast. And those mountains below us looked very dangerous and uninviting. "Try it," said the smiling tempter at my side, and I suddenly found myself holding the knob in a surprisingly steady hand as I gazed out at another curling cloud just ahead.

"Steady now. A little turn to your left." The voice spoke quietly in my ear. "Feel how we move, then stop when we've bypassed that cloud."

It was still coming our way, and I wasn't too keen on getting lost in its billowing folds, so that knob would have to do its stuff.

It gave me an extraordinary feeling of power, almost of recklessness, as I twisted it rather gingerly to my left, and felt the plane respond as it slid easily out of the way of the cloud and into clear blue sky.

"There you are!" said Pete triumphantly. "Couldn't be easier." Then he smiled and added: "You did all right."

I relaxed, and smiled back at him in relief as he took over the controls once more.

He turned his head to glance over to the right. "Look over there," he told me. "That's Shaibah coming up just beyond those mountains. Time for another breakfast."

God forbid! I thought. If anyone offers me eggs and bacon again I'll probably end up being thoroughly airsick.

But they did, and I wasn't, as I had the sense to swallow only two cups of coffee and a slice of toast.

RAF Shaibah was a carbon copy of Lydda and Habbaniyah. We stayed overnight as there was a slight necessary adjustment to be made to the plane, as well as the refuelling for the longer flight across the Persian Gulf to our next stop at Sharjah, one of the Trucial States in Arabia.

April 11th 1945   *en route for Sharjah*
We flew serenely over the Persian Gulf, but by now I was really suffering from the heat. My shirt was sticking to my back which was now distinctly sore from the constant pressure of the hammock hooks, and even though I'd removed my thick stockings while aboard the plane it

didn't make much difference, since solid winter lace-up shoes were never right for hot countries.

Below us, away to our right, off the coasts of Bahrain and Qatar, I could make out an assortment of ships, smaller fishing vessels and the quaintly shaped outlines of what Pete told me were *dhows*, one of the main forms of water transport in this area. These were more numerous as we approached the port of Dubai, then a short while later I saw another familiar lonely airstrip as we came in to land on the hardened sand surface of Sharjah's runway.

It was pleasant to get out and stretch my legs after sitting in such discomfort for so long, and at least the meal we were offered was lunch, though hot tinned steak and kidney pie was hardly the menu for this climate.

As we got back into the plane the navigator, a lean, cheerful young man named Don smiled at me and said: "Next stop India. You'll like Karachi. Maybe you'll find your luggage there."

"Not a moment too soon," I said with a sigh. "I'm absolutely melting."

April 13th 1945   *Karachi, India*
Karachi was a very different story to the RAF bases we'd visited. The airport was a teeming mass of people, many nationalities, both service and civilian, wandering aimlessly about collecting their belongings, porters everywhere handling all sorts and sizes of luggage. The noise was deafening, and the heat and bustle all around me utterly confusing. Where did one begin to hunt for a green suitcase, even though it was clearly marked in white paint with my name and rank?

My Australian friends couldn't have been kinder or more supportive. They accompanied me to the lost luggage office, and one of them, with a totally unpronounceable foreign name introduced himself, then added in an unmistakable Australian accent: "Everyone calls me Joe,

Miss, so you do the same. Now, have you any money?"

I hadn't anything but English pounds, and Joe fished in his pocket and brought out a handful of rupees. "For porters, if you find your luggage," he added.

He wouldn't accept my offer of English pounds, but shook my hand before striding off to join the other members of the crew.

"See you soon," he said as he disappeared into the seething crowd.

Pete had told me that he'd contact me at the WRNS officers' quarters to let me know when we would be taking off again. There were two British Army officers to be flown over to Bombay, but they hadn't turned up yet.

In spite of the pandemonium there was a strange atmosphere in the airport that puzzled me. No one looked cheerful. There were few smiles. Everywhere there was a general air of depression, shoulders and heads drooping. I passed a group of American marines talking quietly together and asked them if they knew why everyone seemed to be looking so sad.

One of the marines spoke in a low voice: "It's President Roosevelt, Ma'am. We've just heard. He's died. Yesterday afternoon – I can't believe it."

And he turned back to his companions as if he couldn't trust himself to say any more.

That was a bitter blow. For someone as valuable to us all as Roosevelt had been, so good a friend in need, to be removed from the scene just when things were beginning at last to go better for us was deeply disheartening. How unfair not be allowed to share in our probable victory! It would be particularly sad for Churchill.

I turned away, feeling as depressed as everyone else, when I saw a sight that drove all other thoughts from my mind. A tall Indian porter was approaching and had almost walked past me when I noticed that he was carrying on his shoulder a familiar green naval suitcase with lettering in brilliant white paint on its lid. With my name and rank! This sort of thing just didn't happen, I thought, paralysed for a moment in utter astonishment. Then I ran forward and stopped him. It wasn't easy to persuade him that the case was mine, but the gift of a few rupees convinced him finally, and he consented to carry it for me to where a battered looking taxi stood at the main entrance. The driver fortunately understood English when I asked him to take me to the WRNS officers' quarters, and in a short while deposited me at the door.

 Oh, the joy and relief to have a bath and a change at last into cool white uniform, white canvas shoes and shady white hat! I was now ready for anything!

April 17th 1945   *Karachi, India*

We had had to wait a few days for the other passengers to arrive. They had been held up somewhere, and I wasn't sorry. It was pleasant to have time to sort out my luggage, to sleep long hours in cool surroundings, and be woken up each morning at six o'clock by a soft-footed, polite Indian servant with tea and what looked like a small orange-coloured melon which he called a paw-paw. It was cold and refreshing, an ideal way to begin the day.

My room was quite large with a narrow balcony outside the window, from which enchanting little green lizards came in and crawled up and down the walls, glancing at me now and then out of their bright round eyes. I much preferred them to the flying black widow beetles which made a sinister clattering noise as they flew against walls or furniture. Luckily they didn't seem interested in me, and anyway I had a mosquito net over my bed, so I just turned over and went back to sleep until it was time for breakfast.

The WRNS officers were very pleasant, and commiserated with me over having to fly so far in an unadapted DC3 aircraft. Most of them had come out by sea, having to endure a long, cramped voyage of nearly three weeks, with the crew very much on the alert for a sight of approaching mines. None of them had been to Ceylon, but one or two seemed envious of my job on Mountbatten's staff.

The two Army officers finally materialised, and we took off again in the comparative cool of a very early morning. They were a pleasant pair, though there were raised eyebrows at the seating arrangements. I was tempted to tell them we'd endured the hooks in our backs all the way from Cairo, but was too tired to pursue the subject. They wouldn't have to bear the discomfort for long anyway.

Arriving at Bombay about three and a half hours later, at nine o'clock, we said goodbye to our two extra passengers, seized a quick second breakfast while the plane was being refuelled, and finally took off again just after ten o'clock. I was told we would be due to land at Colombo round about four o'clock.

Some of the thrill of our journey had definitely begun to wear off. It seemed interminable, and after a couple of hours or so I began to have great difficulty in keeping my eyes open. I decided not to fight it. Someone would be sure to wake me up in time to pull myself together .....

I'd no idea how long I'd been asleep, but suddenly became aware of a hand touching my shoulder, and then a voice invited me to go forward into the cockpit as Pete wanted to give me my first full glimpse of Ceylon. Shaking the sleep from my eyes I obeyed, and Pete looked round at me with a smile as I sat down beside him.

"Not long now," he said. "Last lap." Nodding over to our right he added: "Look over there – in the distance. You'll be seeing it soon. It's a sight I never get tired of. Wait till we're a bit nearer."

A little later he said, with a touch of excitement in his voice: "And there's Ceylon, coming up now. Nice sight, isn't it?"

That was to put it mildly. The sea over which we were

passing was a colour I had never seen or could ever have imagined. It was an incredible sight, a sparkling stretch of the most brilliant, translucent turquoise, tipped with delicate silvery points on its shimmering surface. It bore no resemblance at all to the cool sea–green of our northern seas. As we drew nearer to the island I could see lush green foliage spreading everywhere and the golden beaches round its coast, and thought it was one of the most beautiful views I had seen anywhere since leaving England. What a dramatic change from the Firth of Clyde!

Shortly afterwards we landed in Colombo, at Ratmalana airport, and there I said goodbye to Pete and the others, who all wished me good luck in my new job.

"You'll like Kandy," Pete said. "I've been there several times. It's right up in the hills. A bit cooler than Colombo."

"It's a bonza trip up there," Don added. "Take you a fair time though. It's pretty slow going, but it's worth it for the view."

I glanced rather doubtfully at the elderly engine standing at the platform. It looked as if it had been designed and built a good many years ago, and the wooden seats turned out to be hard and uncomfortable. But at least there was no great hook sticking into my back. The carriages were crowded, and I took the only available free seat beside an RAF wing commander, who obligingly moved over a bit to make room, and helped me put my hand luggage on the rack above our heads.

I smiled and thanked him as we introduced ourselves. His name was Mervyn Horder and he was just returning from leave. He had a long, strongly-boned face which at first looked rather lugubrious, but this expression was lightened by an obvious sense of humour, and when he talked he showed a lively interest in a variety of subjects, one of these being music. In no time at all we were on the easiest of terms, and he told me he was also a keen pianist, and frequently organised concerts for the entertainment of the personnel of SEAC. "There's not much in that line going on in Kandy," he added, "except, of course, the Kandy Esala Perahera in August. That's the big festival up there, with hordes of elephants and the famous Kandyan dancers. It's very impressive. Mountbatten – by the way, he's known as Supremo here – Supreme Allied Commander – has issued strict orders that if we find any of our hosts choosing to sleep on the roadside we are to respect their wishes and give them a wide berth – or else. And no referring to anyone here by an impolite name. He's very tough about this, and I can't say I blame him. They're nice friendly people, the Ceylonese."

As we chugged slowly uphill Mervyn pointed out to me the various places we were passing, and as we got higher he named all the exotic trees like the spreading 'flame of the forest' which, even though it was growing darker now, made the vast hillside look as if it were being swept by fire. "There's one thing about Kandy," he told me. "And that's the incredible colouring. Just wait till you see the botanical gardens at Peradeniya where we all work. You'll hardly believe the colours – and of course the scent, especially first thing in the morning when the air's a bit fresher."

On arrival we shared an ancient taxi to our billets. Mine was the Queen's Hotel just near the Kandy lake, but his, he explained with a faint exculpatory smile, was the King's Hotel which was reserved for the senior staff of SEAC, and visiting VIPs. "But there's nothing much to choose between either of them," he added, "except for the company. I'm told there also seem to be cockroaches in both hotels."

Oh no! Not again! I thought. Had I come all this way to be threatened by the swarming orange horrors?

"By the way," Mervyn said as he climbed back into the taxi, "I'm hoping ENSA may send out a company of artistes to this area fairly soon, people like Leslie Henson or Beatrice Lillie. That's the Entertainments National Service

Association. We could all do with a little comic relief. Failing that, perhaps you'll sing for us sometime. Have you any music with you?"

I said I'd be delighted, as I always travelled with some of my repertoire, and felt lost without it.

"I'll be in touch," he said, "when you've had time to settle in."

The Queen's Hotel was old fashioned and rather shabby, and reminded me a little of the Ugadale Arms. But it also had an atmosphere of its own, as if it had housed untold numbers of visitors of all styles and periods, adapting itself to their various needs and interests without giving way to confusion, and the general impression was a welcoming one.

I sat through a rather unappetising meal in the large dining room with several other WRNS officers, none of whom I'd met before, and though they were pleasant and friendly I made the excuse afterwards that I was very tired after travelling all day, and needed an early night. Before I left them, however, they told me the unwelcome news that Colonel Powell had been taken ill and had been repatriated to England the previous day. They obviously all liked him and were very sympathetic, but had no idea who his replacement might be, but I'd probably hear later on.

Upstairs in my room, mercifully a single one, I paused in my unpacking and went over to the window to look across at the lake. It was quite dark by now, and an enchanting sight with the newly risen moon slanting its beams across the water. It looked enormous as we were so near the equator, and even the stars seemed bigger and much nearer. After a while I began to get attuned to the different noises of the night beneath the constant chatter and activity of people who, in this heat, retired very late to bed. There was a persistent bickering of crickets and full-throated frogs, and the interminable tinkling of bells and other instruments playing their delicate atonal themes made me wonder if I'd ever get any rest. But in fact the sounds were so soothing that I fell asleep as soon as I climbed beneath my mosquito net, and only woke when the sun shone brilliantly into my room.

April 18th 1945   *HQ South-East Asia Command*
                             (SEAC) Kandy, Ceylon (HMS Hathi)
Next morning I went with several others to the Royal Botanical Gardens at Peradeniya, and was momentarily stunned. Mervyn Horder had not exaggerated. The scent from the enormously tall, crimson Canna lilies just inside the entrance was almost overpowering. Everywhere I looked there seemed to be more and more exotic blooms in beautifully designed flowerbeds, as well as shady tree-lined avenues.

It was like a thriving city in an exquisite garden. The rows of office hutments were joined by alleyways with wooden flooring, slightly raised from ground level in order to keep feet reasonably dry during the monsoons. It seemed totally incongruous that anything of such vital warlike importance as the huge task facing Mountbatten should be planned and conducted in such surroundings. One usually associated beautiful gardens with healing silence, but here, from every office section, there was the intrusive sound of intense activity, voices, typewriters and teleprinters in full flow.

Besides the British personnel there were also the American, Dutch, French and Chinese Military Missions, and voices in different languages could be heard arguing, remonstrating, ordering. Even the uniforms were different and colourful, ranging from khaki drill to starched white cotton, either plain or splashed with gold or red or black insignia, almost as colourful as their surroundings.

I was escorted to First Officer Prendergast's adminis-tration office, and found her to be pleasant and friendly. She explained about Colonel Powell, but said someone would

be sent out shortly to replace him as Head of the
Conference Secretariat.

"We were glad to hear you could come," she said.
"You'll be getting promotion to first officer so that you can
attend the conferences. No one under that rank goes to
them. Your job as Colonel Powell's personal assistant would
have been to write up the minutes of these meetings, and
keep them filed and catalogued. I'm sure the first officer,
who was his PA before she returned home on
compassionate family grounds, would have left everything
in good order. Your week's training with Lieutenant
General Kimmins must have been very interesting, and put
you well into the picture."

I assured her that it had, and that I'd been fascinated by
it all.

She smiled and rose to her feet. "Good. Well, I'm sure
you'll fit in very well. I'll take you along now to meet the
others in your section, and they can show you around."

Tony Paget, the Army major temporarily in command
of the Conference Secretariat was pleasant and helpful, and
took me to meet the members of the planning section next
door, as well as several of the foreign military missions. By
the end of the morning my head was spinning. So many
names and titles to remember. There was also a large
American office just close by, where at least eight GIs were
busily at work filing mounds of documents and papers with
great haste and efficiency.

As I was leaving the young man in charge called after
me: "You know where to come if we can be of any help!"
and I thanked him cordially, trying not to catch my
companion's eye. I was sure that remark had not been
intentionally patronizing, just a confirmation of American
superiority over most other nationalities.

My own office consisted of myself and a pretty young
Wren typist named Edna, a very different type to Wren
Hens, rather more sure of herself. Immediately next door,

through an open doorway, was Major Paget who would be joined there by the Colonel when he arrived.

It was a very different kind of job to my previous one at SOASC.

Here there was no sense of urgency. It was all planning ahead at the highest level, all the basic precepts, I supposed, for conducting a war. Not being permitted to attend the daily conferences, there was no possibility of my being allowed to write the minutes, and all I had to do now seemed to be to read through the finished scripts, cross reference the main points of interest, then file them, something any intelligent Wren Hens could have done. I was aware of a faint feeling of disappointment. Perhaps it would be more interesting when the new Colonel arrived, when I was finally promoted to first officer and able to perform my duties properly as his personal assistant.

In the meantime Tony Paget wrote up the minutes with the temporary assistance of an officer from the planning section, and I was left with little to do. I killed time by perusing the minutes of past meetings so as to bring myself up to date when I would be able to fulfil the real job I'd been sent out here to do.

April 30th 1945　　　　　　　　　*in hospital, Colombo, Ceylon*
I had not been feeling well ever since my arrival. I'd found the heat overpowering. What began as a general malaise with sore throat and occasional loss of voice, finally blew up into a full case of serious heat exhaustion, and I was hastily transferred to hospital in Colombo. No one there was surprised when they found out that I'd been travelling so long in the heat, wearing my winter uniform, having come straight from a snowbound Scotland, and I was duly filled up to the eyebrows with cool drinks and vile medicines, and given strict instructions not to attempt to utter a sound till my swollen throat, blocked ears and sinuses had returned to normal. I didn't care. It was so comforting to

lie in a cool atmosphere, not to have to do anything or even think about my new job.

May 2nd 1945   *in hospital*
Through the maze of exhaustion and discomfort I heard the tremendous news that Hitler was dead, and many of his gruesome henchmen with him. It was the end of the infamous Third Reich, and most of the prominent evil-doers were fleeing in all directions from the avenging Allies.

I couldn't quite take it all in. The all-powerful tyrant, leader of the so-called 'master race', who'd subdued and terrorised a whole continent, ruthlessly crushing all resistance, was a threat no longer, though his damaging legacy to the world would take years to obliterate.

A beaming nurse approached with more medicine. "Well, that's a relief anyway," she said. "High time that monster was seen off!"

I drank the vile mixture and smiled back at her, then turned over with a sigh before sinking back to sleep once more.

May 8th 1945   *in hospital*
On this particular morning I was feeling slightly better, and suddenly became aware of an atmosphere of intense excitement in the ward. One of the older nurses came over and sat beside me.

"It's VE Day!" she told me. "Victory in Europe! Can you believe it? The war in Europe's finished – after all this time!"

She was almost incoherent and I thought I saw tears in her eyes.

"Everyone's lost so many friends," she went on, then emotion stifled her voice and she left me rather hurriedly.

My own thoughts flew back to David and my throat tightened. What a dreadful waste it had been! But at least in the end it hadn't been for nothing....

"Now, what's the matter with you?" It was the matron speaking. "You're not to get upset. It won't help you get any better, and you've been quite ill. Yes, I know, and we all feel the same. I'm sorry you'll miss all the celebrations tonight, but if you go on as you're going you should be back on your feet fairly soon."

By the time evening came I was exhausted, and sick of hearing about the celebrations throughout Colombo. Various nurses came and went, all excited and dolled up for the great occasion, and one of them, no doubt thinking it would cheer me up, came and sat on my bed while painting her nails a lurid scarlet and telling me all about her latest American boyfriend.

I didn't mind missing the parties. All that mattered was that half the war was won, and that perhaps it wouldn't be too long before the Japanese were conquered. But I couldn't think far beyond the cessation of hostilities in Europe. How to reconstruct a whole continent and build some kind of permanent peace? It was not going to be easy to sort out the millions of displaced persons, including so many children, left wandering in the wake of battling armies. Nor the desperate inmates of the concentration camps or starving inhabitants of devastated countries. So many people. So much suffering. And how would we begin to trace and punish the many war criminals fleeing to hide from justice? Apart from the noise of rejoicing outside my window I didn't sleep much that night. Why did I have to try and see beyond that first explosion of joy and relief? That was for tomorrow.

May 18th 1945   *SEAC, Kandy, Ceylon*
Well at last, and able to enjoy the warm weather. Still no sign of the new head of the Conference Secretariat, but instead I began to be drawn into the flourishing social life. I took part in a concert which Mervyn Horder arranged,

and dined and danced at a restaurant called Jacob's Folly. We
had been warned either to wear uniform as protection
against mosquito bites and possible malaria, or if in evening
dress to cover neck and arms. Everyone had had the usual
injections before arrival in Ceylon, but once there we all
had to take regular doses of something called Mepacrin.
The worst illness one could suffer from was either amoebic
or bacillic dysentery, for which one had to endure many
painful injections in the stomach. Amoebic dysentery could
lie dormant for years, then attack the liver with dire results
much later on in life.

We also went on pleasant picnics to swim at various
beauty spots. It was such a picturesque country, there was
plenty of choice. Apart from this, one of the Army colonels
named Arthur Bamford possessed an old-fashioned gramophone and a collection of classical records, and there were
musical evenings when groups of us would drive up to
various rest houses where we could order dinner, and listen
to music both before and after the meal. Very civilised!

I even played tennis at six o'clock in the morning on the
court by the King's Pavilion, where Mountbatten lived, and
once even dined at an official dinner with him and Lady
Edwina, to which many exalted officers from his staff were
invited, as well as lesser ranks like myself. This was a rather
daunting occasion, (shades of Villa Brillantmont and our
social training there!), though the ADCs were well used to
keeping the conversation going, and Supremo himself was
a charming and interesting host. Both he and his wife were
adept at making guests feel at home. This was second nature
to them, born of long practice and a genuine interest in
people of all types.

May 21st 1945   _SEAC, Kandy, Ceylon_
It had been a blazing hot day, and Colonel Bamford
suggested we might go up to the rest house at Bandarawela
a little later than usual when it might be cooler. There were

about eight of us that evening, looking forward to hearing Rimsky Korsakov's wonderfully evocative piece 'Sheherazade'. While our ordered curry was being prepared we sat round outside the rest house, sipping our cool drinks and letting minds and bodies relax. As the music played all round us I noticed several pairs of eyes shining out of the surrounding darkness under the trees, and realised we had an audience. 'Sheherazade' had a real eastern feeling to it, the solo violin weaving a delicate melody that caught at the heart. None of us moved for several minutes after the piece ended. We were all so immersed in the Thousand and One Nights and the exquisite section for the Young Prince and Princess.

But the magnificent curry was ready, and almost reluctantly we went indoors to have our mouths and throats pleasantly burnt by hot aromatic spices until we couldn't eat another spoonful.

As we wandered outside again it was almost eleven o'clock, but no one wanted to go back to Kandy straightaway, and Colonel Bamford said: "I don't know about anyone else but I'd like to enjoy the Korsakov entrée again," and promptly wound the ancient gramophone up once more, placing the needle back in its groove.

No one disagreed, and we all settled down again.

This time the surrounding darkness was pierced by literally hundreds of pairs of shining eyes, and the faint moonlight began to reveal the dusky bodies sitting cross-legged and immobile on every patch of empty space around and beneath the trees. Not a sound came from this vast audience. It was completely absorbed, as if spellbound, and at the end a long drawn out sigh floated past us in the air and gradually faded into complete silence.

I don't think I could ever bear to listen to that piece again in a concert hall.

May 23rd 1945   *SEAC, Kandy, Ceylon*
Supremo had arranged for a showing of an unabridged film
of the liberation of the concentration camp of Belsen, and
had ordered as many as possible of the staff of SEAC to see
it. I thought the sight would haunt us for the rest of our
lives. The unbelievable piles of corpses, many thousands of
them, and their living counterparts all too closely
resembling them, the only difference being the dark pits of
their eyes staring blankly out of skull-like faces.

What was it that made people able to carry out such
appalling cruelty? Would they never be haunted, I
wondered, by the tall shadows of the black gas chambers
looming above the lines of wretched huts, or the memory
of what had been done in the torture chambers?

I felt so sick and upset it was all I could do to remain in
my seat, and at the end of the film I stumbled outside to
take in deep breaths of pure, scent-laden air. One thing was
certain. There would be no forgetting this.

May 25th 1945   *SEAC, Kandy, Ceylon*
We had now moved from the Queen's Hotel into a
spacious, newly built WRNS officers' quarters known as
A22, with separate sleeping accommodation called *bashas*,
and a large wardroom with a fantastic view of the river
down below, where we could see the elephants being
brought in to be washed and scrubbed by their *mahouts*. It
was amusing to see these huge animals rolling about in the
water, sometimes disappearing entirely beneath it except
for their trunks waving in the air. The babies especially
were enchanting to watch, as they took in water by their
trunks, then spurted it out again 'at each other. There was
one particular baby I would have loved to have had as a pet.
It was a mischievous creature, and behaved like a young
child playing jokes on its elders. It seemed to enjoy being
swept aside by exasperated adults, and I had an overpowering urge to have a ride on it. We were now a little

further away from the Peradeniya gardens, and I thought what fun it would be to turn up at the entrance astride a baby elephant.

I consulted our houseboy, Stephen, a young lad of about sixteen, and he said he'd arrange to have the elephant brought round next morning somewhere near A22.

"You pay *mahout* few rupees. He lead elephant in case it run away with you," he said reassuringly, and I had a sudden delirious vision of Supremo and General 'Boy' Browning, who often turned up together in a jeep, arriving at the entrance at the same time, to be greeted by a baby elephant ambling towards them with a member of the Conference Secretariat staff on its back.

General Browning was the husband of the famous author Daphne du Maurier, and having met him at the dinner party with Supremo and Lady Edwina, I was convinced of his and Supremo's lively sense of humour. All the same, I wasn't going to risk it, and dismounted some way before reaching the entrance, to make a suitably staid appearance as befitted a second officer in the Senior Service.

May 27th 1945   *SEAC, Kandy, Ceylon*
I repeated this early morning ride, and discovered that the little elephant seemed to know me, for he sidled up to me and touched my shoulder with his trunk, waiting expectantly for another bun and apple I might give him.

But when I mentioned a third ride, the *mahout* told me some of the elephants were being moved to another part of the river and my little friend would be going with them. Perhaps it was just as well. My luck couldn't hold out for ever. Someone would be sure to recognise me.

May 29th 1945   *SEAC, Kandy, Ceylon*
The news came through that a new head of the Conference Secretariat, a Lieutenant Colonel Thomas Coward would be arriving in a week or so. I was glad, as it

meant my job would change for the better. But Tony Paget didn't look very happy, and took me aside.

"What's the matter?" I asked. "Have you met him before?"

"Yes," he answered. "I think I have. And I'm very much afraid it's the same man." He lowered his voice. "It won't be much fun if it is. He's an awful old woman. I don't think anyone likes him."

"Oh heavens!" I exclaimed. "As bad as that?"

"I'm afraid so. Thinks no one can do anything except himself. As pernickety as the devil. It's a great pity Colonel Powell had to leave. He was an excellent chap."

Well, at least I'd been warned. I made one or two discreet enquiries from colleagues in A22 and in other offices in Peradeniya gardens, but no one seemed to have heard of the man. Tony's opinion of him was not exactly encouraging.

Meanwhile another concert was being planned, turning my thoughts away from baby elephants or tiresome lieutenant colonels. I spent some time rehearsing with Mervyn Horder, and it was after one of these sessions that I invited him to come and have a drink at A22. There was a small bar at one end of our large wardroom, and on that particular evening there were quite a few guests as well as the usual occupants.

I had gone over to the bar to collect our drinks from Stephen, our young houseboy who had recently been promoted as barman on occasional evenings. He was very proud of his new position, and wore his crisp white cotton jacket with an air. Not only was he very competent in mixing the drinks, but he had very definite views about protocol and general behaviour from those he served. Just as he was about to pour out the correct measures for my order, a loud female voice from the far end of the room called out "Here, boy! We want some drinks over here!" and a pair of hands clapped sharply.

I looked round, surprised. This was hardly the usual behaviour in our wardroom – *any* wardroom, for that matter. Then I recognised the officer. She was relatively new to Kandy, having come over from Trincomalee on the east coast, and had rather a reputation for drinking more than she could adequately manage.

As I turned back to Stephen I said: "You'd better serve her first. I can wait."

But he didn't attempt to do so, only frowned darkly and muttered: "Her wait. Her not proper Missie."

A subtle judgement from one so young. I wondered if he summed all of us up to the same criteria.

June 5th 1945   *SEAC, Kandy, Ceylon*

The moment our new boss stepped into his office I saw what Tony Paget had meant. Lieutenant Colonel Thomas Coward was not very tall, with sloping shoulders and a sharp-featured face which looked as if a sneer wasn't far away. One of the officers from the planning section had brought him over and performed the introductions. He shook our hands with a cool smile before putting down what looked like a briefcase, all snakeskin and gilt-edged lock and corners, on to his desk. Then he thanked the major who had brought him over, his tone one of dismissal, and sat down to investigate what was in the desk drawers.

I effaced myself and pretended to be searching for something in one of my filing cabinets, while Edna resumed her typing with renewed energy, neither of us glancing at each other. I'd never felt antipathy to anyone I'd ever worked with since I joined the WRNS, but even without the warning I'd received about him I didn't like him. I couldn't quite put my finger on it, but doubtless things might get clearer as time went on. It might be unwise to prejudge him, I thought, but how I longed for Leslie or John at that moment! No nice Colonel Powell either, just this rather unfriendly character.

June 20th 1945   *SEAC, Kandy, Ceylon*
More than two weeks had passed, and still nothing had
been said about my promotion to first officer. Instead,
Lieutenant Colonel Coward seemed to have appointed
himself the only proper person to write up the minutes,
and this he proceeded to do, to Tony Paget's exasperation.
Every sentence was scrutinised, examined step by step and
rewritten, Tony's enthusiastic endorsement being
demanded after every paragraph.

All this took so long that Edna never had the
opportunity to begin typing the finished article until about
four o'clock in the afternoon. It was fortunate that she was
such an accurate and rapid typist, otherwise she would have
had to have stayed on late each day.

I smiled when I read these masterpieces. They might
have been composed for a university thesis or important
public lecture, the wording was so pedantic, the whole
much too long, all of it reflecting the self-styled literary
genius of their creator. I pitied any of the foreign bigwigs
trying to make head or tail of their content.

The fact remained, however, that by this appropriation
of what should have been my job, he was effectively
completely nullifying it.

I mentioned this to Tony who suggested I have a quiet
word with First Officer Prendergast. After mulling this
over, I decided I'd give Lieutenant Colonel Coward a little
more time to get round to the question of my promotion.
Being so new, he might need more opportunity to assess
my job.

June 30th 1945   *SEAC, Kandy, Ceylon*
Things continued as usual. Nothing at all interesting or
memorable happened except for the visit to Supremo by
Major General Aung San, the Commander-in-Chief of the
Burma National Army, a very colourful personality. I
happened to be looking through the open doorway of my

office when I saw this unusual figure come striding past with his entourage.

He was exactly my idea of a brigand, with a somewhat shabby head-dress, loose cotton jacket and three-quarter length trousers above some kind of sandals tied with thin cords round his ankles and calves. He and his entire entourage were well equipped with knives and other weapons thrust into their belts or ankle straps, and looked rather like the cast of some kind of musical stage show.

Nothing at all, however, was done concerning my promotion, and by now, bored and exasperated, I decided to take Tony's advice and see if First Officer Prendergast could hasten things along.

In the event she rang me first, asking me to go and see her straight away.

She was frowning over what looked like some kind of report, and told me to sit down a moment. I could see she was puzzled.

"I've just received this in reply to my query about your promotion," she said. "But Lieutenant Colonel Coward says, among other things, that he doesn't consider you suitable for promotion to first officer. I simply don't understand this. Have you had a row or something with him?"

I shook my head. "A row? No, certainly not. He hardly ever speaks to me. Why? What has he written?"

She avoided answering my question by asking another. "I mean, you haven't possibly done anything he might not approve of?"

This was becoming rather strange. "Like what?" I asked.

Again she avoided answering me. "I don't understand this," she said. "You were very highly recommended for this job with Colonel Powell, and Lieutenant General Kimmins also seemed to think you were ideal for it."

I sat still, racking my brain for a possible misdemeanour on my part. "I can't think of anything wrong I've done," I replied finally. "At the moment, of course, there *isn't* any job for me, beyond being a glorified filing clerk, since Colonel Coward writes all the minutes himself. It's Major Paget who seems to be acting as his personal assistant, not me. And I can't do that until I'm promoted to first officer, so where does that leave me? As things are, he really doesn't need someone like me on his staff at all. Another Wren rating could manage all the filing quite easily."

I asked to see the report, but she shook her head. "I think you should go and see Superintendent Goodenough first. She wants you to go down and talk to her about this. I can't do anything more at present, but this sort of thing isn't very pleasant. I suggest you don't talk about this to anyone till you've seen her." Then she added almost sadly: "Something like this would never have happened if Colonel Powell had still been here. He was such a charming man."

By now, considerably puzzled and indignant, I returned to my office. Both Colonel Coward and Tony were out at the usual morning meeting and Edna was typing. I was careful not to let her see how I felt, but my mind was going round in circles. What did First Officer Prendergast mean by 'among other things' in that report? And why ask if I'd done anything Colonel Coward might disapprove of? I began to feel this must apply to someone else, not to me.

July 1st 1945   *SEAC, Kandy, Ceylon*
Still no wiser I duly presented myself in Superintendent Goodenough's office in Colombo. I'd never met her before, but everyone liked her. She smiled warmly at me as I entered.

"Well now, Roxane," she began, "come and sit down. First Officer Prendergast tells me she has received a rather odd confidential report about you from Lieutenant Colonel Coward. It was marked copy to me, which I received this morning, and I'd like to hear your side of it."

"But I can't tell you, Ma'am, as she wouldn't let me see

it," I answered. "I'm completely in the dark. But I could see she was not only puzzled but rather upset by it."

"I'm not surprised," she said dryly, and suddenly her pleasant' expression changed and became stern. "I don't like something like this happening to any of my officers, and in your case it's all the more inexcusable."

I sat there, frowning, all at sea.

"I had naturally seen all your reports from WRNS headquarters before I recommended you for your present job as personal assistant to Colonel Powell, as it should have been had he stayed on," she continued. "All your reports were excellent, highly satisfactory, also the one from Lieutenant General Kimmins after your week's training with him. So there was never any doubt in my mind that you were the right person for it." She paused and leant forward towards me.

"Now, there must be *some* reason why such a report should have been written about you, so can you enlighten me as to any possible misunderstanding that might have caused this?"

I shook my head. "I spent most of last night trying to work it out," I said slowly. "There are only two vaguely possible, but unlikely reasons I can think of. The first is that he recently came to one of the concerts which Wing Commander Horder organises, at which I sang two groups of classical French songs, and the next day thanked me in a very patronising tone of voice for 'a pleasant interlude'. I told him I intended to make singing my future career. Perhaps he doesn't like singers, or in my case thinks a singer is incapable of taking a wartime job seriously.

"The next reason is more likely. He may have heard that I don't think there's a real job for me now that he has taken over the minutes himself, and that, if a WRNS officer is supposed to be on the strength and there's no job for her, the powers that be might decide to transfer her elsewhere and he may not get his promotion to full colonel. But this is rather a long shot."

"No," the Superintendent said very positively. "Neither of these far-fetched reasons can possibly excuse what he's written about you." She picked up the report and perused it again with distaste." I'm not going to show this to you, but—"

I interrupted her. "But if I don't know what he's said about me how can I possibly refute his accusations?" I demanded.

"I'm not going to upset you by letting you see this," she said evenly, "because it's nothing but personal vindictiveness (for whatever reason), and this is what I do with such filth!"

And to my astonishment she tore the report across several times and flung the bits into her wastepaper bin.

"This will go no further," she said. "I'm transferring you immediately to another job as personal assistant to Admiral Douglas-Pennant, who is very different to Colonel Coward." She rose to her feet as she said this and I followed suit. "It would be another matter altogether, of course, if this was in peacetime," she added. "You could have him up in court for defamation of character."

That last remark nagged at me all the way in the train back to Kandy, and by the time I arrived I was seething with anger. If Superintendent Goodenough imagined I was going to let it rest there she was very much mistaken. Arriving at the Peradeniya gardens I strode purposefully along the wooden walkway and literally stormed into my office. It was about five-thirty, but the office never closed till after six.

Edna glanced up from her typing, mildly surprised, but Tony, next door with Colonel Coward, raised an enquiring eyebrow.

"Excuse me, Tony," I said briskly, not caring what I interrupted, and he saw the danger signals and beat a hasty retreat into my office.

I never saw the massive cohorts of my fierce Scots and

Irish ancestors ranged in a threatening phalanx at my back, but I felt they were there, urging on their maligned descendant to face the enemy, and stand and fight.

My enemy's eyes slid towards mine and as quickly slid away as he saw my face.

"I understand you've written a very damaging report about me," I began, white hot with anger, but my voice ice cold. "I've come to ask you exactly what you said, and for an explanation."

He didn't answer, and never spoke a word during the whole of that interview, while I told him exactly what Superintendent Goodenough had said and done. I then tore his character to shreds, calling him utterly despicable and a disgrace to the British Army, and watched with satisfaction as he still cowered, white-faced, in his chair. I even noticed his hand shaking as it held his pen.

At that moment I didn't care if I was dismissed from the service. But knowing that inter-service disagreements were never popular it was likely that the whole business would be allowed to fade away, but at least I had said my piece, and, I hoped, stripped the enemy of any self-esteem. I added that he had certainly been well named, and with one last searing look at him, now slumped down behind his desk, I swept out through the open door into my own office.

Edna stared at me open-mouthed, frankly astonished, but I caught a glimpse of an appreciative grin from Tony.

"I hope reception was loud and clear!" I snapped as I left, and went back to A22 where Stephen obligingly poured me the stiffest gin and tonic I'd ever had.

July 4th 1945   *SEAC, Kandy, Ceylon*
With all the Navy's tact and discretion, I was given a day off to cool down, while arrangements were made for my transfer as personal assistant to Admiral Douglas-Pennant. To say I was disillusioned and frustrated was to put it

mildly. The whole thing was so unfair, not being allowed to see the report and refute the accusations it obviously contained. I was left imagining all sorts of untrue aspersions and derogatory criticisms, all the more infuriating since for the life of me I couldn't put my finger on anything wrong I could legitimately be supposed to have done.

The Admiral turned out to be a pleasant and attractive man who obviously thought I'd been thoroughly ill-treated, and couldn't have been nicer to work with. I had the impression that anyone who knew anything about my situation was doing their best to placate me. Tony came to have a drink with me at A22 and told me that Colonel Coward, in the face of some obvious but unspoken disapproval, was attempting to pretend none of that unpleasantness had ever happened. No mention of it was being made anywhere. Let sleeping dogs lie. . . .

July 15th 1945   *SEAC, Kandy, Ceylon*
On my way to Admiral Douglas-Pennant's office I had to pass my own original one, and was surprised one morning to see my replacement, a second officer named Margaret, sitting in the doorway, knitting.

She glanced up and said hello, and as there was no one in either her office or the inner one, I stopped and asked her how she was getting on.

"Well, there's not much to do," she told me. "I'd be bored to death, only I'm just sitting it out here till we go to Singapore. My husband's stationed there, you see, so I don't mind."

"There wasn't any real job here, was there?" I remarked casually,

"No, not for a second officer," she agreed. "Can't think why one is needed here at all since the dear Colonel seems to want to do everything himself. He certainly doesn't trust anyone else. There's this silly rule about having to be a first officer before we can go to the conferences, but that doesn't stop me reading the minutes or young Edna typing them. I suppose there's a great deal of talking off the record at the actual meetings, but otherwise I can't see any reason for that ruling at all."

I wondered if she knew why I'd been replaced, but didn't think so, as everything she'd said openly corroborated my own opinion of the way the Secretariat was being run.

"How do you get on with the dear Colonel?" I asked her.

She made an expressive face. "Between you and me and the post," she said, quietly but very positively, "the man's a conceited fool, and I wouldn't trust him further than I could throw him. Don't quite know why, but there it is."

I could have told her. Comforting to have my opinion so thoroughly backed up.

July 29th 1945   *SEAC, Kandy, Ceylon*

My new job was pleasant though unexciting, but at least I was back with the Navy. Admiral Douglas-Pennant certainly didn't overwork me, and allowed me free rein in reorganising several areas of his office, always thanking me for anything extra I had done for him. He showed great interest in my previous job with Combined Ops, and also, rather surprisingly, in my plans for my future career in music. No two men could have been more different than my past and present commanding officers.

Whenever I passed the Conference Secretariat I felt quite sorry for Tony and Edna and my replacement, occasionally wondering who the next victim might be. Margaret obviously was just biding her time, placidly performing the tasks of a filing-clerk, and whenever she happened to see me pass by the doorway would give me an unobtrusive, conspiratorial look. Since I never heard sounds of raised voices or recriminations coming from the inner office I assumed the other members of staff were quietly enduring the dear Colonel's unwelcome presence.

The time was approaching now for the Kandy Esala Perahera, the great festival held there every few years. We were all particularly lucky to be there to see it. The week before was filled with hectic last minute preparations, and Kandy seethed with workmen and visitors, and rehearsals for the Kandyan dancers, which took place frequently along the road. They had a curious movement in their dancing, their legs spread widely outwards, the toes upturned, not pointed, the body bending sideways for each step. It was fascinating to watch, the rhythmic music almost hypnotic.

There were still two days to go, but already cheerful crowds were gathering, and the noise and bustle of their voices and movement provided an atmosphere of growing excitement.

August 1st 1945   *SEAC, Kandy, Ceylon*

I had joined a party of friends to watch the procession from the upper balcony of a Chinese restaurant along the route. It was not due to pass until later in the evening, about ten o'clock, so we ate a wonderful Chinese meal beforehand. The place was packed, as were all the other buildings by the roadside. People of all nationalities were settling themselves at the best vantage points, hundreds of excited, noisy children eager to see what was probably their first festival of this kind.

We hadn't been sitting on the balcony for long when the distant commotion further down the route suddenly increased, with shouts and yells mingling with clapping and laughter as the procession rounded a corner in the road. We could see the coloured lights held high by the *mahouts* on the backs of the enormous elephants leading the cortege, seemingly proudly unconscious of the clamour around them. All the important dignitaries swaying comfortably on the elephants' backs were dressed in a wonderful assortment of styles and colours, festooned with heavy gold jewellery round necks and wrists and ankles. As they drew nearer we heard the jingle of the rows of coloured beads twined all over the bodies of the elephants, and the tinkle of tiny bells round their necks. They were quite the largest elephants I'd ever seen, huge yet graceful animals placing their enormous feet carefully on the road. There must have been almost a hundred of them, from the largest to the smallest of babies, tagging along behind their mothers, their short trunks curled round their mothers' tails in a never-ending line. I scanned them carefully to see if my little friend was among them, but decided he might have grown up a bit since my last ride, and was now probably unrecognisable.

Accompanying them on the sides of the road were groups of musicians, some blowing an assortment of pipes and other strange instruments, others beating a complicated rhythm on small drums; and within the sound of their playing came the Kandyan dancers, small, neat men dressed in colourful costumes and head-dresses, using their feet and hands as if painting a collage of movement. They were incredibly graceful, the tiny bells on their ankles sounding in accord with the music. I had no camera with me, but several of my companions had brought one with them, so we had some record of the event.

It took several hours for the entire procession to pass, and it was very late when we made our way back to A22. As Supremo had predicted the road was lined with weary bodies, whole families settling down to sleep through the rest of the night, and we were very careful not to disturb them as we passed.

August 6th 1945   *SEAC, Kandy, Ceylon*
Unfortunately, the pleasant festival atmosphere of that wonderfully colourful occasion was not to last. News was coming through of an appalling new weapon called an atom bomb having been dropped by the Americans on the

Japanese city of Hiroshima earlier that morning, reducing it totally to rubble and obliterating most of its population. It had spread a lethal pall of radiation which had burnt everything and everyone in its path in a swathe of unimaginable agony.

It was unthinkable, yet it had happened, and everyone seemed stunned and sickened. It was argued that there would have been a far greater number of casualties if the war had had to continue with further fighting in the Pacific, or even with a possible invasion of the Japanese mainland. The Japanese had to be made to surrender, and this dreadful thing was the best way to achieve that.

After the first awful shock had worn off a little everyone began talking of the implications beyond this attack. Where would it lead?

August 9th 1945   *SEAC, Kandy, Ceylon*
No sign of a Japanese surrender, then the news of a second atom bomb being dropped, this time on the important Japanese naval base at Nagasaki. The lurid pictures in the newspapers after the Hiroshima attack had been sickening enough, and now there would be more. The sight of those poor, dazed men, women and children, either wandering aimlessly about or collapsed by the roadside was more than I could bear. My mind was numbed, and I went and sat down at my desk wondering if anything would ever be the same again. I knew none of the blame for this war was on us, but how dreadful that so-called civilised nations should have been brought to inflict such horror upon innocent people. Even if the Japanese surrendered immediately the discovery of this appallingly potent weapon would undoubtedly be a permanent threat to our very existence. Supposing we were unable to control it, or it got into the wrong hands? There'd be no rising from the ashes like the phoenix after five hundred years as there wouldn't be five hundred years ahead of us if this was the way national

arguments were to be settled in future. If the terrifying example of Hiroshima and Nagasaki were anything to go by, how long would it be before our beautiful planet became a bowl of radioactive dust?

August 16th 1945   *SEAC, Kandy, Ceylon*
The Japanese having at last surrendered, the whole situation in SEAC changed radically. Supremo was faced with the enormous task of clearing up the chaos left by the enemy over an unbelievably vast area. The first and most urgent need was to rescue the thousands of prisoners of war and civilians held in Japanese prisons and prison camps. To do this meant being able to locate them, and this was not easy. There were so many of these infamous camps scattered often throughout unknown territory and often very difficult to access. Food and medical supplies had first to be rushed in, since prisoners were close to death through starvation, disease and brutal treatment. And only then could they be safely brought out.

Lady Mountbatten, who was Superintendent-in-Chief of the St John's Ambulance Brigade and Chairman of its Joint War organisation with the Red Cross, had had much experience in the recovery of Allied prisoners of war in Germany, and now embarked on the momentous task of coping with the same situation throughout SEAC. Armed only with a letter signed by Supremo, stating her identity and authority, and accompanied only by a small, intrepid personal staff, she set out on a journey through searing heat and enervating damp that could well have killed a woman of less stamina and determination. Her flair for organisation cut through the endless apathy and confusion she met everywhere, and soon the results of her work began to be seen. We had the greatest admiration for her and her untiring group of assistants.

September 10th 1945   *SEAC, Kandy, Ceylon*
Ceylon has two monsoons every year, obviously
accounting for the wonderful lush greenery flourishing all
over the island. We were approaching the final month of the
south-west monsoon which occurs from June to October.
The other tropical north-east monsoon occurs from
December to March, which leaves only a few months of
really dry season each year. The wet weather must have
greatly added to the general difficulty of dealing with the
prisoner-of-war problem, and we wondered how Lady
Mountbatten and her team were faring. She had already
reported that conditions in the camps she had visited were
terrible, particularly in Sumatra, where prisoners were
literally at their last gasp. It was awful to imagine what they
must have gone through for so long.

September 28th 1945   *SEAC, Kandy, Ceylon*
An unexpected treat! A recital given by a young Polish
concert pianist on his way back to England from a
successful tour through south-east Asia. He charmed us all
with his virtuosity. The old but fairly respectable upright
piano had been rigorously tuned, but still gave away its age
on occasion. Although obviously accustomed to playing on
a concert grand, the pianist nevertheless drew remarkable
depths of sound from this modest instrument, particularly
in his rendering of several pieces by Chopin. He even
managed to ignore the faint spattering of rain on the
corrugated iron roof of the building, adapting his touch to
compete successfully with the irritating interference from
above his head.

   Although the south-west monsoon would shortly be
coming to its end, it was still likely to let loose a really
fearsome downpour, and in the middle of his final piece,
Chopin's powerful and exciting 'Fantaisie Impromptu', the
noise on the roof suddenly became thunderous, almost
completely muffling the sound of the piano. It was then

that I understood the second reason for the pianist's agonized frown. Something appeared to be sticking to the fingers of his right hand, and in sudden exasperation he stopped playing and gave it a quick shake. Several pale thin objects floated down to the floor, but he bravely continued with the piece.

It took only a few seconds for the audience to realise what was happening. The glue attaching the ivory veneers to the actual piano notes had melted in the heat and damp, and every finger was now covered with them. He stopped playing altogether, turned a look of searing reproach upon the audience, and vigorously shook both hands till a shower of ivory veneers landed perilously close to those in the front row, who were giving way to barely stifled mirth.

Mervyn and I sat aghast, in deep embarrassment, but fortunately the pianist suddenly saw the funny side of it, and threw back his head, laughing unrestrainedly. The suppressed amusement of the audience gave way to a great gust of merriment, and the evening broke up with the performer being led away by a throng of admirers, to celebrate the occasion with the strength of alcoholic drink a Pole was undoubtedly entitled to.

October 3rd 1945   *SEAC, Kandy, Ceylon*
Another birthday. My twenty-sixth. How many more, I wondered, would have to pass before I could resume my chosen career? London and the Royal Academy of Music seemed very far off. Might it all be too late? There was so much that stood in the way. Yet there must have been very many others, like me, who had had to put their personal ambitions on hold as long as the worldwide upheaval continued. Music was a peaceful occupation, and had nothing to do with the perpetual and ever present horrors of starvation, killing and bereavement, except perhaps as a lament or requiem.

So shut up and stop moaning, I told myself severely, and

get on with it! There'd be a lot to do before any of us would be freed from our immediate obligations.

It was encouraging to be able to talk to Mervyn about this. He intended to return at once after the war to his previous occupation as director of the publishing firm of Duckworth, and as composer and writer, and nothing was going to stop him.

"If you want to do something enough, you'll do it, whatever it takes," he told me firmly. "You're not going to lose your voice at the age of twenty-six. You might, of course, lose your ambition to pursue a career in singing, but I don't somehow see that happening."

It was pleasant and unusual to be understood so thoroughly, but then Mervyn Horder was a pleasant and unusual person. Although I knew him only as a wing commander in the RAF, I had since discovered that his father, a distinguished surgeon, had been knighted for his services, and that Mervyn had inherited the title.

When I first remarked on this, he had smiled rather quizzically at me. "Did you really expect me to mention my title the first time I opened my mouth? Don't look so surprised. I've never done anything to deserve it, except having a father who had been physician to monarchs from Edward VII onwards, believe it or not. I couldn't be less qualified. All I've done that's been of any real use has been as an intelligence officer in the RAF. I can't even claim to have been one of the Few in the Battle of Britain."

He changed the subject then, and told me that he knew someone high up in ENSA, and through this fortunate connection had managed to get Leslie Henson and Beatrice Lillie to include Kandy in their arranged tour of south-east Asia. So it was that an unexpected birthday treat happened to be a hilarious concert by these two celebrated comic performers, whose absurdities reduced their audience to the sort of helpless laughter that did all of us a lot of good.

October 30th 1945   *SEAC, Kandy, Ceylon*
SEAC Headquarters were preparing to move to Singapore and there was much activity going on in the Peradeniya gardens. Margaret, my replacement in the Conference Secretariat was delighted at the news, and couldn't wait to meet up with her husband in Singapore. I asked her if she could bear to go on working for Lieutenant Colonel Coward, but she just smiled and shrugged her shoulders.

"It may not be for very long," she answered. "And I don't mind anything if only I can be with Ian again."

"Well, I think I've been in the Service long enough," I said. "By the time I get demobbed it'll be almost six years. Everything is winding down now, so there probably won't be so much to do from now on."

"What will you do when this is all over?" she asked curiously. "Get married, I suppose."

"First I'm going to be a professional singer," I told her. "Opera and concerts – that sort of thing. I'll be going to the Royal Academy of Music next September."

"Rather like going back to school," she commented, and smiled almost pityingly.

Strange how few people seemed to understand a dedication to music.

November 19th 1945   *SEAC, Kandy, Ceylon*
Those of us who were not leaving for Singapore would be going down to Colombo to wait for a ship to take us back home. Audrey Clarke, who had been working in Colombo, would be returning with us, and she'd heard that there was likely to be an enormous number of service personnel also on board, so the ship might be very crowded. I almost wished for the Dakota which had flown me out to Ceylon. Even with the hammock hooks in my back it might have been preferable, certainly quicker than the estimated four weeks voyage we'd probably be facing.

November 22nd 1945   *en route for Colombo*
As the ancient train grumbled its cautious way downhill, carefully negotiating the twists and turns of the sharp gradient, I couldn't quite believe my posting in Kandy was over, and that I was on the first stage of my journey home. There might be some time to wait in Colombo for the ship, but no one could tell us for how long.

All I was aware of was an odd feeling of emptiness. Kandy had been an enchanting place, the people colourful and friendly, and if it had not been for the highly unpleasant incident with the loathsome Colonel Coward I would have been able to have remembered it with undiluted pleasure. The beautiful shining lake, the exotic Temple of the Tooth, the magnificent ruins of the ancient city of Anuradhapura, the Peradeniya Botanical Gardens, the rest house at Bandarawela – so many other fascinating places. All these were unforgettable, especially my first view of Ceylon itself, the bright green island nestling in the unbelievable turquoise of the surrounding sea.

There seemed to have been so little time to savour all the memories of the places I'd worked in, and the huge number of colleagues and friends whom I had got to know and like so well.

Several of my friends from Kandy would not be travelling home with me, but we all vowed to keep in touch once the war was over. My address book was full. Mervyn would be working again in London, but so many of my other friends lived miles away, up in Scotland, down in Cornwall, in fact over most of Britain. Our telephone bills were going to be enormous.

November 23rd 1945   *Colombo, Ceylon*
Once down in Colombo we were informed that we'd be leaving in a few weeks in a ship named the *Nea Hellas*, but that in the meantime there were plenty of useful things we could do, such as helping with the cypher watches or in an

administrative capacity, assisting with keeping records up to date. With so much general movement going on this was imperative. But the most necessary help we could give was something very different, but urgent.

Superintendent Goodenough called us together and explained that she had had a request from Lady Mount-batten, asking if some of the WRNS personnel could meet and talk to those of the released prisoners of war who were not yet well enough to be repatriated, but who were responding to medical treatment, such as injections of vitamins and other remedies to improve their general condition. These men would be spending time on the beach at Mount Lavinia, either bathing or just resting on the sand, and were naturally completely out of touch with what had been happening during the last two or three years, having been in a prison camp or working as forced labour on the infamous Siam railway.

"You may find them quite withdrawn," the Superintendent warned us. "And it's possible that some of them may be rather confused. After all, they've just been struggling to keep alive. I agree with Lady Mountbatten that it would do them a great deal of good to talk to you all. Remember, they haven't seen a white woman for all that time."

About six of us were eventually driven to Mount Lavinia, and led towards a group of men who were gathered on the beach in the charge of two medical orderlies, and the shock of that first meeting was something none of us would ever forget.

It was like seeing a cluster of pale ghosts, they were sitting so still, so emaciated and frail there seemed to be no body in them. Their legs and arms were almost like matchsticks, and as they stood up at our approach several of them were unsteady on their feet and had to grasp a colleague's arm. The really awful thing about it was that so many of them were young, and should have been at the

peak of their strength and vigour. Instead they had been
reduced to the final edge of being alive, and I remembered
Lady Mountbatten's report of so many being at their last
gasp. What on earth could we say to them?

After that initial shock we pulled ourselves together and
went forward with a smile to shake their hands and
introduce ourselves. It was pathetic to see what an effort
they were making to appear normal and cheerful when
talking to us, but when they were silent their faces seemed
to fall into an expression of sadness and resignation. It was
difficult to bring them up to date all at once. They had
missed so much of their lives. Some of them were confused
and rather embarrassed by their condition, but this began
to wear off as we chatted. We tried not to be over cheerful
or bracing. The slow and gentle approach was the only way
to get through to them, and if one or two of the younger
ones showed signs of emotion we just turned our attention
quietly to someone else. One of their main worries seemed
to be how their families or loved ones might react to their
changed appearance or wary, uncertain manner. But after a
while we all began to relax, and sitting comfortably round
on the warm sand we did our best to tell them all that had
been going on during their absence.

We were sickened by some of their stories, and after a
couple of hours the medical orderly in charge suggested we
might meet up again the next day. It was obvious the men
were growing tired, and so, in fact, were we.

As we were being driven back to our quarters for lunch
someone was heard to mutter in suppressed fury: "Well, if
this is what the Japs did to their prisoners I'm glad those
bloody bombs were dropped! Serve them bloody well
right!"

But as so often seemed to happen it was not the guilty
Japanese commanders of the prison camps who paid for
their atrocities, but the thousands of innocent men, women
and children of Hiroshima and Nagasaki. I hoped fervently

that the men who had so cold-bloodedly carried out the brutal treatment of prisoners, or their leaders who instigated such a cruel policy, would eventually be branded as war criminals and suitably punished, though no punishment they were likely to suffer could possibly have fitted their appalling crimes.

November 30th 1945   *Colombo, Ceylon*
November was part of the dry season, and the weather was wonderful. We made ourselves useful when required for administrative duties, but could easily have imagined we were on holiday, swimming or playing tennis in the early morning before it grew too hot, having tea with friends on the terrace of the Galle Face Hotel, or going out in the evenings to sample the menus of some of the attractive small restaurants in Colombo. But to bring us down to earth there were always the sobering meetings with the constant stream of prisoners of war and internees from the prison camps. Although the improvement in their general condition was encouraging, there were usually new additions to the groups we met, so that we were always reminded of the real situation and the difficulty of trying to fill in the missed years of their lives. They were always so appreciative and grateful, asking so many varied questions we couldn't always answer. We often felt drained after these sessions. The perfection of our surroundings was marred by the painful, physical evidence of the atrocities these men had been subjected to, and though our indignation at their merciless treatment could never have equalled theirs, it was nevertheless acute.

VI

FINALE

News had come at last that our ship was ready to leave, and
we all gathered on the quay to embark. Our home for the
next month or so, the *Nea Hellas*, was a rather battered
looking liner with a Greek name but British captain and
crew, and we joined the hundreds of passengers who strode
eagerly up the gangway onto the deck. We had been
warned that it might be rather overcrowded, and by the
time we began to move away from the dock we had
discovered the worst.

Our cabins were tiny, obviously originally intended for
a single occupant, possibly two at the most, but now
adapted for four passengers by the installation of two
double-decker bunks. These, together with a minute
washbasin in one corner, completely filled the available
space. There was no room to store anything, and it became

256

obvious we should all have to live entirely out of our suitcases, which could just fit under the lower bunks. It was even worse than our narrow little patch of sleeping accommodation at St Merryn.

June and Christine, who would be sharing the cabin, were cheerful and uncomplaining, but the fourth member worried us a little. Maggie had married a naval officer who had just left for Singapore, and since she was in the early stages of pregnancy was being repatriated. She was not at all happy about the long voyage home as she was invariably seasick, she told us, on board ship, and was afraid that this might affect the baby. We insisted she should have one of the lower bunks, and went out of our way to be supportive.

Fortunately it was totally calm as we moved out from the quay to the open sea, and we all made our way to the dining area to sign on for the first or second serving. There had to be two sessions for every meal as the seating was totally inadequate for so many of us, and the service was accordingly slow. I wondered how Maggie would cope with the food on board. I couldn't imagine the menus would be very appetising, but we found she had been enterprising enough to have brought several bags of fresh fruit with her as a substitute for anything she was unable to eat.

That first evening was tiring, and we all went to bed early. There was no opportunity for a bath, and we had to take it in turns to undress and wash before climbing into the uncomfortable bunks. Heaven help us if the sea got really rough, I thought, before dropping into an uneasy sleep. How could anyone asleep on a top bunk manage to remain there if the ship started rolling?

December 19th 1945   *on board the* Nea Hellas
After an early breakfast an announcement over the tannoy informed us that boat drill would take place at ten, and everyone was to go to their allotted places on deck,

wearing their lifebelts correctly done up. For this exercise we should consult the lists on the ship's notice board so that there would be no confusion.

But where *were* our lifebelts? A more thorough search of our cabin revealed two lifebelts thrust far back beneath each of the two lower bunks, and we spent a rather hilarious twenty minutes deciding what went where and whether we had attached everything in its proper place. But by the time we managed to fight our way within reach of the ship's notice board total confusion had taken over. The *Nea Hellas* had not been designed for three times the intended number of passengers, and it was impossible to find space anywhere near the allotted position for our row of cabins. More and more bodies pressed against each other like the proverbial sardines in a tin, and the naval officer in charge of our section grew extremely irritable.

"Whoever dreamed this up was an incurable optimist," June murmured in my ear. "If ever we have to abandon ship how the hell could we all manage to get into so few lifeboats? Are you a good swimmer?"

I laughed. "We'll just have to hope we don't hit a mine," I answered, then turned as Christine uttered an exclamation and nodded across at Maggie, who was paper white and looked as if only the press of people round her was keeping her upright.

"My God! Poor Maggie!" Christine said, trying to move nearer to her. "We must get her out of here. Can't have her passing out in the middle of all this. That poor man will have a fit," she added, glancing across at the harassed officer in charge.

But extricating Maggie from the crowd proved impossible for the moment, and it wasn't until a quarter of an hour later that we managed to form a sort of protective cortege around her and push our way through the milling crush, loudly demanding passage.

The ship's doctor, a reassuring character, called round a

little later to see how she was, and suggested that she stay in bed for the rest of the day and have her meals brought in to her.

This was a relief, but the boat drill brought home to us how vulnerable we would all be in the event of striking a mine, and we decided not to think about it, but perhaps to keep a weather eye open for anything suspicious floating near by. We weren't the only ones to be on the alert. Hundreds of pairs of eyes constantly scanned the surrounding water. The war was over, but now more than ever caution was the only watchword.

Christmas Eve, 1945   *on board the* Nea Hellas
There was something magical about night-time in the Indian Ocean, with a brilliant moon piercing the darkness of the water. I discovered that almost the entire quota of service personnel preferred to sleep on deck rather than far down below where it was not only stiflingly hot, but far less easy to escape from if we ever had the bad luck to strike a mine. Having come so far through nearly six years of war, no one wanted to risk losing his life at such a late date.

Christmas Day, 1945   *on board the* Nea Hellas
For all the difficulties and discomfort of an overcrowded ship, the Captain and crew organised an almost normal Christmas lunch for us. The usual Sunday church service took place beforehand, and although the *Nea Hellas* was a 'dry' ship (no alcohol) we still spent an enjoyable day, ending with an evening of Christmas carols led by the Army padre, and sung by a far more numerous and vociferous congregation than he could ever have heard.

December 27th 1945   ·   *on board the* Nea Hellas
After that first week I had got to know the purser quite well. He was a nice, friendly individual, very ready to chat to everyone. It was very hot that morning, and I had gone

up on deck for some fresh air, and was leaning over the deck rail gazing abstractedly down into the water when he approached and asked me how I was enjoying the voyage.

"Very much," I answered. "I had no idea how big the *Nea Hellas* was."

He smiled. "Oh, she's big enough, almost seventeen thousand tons. She was built in Glasgow, you know, by a British company, and commissioned originally as a passenger liner called the *Tuscania*. Very smart and luxurious. In 1921, that was."

He saw that I was interested and added: "But she's not a Greek ship in spite of her name. Early in 1939 she was sold to a Greek navigation company who renamed her the *Nea Hellas* – the 'New Greece', and went on her first trip to the United States amid tremendous publicity and ballyhoo. That didn't last long, of course, as the war started and in 1941 she was taken over by the Allies as a troopship. They had a pretty rough time of it, what with enemy submarines and being attacked by German aircraft in the Med. But they never lost a soul."

He looked round him almost with affection, and I asked him how long he'd been with the ship.

"Since she was placed under Allied control again," he said. "She's been like a second home to me really. The troops were very fond of her too, and used to call her the 'Nelly Wallace'." I must have looked rather blank, for he went on: "She was that old vaudeville artiste who used to be very popular back in the twenties. You wouldn't have heard of her, you're too young."

After that, I saw the *Nea Hellas* through new eyes, and tried to imagine how she would have looked in her prime, with important business people and fashionable society passengers on board. Very different.

"You might think she's come down in the world," the purser went on. "But to my mind she's performed a far more useful service during these last few years."

December 28th 1945   *on board the* Nea Hellas
The carol concert was not the only musical entertainment
on board. There was a really deplorable piano in the main
mess, and anyone who could supply the sort of music
which could be danced to was dragooned into playing for
hours on end, or till relieved by another suitable pianist.
There were few enough of these, and I was frequently
called upon to fill the gap. The ship's doctor had a rather
pleasant baritone voice and I sometimes accompanied him.

One beautiful calm night everyone was comfortably
settled up on deck, filling every corner, when someone
took my arm and asked me to sing to them.

"But there's no piano up here," I objected.

"Oh, you needn't bother about that," said the voice, and
I realised it was the First Lieutenant, a man named
Henderson. Objection was useless, and I soon found myself
standing high up on the bridge, staring down at a vast
crowd of upturned faces and knew there was no escape. I
longed for the two excellent accompanists I had sung with
at St Merryn, Margaret Blackwell, a first class musician and
pianist, and Pat Adams, a brilliant jazz pianist who could
also sight-read more or less anything I gave her to look at.

But now there was nothing for it, and as I launched into
one or two of the songs which had been most popular in
many other places, my mind flew back to that dangerous
night in the shelter outside Bruce Hut during one of the
worst air raids at St Merryn, and I remembered the aria I
had sung then from Puccini's opera 'Madam Butterfly'. All
right, I thought, glancing at Lieutenant Henderson, you've
asked for it, so you're going to get it! 'One fine day' with
top B flat and all, the only trouble being that, not having
perfect pitch and no piano to pitch from, I set it too high,
so that the final note was a top C sharp. Happily, once
comfortably and safely up there, I found it easy to hold the
note until a prolonged burst of applause reassured me that
Puccini was not turning in his grave.

New Year's Eve, 1945   *on board the* Nea Hellas
Still the weather remained calm, and Maggie was not upset
by any violent movement of the ship. We had got into a
well organised routine in our cabin which, though not
exactly comfortable, worked quite well. I spent a long time
up on deck, gazing down into the sparkling wash of the
passing waves, not thinking of anything in particular but
just letting my thoughts roam idly, registering the colourful
sights and sounds of the busy bank of the Suez Canal which
we were just entering.

There would be great celebrations that evening with the
many Scots on board preparing for Hogmanay. Auld Lang
Syne would have a special meaning, a sort of fin de siècle
ending to the life we'd become accustomed to, before we
embarked on the beginning of another very different one.
It would be a plunge into an unknown, unplanned
existence for many of us when everything would depend
on our own efforts. I could tell that a lot of us were
uncertain of our futures, and was reminded of that
marathon drive from St Merryn up to Cheshire, when
there were no signposts anywhere. But at least there had
been a familiar destination at the other end of our journey.
This time we might land up anywhere, so many of us
without the comforting presence of loved ones. How
would we all cope?

But New Year's Eve was upon us, and by ten o'clock the
celebrations were mounting to a frenzy, a certain amount of
alcohol having been successfully smuggled on board, with
everyone determined to enjoy a last fling.

As usual I had been dragooned into playing on that
appalling piano so that everyone could dance. People kept
coming up to me with requests for tunes they liked, half of
which I didn't know, but even though I was playing by ear,
probably with handfuls of wrong notes, nobody noticed,
nobody seemed to care, everyone was singing along happily
and the noise was terrific.

A merry young Army lieutenant approached me with a glass in his hand. "I say," he said, "you've been working so hard you haven't even had time for a drink! You must be exhausted. Try this one. It's one of Charlie Dent's specials called Moselle Mist. Guaranteed to bring anyone back to life."

I supposed I should have been warned, but I only half heard him above the din. It was very hot in the overcrowded space and I was very thirsty, so I thanked him and took a sip. It was cold and refreshing, though with a rather peculiar taste. He waved at me cheerfully and returned to begin an energetic session with a bright, red-haired Wren.

After a while I felt I needed a short break, so a few minutes later I stopped playing and drank the rest of the Moselle Mist. But just as I was deciding which tune to play next, the walls and ceiling astonishingly began to change shape and lean inwards towards me, while all the waiting dancers were suddenly swaying to and fro in a weird, mad pattern. A loud, frightening roaring sounded in my ears. I felt about to faint, but managed to stand up and make my way unsteadily through the throng towards the companionway down to the cabins. I never reached mine, but instead dived into the nearest ablutions section where I was violently and gloriously sick. I was lucky to have the kind of stomach which firmly rejected any indigestible or excessive intake, and after that horrendous convulsion was just able to find my way to my cabin. I still felt very peculiar, but at least the walls stayed still and the floor had stopped heaving beneath my feet.

Thank God the cabin was empty. After clambering up into my bunk I must have passed out, for when I next woke my watch said twelve thirty, half an hour into the year 1946. Climbing carefully out of my bunk I washed and changed, and finally made my shaky way up towards the rumbustious din that indicated the party was still in progress. I could have strangled Charlie Dent, whoever he was, who'd created that revolting mixture. If ever a drink had been well and truly spiked mine had. To be fair, of course, somebody else might inadvertently have added the final lethal ingredient only to my glass. If many of the other merrymakers had drunk the same concoction as mine there surely would not have been many dancers left standing. Admittedly most were pretty far gone, but nobody seemed to have passed out.

I was greeted with loud cheers and almost dragged to the piano, though I tried in vain to make them understand I'd only come back to wish everyone a happy new year. But in the end, stone cold sober, I played for them until the party broke up riotously at two o'clock. It had all been a disaster as far as I was concerned, but at least I'd seen in *something* of the new year.

January 8th 1946   *on board the* Nea Hellas

The voyage so far had been uneventful, but as we began to reach cooler waters with the resulting weather change the whole atmosphere on board seemed to change with it. People began to join up in small groups, talking earnestly together, mainly about politics, about jobs, but most of all about the kind of world they'd be returning to.

"I'll not be going back to my old job, that's for sure," I heard one burly Army sergeant state very firmly. "That sort of life's not for me any more. And I've had enough of Army life too. No, I'm going to find something else, and it'll bloody well have to be better than anything I've done before!"

There were murmurs of agreement. "We've seen too much of the world to go back," another voice chimed in.

"Things are going to be different now," someone else said.

"Well, I'm going to tell my old boss to take a running jump!" a young Air Force man interposed forcefully and there was laughter. "Never could stand him."

"He's probably died of old age by now," the first speaker said. "Anyway, what you need, my boy, is a proper education. Stay in the RAF, why don't you? You could rise to air vice-marshal one day if you put your mind to it."

More laughter, then Audrey Clarke came up to me at that moment, so I lost the remainder of that overheard conversation. Bright and sparkling as ever, she didn't seem worried about anything, but leant beside me over the rail, staring down into the water.

"Are you really going to the Royal Academy of Music?" she asked.

I answered, yes, of course I was. It was the only thing I'd ever planned to do way back in 1939.

"Nobody seems to know what they'll do next, except dive into matrimony," she said. "But I haven't met the right man yet. You're lucky to know what you want."

"Well, I can always get married later," I said. "But it'll have to be to someone who wants to have a wife who's a professional singer. Maybe that won't be easy. It's frightened off several people already."

I asked her what she would do, but she said she hadn't made up her mind yet. She was silent for a moment, then said suddenly: "It's rather like being on a bus, isn't it? When it stops suddenly, and the conductor calls out 'All change here for a new life!' and you haven't a clue exactly where the bus has stopped."

She sighed, and smiled at me. "But whatever happens we must all keep in touch somehow. It'll be pretty lonely if we don't, after always being with so many people."

That was what had also worried me, the sudden silence and emptiness, the lack of voices and laughter, particularly the laughter. But I remembered what Mervyn had once said to me. If you want anything badly enough, you'll do it, and nothing will stop you.

And I knew my decision was right.

January 15th 1946   *on board the* Nea Hellas
Suddenly we had passed Ailsa Craig on our port side and
were entering familiar waters. The Firth of Clyde looked
wonderful in the cold, bright January sunshine, and as we
approached Troon over to our right I was seized in the grip
of nostalgia. Would I ever forget that afternoon when I had
recklessly steered our small boat underneath the anchor
chain of one of the aircraft carriers in the Fleet anchorage,
to the horror and disapproval of that poor young Scottish
seaman in charge? At the sight of Largs, Gourock and
Greenock memories came flooding back of SOASC, of
Leslie Wintle and John Norton, young Wren Hens and
Lieutenant Jim Ewing, and that memorable summer
morning when Admiral Warren couldn't contain his
excitement and emotion at the announcement of our
invasion of Europe. Of all the bases I had been in I knew
Greenock would probably hold pride of place in my
memory, although St Merryn would run it a close second.

I suddenly felt alone, in an odd way bereft of my
identity. I could hardly believe the sort of person I'd once
been in August 1940, when I had first joined the WRNS,
someone so full of outdated ideas of how one should live,
so closely confined within the taboos of class and the safe
little circle of friends and acquaintances who met our
narrow standards. And then I thought of Ada, the Eliza
Doolittle of Bruce Hut at St Merryn, and felt ashamed at
the memory.

But that had all gone now. Soon I wouldn't even be a
part of the great naval service whose traditions and
regulations had governed my life for so long. I would
become a separate person, going her own separate way,
making her own decisions. I had joined the others on board
the *Nea Hellas* who would be looking for new identities,
new jobs, new standards of living.

I wondered what David would be doing now if he were
alive. So many of his term at Dartmouth had been lost in

the voraciously hungry sea, all their courage, youth and laughter stilled for ever except in painful, never-to-be-forgotten echoes. What might they all have achieved?

Then we had arrived at Glasgow, and there was no time for further introspection. Packed up and ready to disembark, all goodbyes said. No good looking back, at least for the moment. My nostalgic memory of SOASC was merely a single echo out of a whole chorus of echoes which would never leave me entirely.

January 15th 1946 – later   *en route for Garden Cottage,*
                                                 Hook, Hampshire

As the train chugged wearily southward I lay back in my seat and closed my eyes. I was very tired, but my mind was full of confused thoughts and ideas and would not let me rest.

On board the *Nea Hellas* we had all talked endlessly about being back home with our families, but now I began to realise that nothing would be the same as I'd remembered it. I was going to a new home in unfamiliar surroundings, from which two precious members of my family would be absent. Tony, thankfully, had survived, but at the moment my gallant mother was there alone, struggling, like so many thousands of others, to adjust to a painfully different life. I would feel almost a stranger. I had a disturbing conviction that all of us who had come through the last six years had unknowingly undergone a subtle transformation in a sort of mild social revolution. It seemed as if the whole country was like a great ship which had been gradually changing course, so gradually that none of us had fully realised it. And now, even the restored signposts might be found to be pointing in quite different directions, and we would have to make up our own minds which one to follow. Six years was a long time. Six years of obeying orders, following the designated route laid out for us without ever having to question or make difficult decisions for ourselves. No wonder many of us were finding it confusing!

But in one way I was lucky, I suppose, for I knew exactly where my particular signpost was pointing. I had become aware of the pull of almost forgotten echoes of my past, reminding me of long-neglected friends who spoke my language, and whose musical genius had been the underlying mainspring of my life. So many, like Purcell, Bach, Schubert, Puccini and of course, Mozart – all waiting to welcome me.

I leant back against my seat and closed my eyes. Although deeply thankful that peace had come at last I'd never felt less like celebrating, when thinking back to all the dreadful things we'd had to do to win the war. Of course, *then* there had been no choice, but now we could, and *must* put all our energies into the monumental task of ensuring the safety of the future that had been so bitterly fought for, and for which so many sacrifices had had to be made ....

Well, that was for tomorrow, I thought, half asleep. At least music had the power to override national boundaries, and now its echoes could travel freely throughout our tired and troubled world, and perhaps, before too long, bring it nearer to safe harbour and sanity.

EPILOGUE

The return to peacetime in a severely battered and weary London was neither easy nor straightforward. We found ourselves living through many disastrous and often hilarious happenings as we struggled to adjust to such a very different lifestyle. With rejoicing over, naval uniforms and identities shed, and Royal Navy 'big brother' protection withdrawn, many of us were left anxiously searching for direction from our own personal signposts.

Mine, however, was easily found, since it led directly to three satisfying years at the Royal Academy of Music, followed by a further thirty years as a professional opera and concert singer, performing throughout Great Britain and abroad. I eventually got married and had a delightful daughter and son, and now have four equally enchanting grandchildren.

There are so many times and events in my life which will never be forgotten, throughout which the enduring strand of music has woven a special counterpoint; from that magical evening in the Indian Ocean singing to returning troops on board the *Nea Hellas*, to the soft scent-laden air after a summer evening performance of 'The Magic Flute' at the Glyndebourne opera in Sussex, and –

but that is another story...

DRAMATIS PERSONAE